Jennifer Lee

Paris in Mind

Jennifer Lee is an experienced editor with two previous anthologies, *Martial Arts Are Not Just for Kicking Butt* and *2sexE: Urban
Tales of Love, Liberty, and the Pursuit of Gettin' It On*. She lives in
the Bay Area in California and is happy to trade Paris and San
Francisco restaurant tips.

Paris in Mind

Paris in Mind

Three Centuries of Americans
Writing About Paris

EDITED AND WITH AN INTRODUCTION BY
Jennifer Lee

Vintage Departures

VINTAGE BOOKS

A DIVISION OF RANDOM HOUSE, INC.

NEW YORK

FIRST VINTAGE DEPARTURES EDITION, JULY 2003

Copyright © 2003 by Jennifer Y. Lee

Permissions credits for *Paris in Mind* appear at the end of the book.

Library of Congress Cataloging-in-Publication Data
Paris in mind : three centuries of Americans writing about Paris / edited and with an introduction by Jennifer Lee.
p. cm.—(Vintage departures)
Includes bibliographical references.
ISBN 1-4000-3102-8 (trade paper)
1. Americans—France—Paris—History.   2. Paris (France)—Social life and customs.   I. Lee, Jennifer, 1971–
DC715.P2545 2003
2002192282

Author photograph © Robert Foothorap, 2003.
Book design by Matt Songer

www.vintagebooks.com

Printed in the United States of America
10 9

This book is dedicated
to my mother and father,
who gave me Paris as a child,
long before they could afford it themselves.

Contents

Food

(How to Eat Like a Parisian)

The Art of Living
(*How to Live Like a Parisian*)

Tourism

(How You Can't Help Being an American in Paris)

Introduction

If you are lucky enough to have lived in Paris as a young man, then wherever you go for the rest of your life, it stays with you, for Paris is a moveable feast.

—Ernest Hemingway

The New Yorker dreams of Paris while the Parisian wonders about New York.

—Anaïs Nin

There's an Oscar Wilde maxim that goes something like this: When good Americans die, they go to heaven; if they've been *very good,* they go to Paris. Americans have been heeding those sentiments for more than three centuries, from Benjamin Franklin, Mark Twain, Anaïs Nin, to Dave Barry and David Sedaris, all of them collected here. Many of us cheat and get there a little before we've actually earned it.

I first saw Paris when I was twelve years old. I was on a chaperoned school tour of the great (read: *old*) cities of Europe. Paris felt like a respite from Europe's ancient ruins. In Paris, we kids went gallivanting in parks, checked out bookstalls near the Seine, ate too many pastries, and tried to pass as older than we were. We snuck out of our hotel at four in the morning and walked to the Eiffel Tower unchaperoned. The city was still and quiet, and we could hear the crunch of dirt and gravel beneath our feet. We felt powerful to be alone, except for the few elderly people walking their tiny French dogs or feeding the city's many pigeons.

I realize now that my youthful excitement didn't just come from being in a beautiful city. Racing like wild children along the banks of the Seine, or weaving through a crowd of people on the Champs Élysées, and watching adults sitting and talking in cafés, I sensed then that there was a way of life different than the one I knew back in my dusty, rural California hometown.

The second time I saw Paris, I was in love. We had flown to Paris on a whim. This time Paris felt like a respite from the daily grind. We strolled along the Seine, ate too many pastries, and behaved more youthful than our age. In her book, *The Gastronomical Me*, M. F. K. Fisher advises that Paris "should always be seen, the first time, with the eyes of childhood or of love." We're especially lucky if we've seen Paris both ways.

So seductive is the idea of Paris that even those who have never set foot in the city fall in love with it. You don't even have to be a Francophile. Paris is one of the few cities in the world that defines an entire country, yet stands singular and apart from it. To some, their love for Paris is part of a broader love of all things French. To others, it's discrete. They love Paris and only Paris.

Gertrude Stein believed that when we talked about France, we were really talking about Paris. She wrote, "Paris is where the twentieth century was." She was writing not so much about political power or technological progress, but of contributions in the arts and in the things more loosely called civilization, the art of living well. It was perhaps more true in the early twentieth century than it is today. Today, art, literature, culture, and fashion are no longer the sole domains of haute Paris, and Paris is no longer the only French destination for Americans and other travelers. When people talk about Paris, it's no longer a given that we mean France in general and vice versa. Yet to so many, by the power of imagination or myth, Paris remains *sui generis*, and the most seductive of cities.

How seductive is Paris?

So seductive is it that God is seduced in Saul Bellow's essay "My Paris." Bellow writes, "God would be perfectly happy in France because he would not be troubled by prayers, observances, blessings and demands for the interpretation of difficult dietary questions. Surrounded by unbelievers He too could relax toward evening, just as thousands of Parisians do at their favorite cafés."

So seductive is Paris that long after one's affair in Paris has ended, many continue their affairs with the city itself.

So seductive is Paris that even its winters can't hide its charms for long. Irwin Shaw laments the cold season. He writes in "Paris in Winter," "The most openly loving of cities, it is the coldest when the lovers are driven indoors. [In Paris] it is impossible to overlook the unheroic fact that not enough people kiss in the rain or at five degrees below zero." Shaw describes the anti-Paris, and still, he can't help being captivated all over again when the sun comes out for the briefest of moments.

Much of the seduction comes from the long history of U.S.–French relationship: we revolt against the British—the French give us ships and money; they're occupied by the Germans—we invade Normandy and liberate them; they invent film—we make an industry out of it; we make B-action flicks—they name it "film noir"; they're crazy about Jerry Lewis—we fall in love with Catherine Deneuve. They gave us the most American of American icons, the Statue of Liberty. The Americans and French have held a political, cultural, economic, and artistic dialog for more than three centuries. In many ways, we—Americans and Parisians—are both our best and worst reflections.

The stories about Paris that I read as a teenager made at least as big an impression as my first visit to the city. In general, Paris isn't a city for twelve-year-olds the way some cities are—cities like, say, Orlando, Florida—even now, despite Euro Disney. The first book about Paris that I read was Ernest Hemingway's *A Moveable Feast,* and I haven't yet outgrown the love it first inspired for the City of Light. Reading about grown-up Parisian adventures revealed future possibilities for this restless teenager, and it made me aspire to see Paris as a grown-up.

I suspect many Francophiles have a similarly worn and beloved book about Paris. Without a doubt, the American artists, writers, and musicians who went to Paris have influenced much of our fascination and love for this city. It is they who inspired this collection in that they first sparked my love of Paris.

I'm not alone in my fondness for the City of Light. Travel between the United States and France has always been strong. Americans still comprise the largest group of tourists to Paris annually despite the significant decrease immediately following September 11, 2001. The Travel Industry Association of America expects air travel to return to normal levels by late 2004 or 2005. The history of travel between Americans and French, which spans centuries, not decades, attests to our mutual strange fascination with each other.

One of the legacies of this long relationship has been great American literature about Paris and about being an American in Paris.

A few words about how this book was put together and what you'll find here: though I searched far and wide to collect the pieces in *Paris in Mind,* I also relied on the familiar literature on Paris. This is not a collection of unknown, never-before-seen Paris dispatches, and you'll find some familiar suspects such as Ernest Hemingway, Gertrude Stein, and Thomas Jefferson. Some Americans have been so important to the way we imagine Paris, that without them no Paris collection could offer a full sense of Franco-American relationship.

Secondly, many pieces are presented here, but many more have been left out. As an editor, I naturally wanted readers to have a chance to read everything I read. As a fellow *reader*, however, the process of editorial research wasn't the reading experience I'd wish to inflict on innocent readers, simply because not everything you read turns out to be a find.

Lastly, I followed two goals for this collection: pleasure and variety. A selected piece had to be a pleasure to read or offer a perspective, or examine a topic, that testified to the breadth of American interests and experiences in Paris. That is, admittedly, a subjective process. In general, I found that people for whom writing was their vocation wrote more vividly and thoughtfully about their experiences in Paris than those whose lives didn't depend on their prose. So, the book includes pieces that are almost all by professional writers, rather than by celebrities, musicians, politicos, and so forth.

In some cases, I included pieces that played off of other selections, and thus provide a sense of dialog between eras or between writers. The two pieces by Edith Wharton (from *A Backward Glance*) and E. B. White ("Liberation of Paris") are good examples. They're both about Paris and the end of a war, for Wharton the First World War and for White the Second World War: two different wars and writers, but the same overwhelming sense of emotion surfaces when each writer learns that the city they love so much is finally out of danger.

T. S. Eliot's and Anaïs Nin's pieces are another example. In his letter to the American poet, Robert McAlmon, Eliot admires French literary tradition because of its overarching sense of history, whereas Nin complains, "There is a monster in Paris called the Literary Tradition." Eliot is the scholar and great critic, while Nin the mystic and bohemian. Two American writers with different opinions about French literature reveal vastly differing sensibilities about life. In turn, they give away diverging approaches to their own literary work.

A friend asked: If I read this book, will I quit my job and move to Paris? Will I hate the French for being better at everything, and skinnier? Will I finally be convinced that frog tastes just like chicken? Will I understand myself better as an American?

If you've picked up this book, you might be someone who has already once quit his or her job and moved to Paris. You might be someone who already knows that frog doesn't taste just like chicken, it tastes *more like rabbit.* Just as likely, you might be someone who has never visited Paris except through movies, Cole Porter songs, and the travel articles of your local Sunday paper. In any case, you probably already hate the French for being skinnier. We all do. This book won't really change that because—bad news—they're even thinner in Paris, as Dave Barry will confirm. Barry writes in the two-part article collected in this book, "It's odd that the French appear to be in such good shape, because the major activity in Paris . . . is sitting around in cafés for days at a time looking French."

As for my friend's question, Will I understand myself better as an American? I hope so. These American stories about Paris comprise a catalog of tastes, fashions, social rules, and expectations, not only of what we think it is to be Parisian but also what we think it is to be American.

Finally, if you've never been an American in Paris, I think you'll want to be.

If you already have been, you'll want to again. When M. F. K. Fisher wrote that Paris "should always be seen, the first time, with the eyes of childhood or of love," she assumed we'd see Paris again and again.

Paris in Mind

Love

How to Seduce and Be Seduced Like a Parisian

E. B. White
(1899–1985)

E. B. WHITE, born Elwyn Brooks, is most famous and loved among bookish children all over the world for *Charlotte's Web, Stuart Little,* and *The Trumpet of the Swan*. Among prose purists, he is known for *The Elements of Style* with William Strunk and his *New Yorker* essays. By his own accounts, White began his career as a not very good newspaper reporter. Then, while working as an advertising copywriter, he began submitting pieces in 1926 to a brand new and struggling magazine called *The New Yorker*. The editor, Harold Ross, immediately hired him. White wrote the "Talk of the Town" section for almost eleven years, and afterward many poems, sketches, and essays as a contributing editor. White is often credited with having shaped the unique cadence and voice of *The New Yorker*. Among White's many accolades, he received the Laura Ingalls Wilder Award for his work in children's literature; honorary doctorates in literature from both Yale and Harvard Universities; and a Pulitzer Prize citation for his lifetime body of work.

⚜ Liberation of Paris ⚜
9/2/44

Probably one of the dullest stretches of prose in any man's library is the article on Paris in the *Encyclopædia Britannica*. Yet when we heard the news of the liberation, being unable to think of anything else to do, we sat down and read it straight through from beginning to end. "Paris," we began, "capital of France and of the department of Seine, situated on Ile de la Cité, the Ile St. Louis, and the Ile Louviers, in the Seine, as well as on both banks of the Seine, 233 miles from its mouth and 285 miles S. S. E. of London (by rail and steamer via Dover and Calais)." The words seemed like the beginning of a great poem. A feeling of simple awe overtook us as we slowly turned the page and settled down to a study of the city's weather graph and the view of the Seine looking east from Notre Dame. "The rainfall is rather evenly distributed," continued the encyclopædist. Evenly distributed, we thought to ourself, like the tears of those who love Paris.

Edith Wharton
(1862–1937)

EDITH WHARTON is best known for her novels such as *Ethan Frome* (1911), *House of Mirth* (1905), *The Custom of the Country* (1913), and *The Age of Innocence* (1920). She received a Pulitzer Prize for the latter despite the opinion of some, including herself, that the prize should have gone to a new writer named Sinclair Lewis. Characteristically, Wharton wrote to him and told him so, and he dedicated his next novel, *Babbitt*, to her. Wharton was an avid traveler, and she left a substantial body of travel writings and other nonfiction works inspired by her wanderlust and her love of French culture including *A Motor-Flight through France* (1908), *Fighting France, from Dunkerque to Belfort* (1915), and *French Ways and Their Meaning* (1919). She lived in France after she and her husband, Edward Robbins Wharton, divorced in 1913. She divided her time between her homes just outside Paris and in the Riviera.

During World War I, she organized an American committee of the Red Cross in Paris. For her war relief work, her love of France, and her literary talents, she was made a member of the Cross of the Legion of Honor by France and a Chevalier of the Order of Leopold by Belgium.

from

✣ A Backward Glance ✣

When I am told—as I am not infrequently—by people who were in the nursery, or not born, in that fatal year, that the world went gaily to war, or when I have served up to me the more recent legend that France and England actually wanted war, and forced it on the peace-loving and reluctant Central Empires, I recall those first days of August 1914, and am dumb with indignation.

France was paralyzed with horror. France had never wanted war, had never believed that it would be forced upon her, had proved her good faith by the absurd but sublime act of ordering her covering troops ten miles back from the frontier as soon as she heard of Austria's ultimatum to Servia! It may be useless to revive such controversies now; but not, I believe, to put the facts once more on record for a future generation who may study them with eyes cleared of prejudice. The criminal mistakes made by the Allies were made in 1919, not in 1914.

I have related, in a little book written during the first two years of the war, the impressions produced by those dark and bewildering days of August 1914, and I will not return to them here, except to describe my personal situation. This was rather absurdly conditioned by the fact that I had no money—a disability shared at the moment by many other foreigners in France. When I reached Paris I had about two hundred francs in my pocket, and was preparing to call at the bank for my usual remittance when I learned that the banks would make no payments. I borrowed a small sum from Walter Berry, who happened to have some cash in hand; but other penniless friends assailed him, and I could not ask for enough to send to my servants in England, who were expecting me to arrive with funds to pay the previous month's expenses. My old friend Frederick Whitridge was staying at his house in Hertfordshire, close to the place I had hired, and I wired him to give my servants enough to go on with. He replied: "Very sorry. Have no money." I cabled to my bank in New York to send me at least a small sum, and the bank cabled back: "Impossible."

At last, after a long delay—I forget how many days it took— I managed to get five hundred dollars from New York, by paying another five hundred for the transmission! To re-transmit to England what remained would have been, if not impossible, at any rate so costly that little would have been left to settle my tradesmen's bills. I had never had a house in England before, and accustomed to the suspiciousness of French tradespeople I was wondering how much longer my poor servants, who were totally unknown in the neighbourhood, would be able to obtain credit, and I realized that the only thing to do was to get to England myself as quickly as possible—not an easy undertaking either.

As I had no money to pay any more hotel bills I moved back to my shrouded quarters in the rue de Varenne, and camped there until I could get a permit to go to England. At that time it was believed in the highest quarters that the war would be fought out on Belgian soil, that it would last at the longest not more than six weeks, and that one decisive battle might probably end it sooner. My friends all advised me, if I could get to England, to stay there "till the war was over"—that is, presumably, till some time in October; and the first news of the battle of the Marne made it seem for two or three delirious days as though this prediction might come true.

While I was waiting to get to England I was asked by the Comtesse d'Haussonville, President of one of the branches of the French Red Cross (*Secours aux Blessés Militaires*) to organize a work-room for such work-women of my *arrondissement* as were not yet receiving government assistance. Almost all the hotels, restaurants, shops and work-rooms had closed with the drafting of the men for the army, and there remained a large number of women and children without means of livelihood, for whom immediate provision had to be made. I was totally inexperienced in every form of relief work, and not least in the management of anything like a work-room for seamstresses and *lingères*; and I had no money to do it with! But by this time it was possible for those who had a deposit in a French bank (which at the moment I had not), to draw it out in small amounts, and I assailed all my American friends who were either living in Paris, or still stranded there. I collected about twelve thousand francs (the first of many raids on the pockets of my compatriots), someone lent us a big empty flat in the Faubourg Saint-Germain, and luckily I came across two clever sisters (nieces of Professor Landormy, the well-known musical critic), who gave the aid of their quick wits and youthful energy. All this did not teach me how to run a big work-room, where we soon had about ninety women; but there was an ardour in the air which made it seem easy to accomplish whatever one attempted. There were several skilled *lingères* among our workers, and we decided to try for orders for fashionable *lingerie*, instead of competing with the other *ouvroirs* by making hospital supplies; and by dint of badgering my friends I extracted from them a rush of orders later supplemented by more from America. Our *lingerie* soon became well-known, and as I had told my assistants never on any account to refuse an order, whatever might be asked for, we were soon doing a thriving trade in unexpected lines, including men's shirts (in the low-neck Byronic style) for young American artists from Montparnasse!

[. . .]

One evening at the end of July 1918 Royall Tyler and I were sitting in my drawing-room in the rue de Varenne. He had been staying with me for a few days; and I suppose that as usual we were talking of the war, though his responsible position in our Paris Intelligence Bureau made confidential communications impossible. At any rate, as we sat there our talk was suddenly interrupted by the sound of a distant cannonade. We broke off and stared at each other.

Four years of war had inured Parisians to every kind of noise connected with air-raids, from the boom of warning maroons to the smashing roar of the bombs. The rue de Varenne was close to the Chamber of Deputies, to the Ministries of War and of the Interior, and to other important government offices, and bombs had rained about us and upon us since 1914; and as we were on Big Bertha's deathly trajectory her evil roar was also a well-known sound.

But this new noise came neither from maroon, from aeroplane nor from the throat of the dark Walkyrie; it was the level throb of distant artillery, a sound with which my expeditions to the front had made me painfully familiar. And this was the first time that I had heard it in Paris! The firing along the front was often distinctly audible on the south coast of England, and sometimes, I believe, at certain points in Surrey; but though familiar to dwellers in the southwestern suburbs of Paris, it had never before, to my knowledge, reached the city itself. My guest and I sprang up and rushed to a long window opening on a balcony. There we stood and listened to that far-off rumour, relentless, unbroken, portentous; and suddenly Tyler turned to me with an illuminated face. "It's the opening of Foch's big offensive!"

Some three months later, on a hushed November day, another unwonted sound called me to the same balcony. The quarter I lived in was so quiet in those days that, except for the crash of aerial battles, few sounds disturbed it; but now I was startled to hear, at an unusual hour, the familiar bell of our nearest church, Sainte Clotilde. I went to the balcony, and all the household followed me. Through the deep expectant hush we heard, one after another, the bells of Paris calling to each other; first those of our own quarter, Saint Thomas d'Aquin, Saint Louis des Invalides, Saint François Xavier, Saint Sulpice, Saint Etienne du Mont, Saint Séverin; then others, more distant, joining in from all around the city's great periphery, from Notre Dame to the Sacré Cœur, from the Madeleine to Saint Augustin, from Saint Louis-en-l'Ile to Notre-Dame de Passy; at first, as it seemed, softly, questioningly, almost incredulously; then with a gathering rush of sound and speed, precipitately, exultantly, till all their voices met and mingled in a crash of triumph.

We had fared so long on the thin diet of hope deferred that for a moment or two our hearts wavered and doubted. Then, like the bells, they swelled to bursting, and we knew the war was over.

Art Buchwald

(1925–   )

ART BUCHWALD has been called the "breakfast table Voltaire" for his biting satires dressed in simple prose. Today, his political humor column appears in more than 500 newspapers worldwide. But his career began as an American in Paris. In 1948, Buchwald bought a one-way ticket on a ship to France to study French in Paris using his GI Bill. But instead of attending classes, he bribed the attendance taker to mark him present each day, so he could spend the rest of his GI Bill to live *la vie bonhomie*. Only months later, he talked his way into his own column on Paris nightlife for the Paris edition of the *New York Herald Tribune*. By the time he was thirty-one, he had two Paris columns syndicated throughout the United States. Here, we've reprinted his interview with Vernon Duke, the composer of "April in Paris," a song that has inspired many an American romance with the City of Light. As the interview reveals, the song's strength doesn't lie in its accuracy about the weather in Paris in April.

Art Buchwald has received the Prix de la Bonne Humeur for his French translation of *A Gift from the Boys,* an honorary doctorate from Yale University, and a Pulitzer Prize for commentary. In addition to many books on American political foibles, he has written several books about Paris including *Paris After Dark, I'll Always Have Paris: A Memoir,* and *Art Buchwald's Paris.*

⚜ April in Paris ⚜

from Art Buchwald's Paris

I finally caught up with the man who is responsible for bringing more American tourists to Paris in April than any other person. His name is Vernon Duke and he is the composer of the great romantic song "April in Paris." The fact that it had been raining in Paris all month didn't seem to faze Mr. Duke at all. He carries an umbrella and raincoat with him at all times.

Mr. Duke told me: "The whole song is a hoax, because I knew the weather was like this. They're talking about giving me the Legion of Honor for getting so many tourists to Paris so early in the season."

"Have you ever had any romances in Paris in April?"

Mr. Duke, who is a bachelor, replied: "Never. You always have to wait until May before things start popping."

I asked the composer to tell how he came to write "April in Paris."

"I was living with George Gershwin in New York at the time. Incidentally my real name is Vladimir Dukelsky and it was Gershwin who gave me the name Vernon Duke. We were preparing a show called *Walk a Little Faster*, which was to star Beatrice Lillie, in April, 1932. At the time, we needed a romantic number for Evelyn Hoey. I was sitting in Tony's, on 52nd Street, with Dorothy Parker, Bob Benchley, Monty Woolley, who staged the revue, and John McClain, the theater critic. We were all drinking and reminiscing about Paris and there was a lot of crying going on.

"Dorothy Parker or somebody said something like: 'Oh to be in Paris now that April's here.' I, in my unsobered condition, replied: 'What a wonderful title for a song.'

"Tony told me he had a piano upstairs, and I was high enough to say okay I'd write it right then and there. I went upstairs and came down ten minutes later with the music.

"The next day I told E. Y. Harburg, who was writing the lyrics for the show, that I had a song about Paris. Harburg had never been to Paris and said: 'Who the hell cares about "April in Paris." I don't know what happens there.'

"I told him I'd bring him a lot of guidebooks from the library. I gave them to him, but after he read them he called me and said: 'I still don't know what goes on in Paris in April. You better get over here and tell me!' So I went over to his apartment and he said: 'Now, exactly what happens?'

"I said I didn't know exactly, but I thought the French people went out into the open and sat under the trees. 'Great,' said Harburg. 'Now we're getting somewhere,' and he wrote the first lines of the song:

> *April in Paris*
> *Chestnuts in blossom*
> *Holiday tables under the trees*

"Then Harburg said: 'And what's the feeling there in April?' and I replied: 'I always had the feeling that in Paris in the spring something wonderful should inevitably happen, but it never did,' which took care of the last part of the song:

> *April in Paris*
> *Whom can I run to?*
> *What have you done to my heart?*

"The song was rehearsed and put into the show and it had a beautiful reception when it was done in Boston. But when the show opened in New York, no one mentioned it except Robert Garland of the *Telegram*, who said there were several unnecessary items in the score, particularly something called 'April in Paris.'

"It caught on only two years later, when Marian Chase started singing it in nightclubs and made a recording of it. Last year Warner Brothers made a picture called *April in Paris*, and several good records of it have been made by Frank Sinatra, Doris Day, and Sauter and Finnegan.

"I like the song, but it's plagued me for the last twenty years. I usually keep meeting plump matrons who say: 'So you wrote "April in Paris." I remember when I was in Paris and Frank and I heard the song.' It seems to me all the pretty girls have had their romances some place else.

"I guess I'll have to live with it for the rest of my life."

It was raining as Mr. Duke got up to leave. He put on his raincoat, got ready to open his umbrella, took one look out the window and said: "My God, what weather!"

A. J. Liebling
(1904–1963)

A. J. LIEBLING, born Abbott Joseph, was the son of a New York furrier. He received a B.A. in literature from Columbia University and studied for a year at the Sorbonne in Paris during the 1920s. His first love was New York City, on which he reported for various papers including *The New York Times* and *The New Yorker*. His second love was Paris, and in 1939, *The New Yorker* sent him abroad to be their Paris correspondent. With the outbreak of World War II later that same year, he became their war correspondent as well, sending dispatches from France, England, and North Africa. As a reporter, Liebling crossed the English Channel with Allied troops, landed on the shores of Normandy on D day, and participated in the liberation of Paris. Here, Liebling poignantly recalls his days in Paris before the war, and in particular, Angèle, the working girl and friend with whom he explored Paris while he was a distracted student of medieval history.

Liebling published three books about Paris: *The Road Back to Paris, Normandy Revisited,* and *Between Meals: An Appetite for Paris* from which the excerpt comes. For his love of France, he was named a Knight of the French Legion of Honor.

❧ Passable ❧

from Between Meals: An Appetite for Paris

Following the publication of some of the foregoing papers I had an avalanche of letters—perhaps a half dozen—asking scornfully whether, in my student days in Paris, I did nothing but eat. I tried conscientiously to think of what I did between meals in the years 1926–27, when I was twenty-two–three, and it seems to have been quite a lot. For one thing, in those days young men liked women. We did not fear emasculation. We had never heard of it. This would today be considered a subliterary approach, but there it was. Havelock Ellis was the sage who made authority in the dormitories. Freud had not yet seeped down to the undergraduate level. Molly Bloom was the pin-up girl of the *nouvelle vague*, and we all burned to beat out Blazes Boylan.

Women offered so much fun from the beginning that further possibilities appeared worth investigating. For this we considered acquaintance, or even marriage, with an undergraduate of the opposite sex insufficient. We assumed, perhaps overoptimistically, that the possibilities of the subject were limitless. They may not be, but no finite man will ever be able to brag that he has exhausted them.

For the beginning student of all essential subjects, the Latin Quarter was an ideal school. The Restaurant des Beaux-Arts, as I have indicated, was a great place to learn to eat because the items on the menu were good but simple. The cafés on the Boulevard Saint-Michel offered self-instruction of another kind, but similarly within the grasp of the beginner. You could find any feature of a beauty queen in our cafés, but they were all on different girls. A girl who was beautiful all over would pick a better neighborhood. So, just as at the restaurant, you had to choose a modest but satisfying agenda. In doing that you learned your own tastes.

It was trickier than that because a woman, unlike a *navarin de mouton*, has a mind. A man may say, when he begins to recognize his tastes, "Legs, on a woman, are more important to me than eyes." But he has to think again when he must choose between a witty woman with good eyes and a dull one with trim legs. Give the witty woman a bad temper and the dull one constant good humour and you add to the difficulty of the choice. To multiply the complexity the woman, unlike the *navarin*, reacts to you. She may be what you want, but you may not be what she wants. In such a case she will turn out to be not what you wanted at all.

The unimaginative monogamist has none of these perplexities, but I doubt that he has fun either. I attribute the gloom of many young novelists to an adolescent mistake made at a church. Afterward belated curiosity clashes with entrenched ignorance and produces that *timor mundi* which is the *mal de siècle*. "Ain't It Awful, Mabel?" is their strange device, instead of "Up in Mabel's Room."

The girls would arrive at their customary tables soon after lunch, in late afternoon, and establish themselves with a permanent *consommation*, something inexpensive and not tempting, for they would make it last until somebody treated them to something better. This might be a long time, and they had a skill in husbanding the drink that would have stood them in good stead if they had been airmen downed in the Sahara. When treated, they exhibited another desert talent, the opportunism of the camel. They drank enough to last them to the next oasis.

They spent the afternoon writing on the house stationery. If the waiter caught them doodling or doing ticktacktoes he would cut off their supply. With the hour of the *apéritif* came animation and hope. After the dinner hour, if they had not been invited to eat, there remained animation. It could always happen that, if they kept up their spirits, some late customer would offer them a sandwich. The girls were like country artisans; they took money for their services, but only when they felt like working. On occasion they would accept payment in kind—a dinner or a pair of stockings—but then, as often as not, they would ask you to lend them their current week's room rent.

I suppose some of them had sweet men, but these must have been *dilettanti* too. No protector worthy of the name would have tolerated such irregularity. He would have said the girls of the Boulevard Saint-Michel were not serious. And he would have starved on a percentage of their earnings, like a literary agent who depended on poets. All the girls were young. It was easy to comprehend that this was a phase without a future; there was no chance to accumulate. Where they went after they disappeared from the Quarter I do not know. They were brisk rather than chic, and they made up without exaggeration. My memory is not tenacious in matters of dress, but I am sure the girls wore short skirts—I remember the legs. One girl helped me select a hat for a woman in America, and this would not have been possible except in a period when all hats were essentially alike. It was the age of the face *sous cloche*.

The *cloche* was an enlarged skullcap, jammed down on the head like an ice-cream scoop on a ball of vanilla. For the rest, their clothes were not elaborate, with the short skirt, a short blouse and short jacket, and underneath a *soutien-gorge* and *pantalon*. Having the *points de repère* once well in mind, one saw at a glance what was what.

Sometimes a girl would enter *en menage* with a student, usually a Romanian or an Asiatic. If it was one of the latter, with an allowance from home, the girl would disappear from her customary café for a while or appear there only with him. If it was a Romanian, she would be on the job more regularly than before. Often a girl would make such an arrangement to gain the status of a kept woman, which would protect her from the jurisdiction of the *police des moeurs*.

Once the cops of this unsavory group picked up a girl without visible means of support they would force her to register. Then they would give her a card that subjected her to a set of rules.

"Once a girl has the card she is bound to infract the rules," the girls said. "We are all so lazy. She misses a couple of visits; she is subject to heavy penalties. Then comes blackmail. The police put her to work for chaps who give them a cut. *Hop*, then, no more chattering with student friends who have no money.

"It's the pavement for her, and turn over the receipts to the mackerel at five o'clock in the morning. The police have opened another account."

I was glad to know how things were. It made me feel like an insider, and it helped me understand cops, who run to form everywhere.

Our girls were not intellectuals. None was a geisha primed with poems, nor were there hetaerae who could have disputed on equal terms with Plato, or even with Max Lerner. But all served as advisers on courses of study. They knew the snaps and the tough ones in all faculties, which professors were susceptible to apple polishing and which the most resolutely *vache*. Above all, they had anticipated a theory that was to be imparted to me later as a great original discovery by T. S. Matthews, an editor of *Time*, who told me that the content of communication was unimportant. What did count, Matthews said, was somebody on one end of a wire shouting, "My God, I'm alive!" and somebody on the other end shouting, "My God, I'm alive too!"

It was a poor prescription for journalism, but a good program for conversation between the sexes. (The girls did not keep us at the end of a wire.)

To one I owe a debt the size of a small Latin American republic's in analysts' fees saved and sorrows unsuffered during the next thirty-odd years. Her name was Angèle. She said: *"Tu n'es pas beau, mais t'es passable."* ("You're not handsome, but you're passable.")

I do not remember the specific occasion on which Angèle gave me the good word, but it came during a critical year. I am lucky that she never said, *"T'es merveilleux."* The last is a line a man should be old enough to evaluate.

My brain reeled under the munificence of her compliment. If she had said I was handsome I wouldn't have believed her. If she had called me loathsome I wouldn't have liked it. *Passable* was what I hoped for. *Passable* is the best thing for a man to be.

A handsome man is so generally said by other men to be a

fool that in many cases he must himself begin to believe it. The superstition that handsome men are dull is like the prejudice that gray horses quit. Both arose because their subjects were easy to follow with the eye. The career of the late Elmer Davis, a handsome but intelligent man, was made more difficult by his good looks. Favored with a less prepossessing appearance, he would have won earlier acceptance. There are homely fools too, and quitters of all colors.

Women who are both randy and cautious, and therefore of the most profitable acquaintance, avoid handsome lovers because they are conspicuous. He who is *passable* escapes attention. To be *passable* is like a decent suit. It gets you anywhere. *Passable* and *possible* are allied by free association. A young man wants desperately to be considered at least a possibility. But it is the only game in which there is no public form, and he can't present a testimonial from his last employer. He is like a new player in a baseball league where there are no published batting averages. To be *passable* gets him in the ballpark without arousing inflated expectations. The ugly man is the object of a special cult among women, but it is relatively small. He runs well only in limited areas, like a Mormon candidate in Utah.

A heartening fact, if you are *passable*, is that there are more *passable* women than any other kind, and that a *passable* man establishes a better rapport with them. Very pretty girls are preferable, of course, but there are never enough to go around. Angèle was *passable* plus—a woman who looks pretty at her best and *passable* at her worst. Her legs, though well-tapered, were a trifle short and her round head a trifle large for good proportion with her torso, in which there was no room for improvement. It was solid Renoir. Her neck was also a bit short and thick—a good point in a prizefighter but not in a swan. She had a clear skin and a sweet breath, and she was well-joined—the kind of girl you could rough up without fear of damage. Angèle had a snub nose, broad at the base, like a seckel pear tilted on its axis.

It was a period when the snub nose enjoyed high popular esteem. The fashions of the day called for a gamine, and a gamine cannot have a classic profile. A retroussé nose, for example, looked better under a cloche. The cloche made a girl with an aquiline nose look like the familiar portrait of Savonarola in his hood. It gave her the profile of that bigot or a spigot.

I had an early belief that I could get along with any woman whose nose turned up. This proved in later life to have been a mistake based on a brief series of coincidences, but when I knew Angèle it still influenced me. Among snub-nosed idols in the United States we had Mary Pickford, Marion Davies, Mae Murray, and Ann Pennington, to name a few I remember. The last two were dancers, and when they kicked, the tips of their noses and their toes were in a straight line. In France they had Madge Lhoty and a girl named Lulu Hegoboru.

Here memory, furtive and irrelevant, interpolates a vision of La Hegoboru taking a refrain of "Tea for Two" in English, in the Paris production of *No, No, Nanette:* "I will back a sugar cack—" as she jumped right, kicked left.

We have no such artists today. The profession of ingenue exists no longer. There was a girl in *Little Mary Sunshine* who had the gist of it, but she will have no chance to develop. In her next job she may have to play an agoraphobic Lesbian in love with her claustrophobic brother. The tragic siblings will be compelled to tryst in a revolving door. It is the kind of play people like to write now, because it can be done in one set, in this case the door.

Angèle had large eyes with sable pupils on a pale-blue field, and a wide mouth, and a face wide at the cheekbones. Her hair was a black soup-bowl bob, as if she had put a cloche on and let a girl friend cut around it. (Girls in the United States went to barber shops for their haircuts.) The corners of her mouth were almost always turned up because Angèle was of a steady, rough good humor. Angèle was a Belgian; half the girls in Paris were Belgians then, and all of them said their parents had been shot by the Germans in World War I.

I met Angèle at Gypsy's Bar on the Rue Cujas, a late place outside the circle of tranquil cafés in which I usually killed my evenings. Most of the time I tried to live like a Frenchman, or, rather, like my idealized notion, formed at home, of how a Frenchman lived. The notion included moderation: I would drink only wine and its distillates, cognac, Armagnac and marc. I did not class French beer among alcoholic drinks. In the United States I had been accustomed to drink needle beer, reinforced with alcohol; a six-ounce glass for twenty-five cents hit as hard as a shot of whiskey for half a dollar.

I did not get drunk as long as I followed what I imagined was the French custom. I thought a sedentary binge effeminate. Now and then, though, I would suffer from a recurrent American urge to stand up and tie one on. It was like the *trouvère*'s longing to hear the birds of his own province:

> *The little birds of my country,*
> *They sing to me in Brittany;*
> *The shrill-voiced seagulls' cries among*
> *Mine ears have heard their evensong,*
> *And sweet, it was of thee.*

When this yearning struck during the solvent week of my month—the first after receiving my allowance—I would go to Gypsy's and drink Scotch. The bar was in the Quarter but not used by students. It was too dear. There were even gigolos there—what student would tip a gigolo? I shall not try at this distance in time to guess the nature of Gypsy's sustaining clientele. There may have been a *spécialité de maison*, but I never learned what. I would stand at the bar and think my own thoughts, clear and increasingly grandiose as the level dropped in the bottle. People whose youth did not coincide with the twenties never had our reverence for strong drink. Older men knew liquor before it became the symbol of a sacred cause. Kids who began drinking after 1933 take it as a matter of course.

For us it was a self-righteous pleasure, like killing rabbits with clubs to provide an American Legion party for poor white children. Drinking, we proved to ourselves our freedom as individuals and flouted Congress. We conformed to a popular type of dissent—dissent from a minority. It was the only period during which a fellow could be smug and slopped concurrently.

Angèle impinged on my consciousness toward the end of one of these reveries. She said that I needed somebody to see me home. In Tours the previous summer, a girl making a similar offer had steered me into the hands of two incompetent muggers. Angèle was of a more honorable character. She came home with me. In the morning, when we had more opportunity to talk, we found that we were almost neighbors. She had a room in the Hôtel des Facultés, where the Rue Racine and the Rue de l'École de Médecine form a point they insert in the Boulevard Saint-Michel. My room, one of the pleasantest of my life, was in the fifth (by French count) floor, front, of the Hôtel Saint-Pierre, 4 Rue de l'École de Médecine, next door to a Chinese restaurant that had dancing. At night, while I read, the music from the dancing would rise to my window and a part of my brain would supply the words to the tune as I tried to maintain interest in the *Manual of Provençal Documents* of Monsieur Maurice Prou. One that recurred often was *"Oh, les fraises et les framboises, le bon vin qu'nous avons bu,"* from *Trois Jeunes Filles Nues*, one of Mirande's great hits.

It was an atmosphere not conducive to the serious study of medieval history, which was my avowed purpose in the Quarter.

Angèle not only lived by day on the same street, but frequented by night the same cafés I did—the Taverne Soufflet, La Source, the Café d'Harcourt, all strung along the Boulevard Saint-Michel. She made her headquarters in the d'Harcourt, where it was the merest chance that she had not remarked me, she said. She had so many friends, she explained, there was always somebody engaging her attention.

I said that in any case I spent most of my time in the Soufflet, where the boss was a pal of my landlord. But after that I would go to the d'Harcourt whenever I wanted to see her. It had a favorable effect on her standing if I bought her a drink there, and none on mine if I took her to the Soufflet. If she was not at her post, her waiter would take her messages. He would also tell her to dress warmly in winter and not get her feet wet, to take sufficient nourishment to keep up her strength, and not to be beguiled by clients who had to his experienced eye the aspect of musclemen recruiting for a brothel. It was a relationship already familiar to me from New York, where a waiter was the nearest thing to a mother lots of girls had.

When we had established the similarity of our *fréquentations*, Angèle and I marveled that we had to go all the way to Gypsy's, a good fifty meters from the Boulevard, to find each other. We sounded like the traditional New Yorkers who inhabit the same apartment house but meet for the first time in Majorca.

After that I was with her often. I do not know if she had a heart of gold, but she had what I learned long years later to call a therapeutic personality. She made you feel good.

When I took her out in the evening we sometimes strayed from the Quarter. This was like taking a Manhattan child to the Bronx Zoo. Girls did not shift about in Paris. Clienteles were localized, and so were usages. Montparnasse, although not a long walk away from the Quarter, had all the attributes of a foreign country, including, to a degree, the language.

In Montparnasse the types in the cafés spoke English, American, and German. The girls there had to be at least bilingual. In the Quarter, the languages, besides French, were Vietnamese, Spanish, Czech, Polish and Romanian. But the specimens of all these nationalities spoke French at least passably. The girls consequently could remain resolutely monolingual. The clients were students, or simulated students, at the University. Those were the days of the Little Entente, and France set the cultural and military pattern for the East Europe that is behind the Curtain now. Romanian students came to French universities as freely as if they had done their secondary work in France.

The pre-eminence of the University of Paris was acknowledged as it had been in the Middle Ages. All the tribes rescued from the Austro-Hungarian and Turkish Empires flocked there—Serbs and Croats, Egyptians, Greeks, Armenians, along with Haitians and Koreans, Venezuelans and Argentines. There were also, of course, the North Africans. It would have been a great place to form friendships that would serve in the convulsive years to come. But I thought, if I thought about it at all, that regional convulsions were as out-of-date as *écriture onciale* or horse armor.

Our foreignness made each more confident of his speech than he would have been among the French. From my first appearance in the Quarter, my French was no worse than that of a White Russian or a Czech, and I rose rapidly and successively through the grades of being mistaken for a Hungarian, German Swiss, Alsatian, and Belgian from the Flemish-speaking provinces. Beyond that point I have not since progressed, except in Algeria, where I am mistaken for an old lag of the Foreign Legion who has all kinds of accents so inextricably mixed that it is hopeless to attempt to disassociate them.

Angèle did not like Montparnasse. Neither did I. I had come to France for the same reason that at home I would go out to a beach and swim out just beyond the breakers. There I could loaf. Lying on my back, I would paddle just enough to keep out of the pull, and draw my knees up to my chin and feel good. The Americans in Montparnasse, sitting at their tables in front of Le Sélect and talking at each other, reminded me of monkeys on a raft. They were not in the water at all. One reason I didn't think I liked them was that they had all decided they were writers, or painters, or sculptors, and I didn't know what I was. During my residence in the Hôtel Saint-Pierre I never heard of Gertrude Stein, and although I read *Ulysses*, I would as soon have thought of looking the author up as of calling on the President of the Republic.

Angèle disliked Montparnasse because the people looked at the same time too prosperous and too bizarre. The American women, she said, did not look like Frenchwomen and the Frenchwomen did not look like other Frenchwomen. There were no serious bookstores stacked with doctoral dissertations and tributes to deceased savants. (She herself was not a reader, but she liked academic surroundings.) The types appeared smug and possibly addicted to narcotics. The waiters in the cafés were insolent and Italian, and the *consommations* were overpriced. There were too many fairies and they gave her *drôles* of looks. Let them not fear, she was not in competition. We wound up our tour at the Closerie des Lilas, the border post, at the corner of the Boulevard Montparnasse and our own Boulevard Saint-Michel. The Montparnassiens occupied the post—its tariff was too high for the Quarter. I offered her a whiskey there, but she said it smelled of bedbugs. Now all the French drink Scotch.

Angèle could not get back to the d'Harcourt with sufficient celerity, but once there, it pleased her to have voyaged. She talked as if she were home from a world cruise. But when we went to Montmartre, she was in her glory. She had talked all her life about the *nuits blanches* of Montmartre but had never been there. I took her to Zelli's and we drank several bottles of champagne. She was a solid drinker. All her appetites were robust. In bed she was a kind of utility infielder. She made me buy half a dozen flashlight photographs of us and the bottles, like sportsmen and sailfish, to serve as documentation when she recounted our adventure. Her room, in the prow of a ship-shaped building, was barely wide enough for a single bed. I was there only once, in September of 1927, when she was ill. Half of the mirror was covered with photographs of us at Zelli's.

Aside from her concession that I was passable, which is wrapped around my ego like a bullet-proof vest riveted with diamonds, I retain little Angèle said. The one other exception is a report so vivid that I sometimes confuse it with a visual memory.

Angèle told me one morning that she and a number of her colleagues had been playing cards in her room. There were a couple of girls sitting on her bed, a couple more on the bureau, one on the only chair and another on her trunk, when one took off her shoes.

A second girl said, after a moment, "It smells of feet in here!" The shoeless girl said, "Say that once more and you will say *Bon jour* to the concierge."

"You get it?" said Angèle. "The concierge is on the ground floor, we are on the sixth. She will throw her down the stairs. The other comrade who commenced says again, 'It smells of feet.'

"So the other hooks on and drags her out on the landing, and they roll down the stairs together, interscratching with all claws. On the fifth, two law students, interrupted in their studies, pull them apart from each other. The girls couldn't work for three nights afterward.

"One student took up for the girl he had pulled upon, and the other took up for the adversary. Now the students have quarreled, and the girl whose feet smelled has moved in with one of them at the Facultés, while the other student has moved in with the girl whose nose was delicate. It is romance in flower."

Life in the Quarter was a romance that smelled of feet.

I am afraid that I do not succeed in making Angèle's quality come clear. To attempt a full description of a woman on the basis of a few fragmentary memories is like trying to reconstruct a small, endearing animal from a few bits of bone. Even some of the bits are not much help. My arms try to remember her weight— I should say 118, give or take two pounds.

It makes me wince, now, to recall that she used to butt me in the pit of the belly, quite hard, and that we both thought it chummy. My point of view has changed with the tone of my muscles.

Yet she existed. The proof is that my old landlord, Perès, remembers her well. I sometimes meet Perès at a brasserie called l'Alsace à Paris. The proprietor there is M. Perès' old friend, the former owner of the Taverne Soufflet, which failed in 1931 because he had a wife who did not keep her mind on the business. (It is too much to expect the *patron* of a café to keep his mind on the business himself.) Now M. Robert, whose last name I have not learned in thirty-six years of greeting him, has an excellent wife who does not have to keep her mind on the business. It goes as if on rollers.

M. Perès, who retired from the management of the Hôtel Saint-Pierre shortly after World War II, continues to live in the Quarter because, he says, it keeps him young. He has recently been made an Officer of the Legion of Honor. He was a Chevalier, *à titre militaire*, as I have said before, when I first came to live under this roof in 1926, having distinguished himself by courage in World War I. I always suspected him of trying to give the impression, however, that he had won the ribbon for some discovery in Aramaic intransitive verbs or the functioning of the gall bladder. This would have been more chic in his neighborhood. During World War II he served as a captain of infantry, at fifty-one, and distinguished himself again.

"I was a bit put out," he said to me when I congratulated him on his new rosette, "because my promotion was slow in arriving. A man of seventy in the vicinity of the University who has only the ribbon has the air of a demifailure. But the delay was occasioned by the nature of my business. The Chancellery of the Legion is cautious in awarding the higher grades to hotelkeepers, because the hotel may be a *maison de passe*. Once I announced my retirement, the rosette was not long on the way."

M. Perès, in thirty years at the Saint-Pierre, lodged an infinity of students. It makes him think of himself as a housemaster. "One of our fellows is raising the question of confidence in the Chamber today," he may say when you meet him, meaning a Deputy who used to live at the Saint-Pierre as a student. "He has gone farther than I would have predicted." Or, "One of our fellows is now the leading internist in Port-au-Prince—I had a card last week." Or, "One of our chaps who is the professor of medieval history at the University of Jerusalem has, it appears, achieved a remarkable monograph on secular law in the Latin kingdom of Acre. He had your room about ten years after you left. He, at least, worked from one time to another." It is M. Perès' contention that I was a *farceur*, a do-nothing, because we sneaked out so often for a drink at the Soufflet when his wife was in bad humor.

The Anciens de l'Hôtel Saint-Pierre is the sole alumni association of which I would willingly attend a reunion; unhappily it does not exist. If it did, it would include the ladies' auxiliary, *bien entendu;* the girl who lived with the Korean on the floor below me, the mistress of the Dane upstairs, Angèle and subsequent and preceding Angèles of all promotions, and the two little maids from Dax, Lucienne and Antoine, who led the way to the bathroom, which was on the third floor, when the client had ordered a bath. They then allowed themselves to be trapped long enough for an invigorating tussle.

M. Perès remembers Angèle almost as well as if she had made a name for herself as a comparative zoologist in Peru.

She died in the winter of 1927–28, not of a broken heart, but flu. I was no longer in Paris, but in Providence, Rhode Island, where I had returned to a job on the Providence *Journal* and *Evening Bulletin*, and Perès included word of her death, along with other neighborhood news, in a letter that he sent me.

"She had a felicity of expression," he said of her one day thirty years later. "Once she said to me, 'Head of a ruin, how much do you extort for your cubicles?' There wasn't a sou's worth of harm in her. What a pity that she had to die. How well she was built!" he said in final benison.

"She was *passable*," I said.

I could see that M. Perès thought me a trifle callous, but he did not know all that *passable* meant to me.

Maxine Rose Schur
(1948–   )

MAXINE ROSE SCHUR is an award-winning travel writer and the author of ten books. She has twice received the Lowell Thomas Award for excellence in travel writing from the Society of American Travel Writers. Her articles have appeared in many national publications including the *Christian Science Monitor,* the *Los Angeles Times,* and *Escape.* Currently, Ms. Schur is a columnist and feature writer on Caribbean art and culture for *Caribbean Travel & Life.* Her books include a travel memoir, *A Thirst for Faraway Things,* and several children's books, *The Peddler's Gift, Sacred Shadows,* and *Day of Delight* among others. Ms. Schur lectures and teaches travel writing and children's fiction writing at universities and conferences nationwide. She is currently working on a book about the Loire Valley.

❖ Passionate and Penniless in Paris ❖

We kept very still of course, and were satisfied with the idea of Paris.

—Elizabeth Barrett Browning

I sure know what Elizabeth meant. We've been to Paris five times, but the very idea of Paris still seduces. I hunger for Paris and lust over memories. Yet at night, when I lie in my husband's arms, it isn't the recent, sybaritic images I conjure to lure him into that intimate realm of memory. No. At night, fancy restaurants, scenic boat rides, chateaux and boutiques evaporate. In their place float up memories, strange and strong. Up floats an idea of Paris from my first visit a quarter century ago, when I was twenty-two and newly wed.

Of course, even then I had an idea of Paris. That's why, driving into the city in our VW van, I dressed in what I fancied were "Parisian clothes." Never mind they were Parisian clothes of some other century. In my long black skirt, black boots, hoop earrings, flea market scarf of pink silk, I felt like Paris personified.

The moment I arrived in the City of Light, I was lit. "We must stay at least a month," I told Stephen, my husband. "Let's enjoy Paris!"

Paris was expensive and we had little money, but I made a fuss so at last he said, "All right, we'll stay—but we'll have to camp."

"Camp!" I cried. "In Paris? Nobody camps in Paris!"

We did.

That night we rolled our van, outfitted with no more than a mattress, down the ramp to the Quai de la Tournelle, where vehicles are forbidden. We parked at the edge of the river, just past the Pont de la Tournelle. When we looked left, we could see the stone bridge with its little statue of St. Genevieve, and beyond, the floodlit Cathedral of Notre Dame. Looking right, we saw our quay merge with the next, then vanish in murky shadows. In front of us, across the narrow arm of the river, rose the elegant apartments of the Ile St. Louis.

We climbed in the back of our van, lay face up on the mattress and looked out the windows.

Magic.

The effect was as if we were both inside the van and out of it too. At once cozy in an enclosed, secret place, and also right out in the city. In its very heart. Above us, apartments loomed into the stars, their lacy iron balconies bathed in light, and at our feet, the Seine flowed discreetly southward.

"Let's enjoy Paris," Stephen murmured.

Now, a lot of practical things can get in the way of romance—
such as the need for a bathroom. But we had the courage of youth
and didn't let it. The next afternoon we sat on the riverbank plan-
ning just which cafés we would discreetly visit at what times of
day when a van, big and white as an ambulance, pulled up next to
ours. A young man stepped out. He wore no shirt and balanced a
hammer vertically on his nose.

"Gidday," he said.

This was Basil Didier, a Mormon New Zealander who'd come
to Paris to research his genealogy.

His trick turned the wheel of camaraderie. We had a few
laughs together, then seeing our interest in his Citroen delivery
van, he asked, "Would you like a perv?" which is New Zealandese
for "Would you like to take a look?"

We were awed by the ingenious cabinetry: the seat that
evolved into a bed, the stove built into the counter, the table hung
on the wall like a picture, and the sink with its clever foot pump,
small as a piano pedal.

"I'm a carpenter," Basil said with Down Under modesty. But
when I opened the narrow door and discovered a flush toilet, I
knew he was more than a carpenter. He was our friend.

There must have been something in the air that August 1971.
The next day two more vans arrived. One was inhabited by a
young New York couple who'd just returned from North Africa.
The other, a rusted black Fiat, contained a bearded artist from
Hawaii named Hayden and his black dog, Mahler.

Of an evening, the couple would regale us with their adventures in Morocco and Hayden would recount the curious theatrics
performed by a tribe of gypsies he'd lived with in Toulouse. For
the next month, the six of us shared food, opinions, toilets and, at
sunset, *vin rouge*. Surely there was alchemy at work, for though it
was totally *défendu* to camp there, directly across, as we learned,
from the island home of Prime Minister Pompidou, the gendarmes never told us to leave.

Au contraire! Each night a gendarme would stop by our van to check passports and to see that we were all right.

"*Ça va, jeunes Americans?*"

"*Ça va.*"

One warm evening, as Hayden was inside his van painting on its walls by candlelight what he called his "private vision of Paris" and the New Yorkers were playing gin rummy and Mahler was barking at every kerosene barge that chugged up the river, Basil, Stephen and I sat on the quay, dangling our feet over the water. Stephen and I were drinking wine and trying in vain to get Basil to taste the marked-down cheese we'd bought from the Monoprix. But Basil was too busy preaching how French cheeses were decadent.

"Food should be just matter to fill up space," he said.

Then he went on about sex.

Mormonism forbids sex before marriage and in his opinion that was "too right," for any fool could see sex is merely a fad. A style! A kind of fashion!

"Sex," Basil explained, "is just Gucci Hootchie-Kootchie."

Bored with his ideas, we told him one of ours: to drive from France to India. "And what we need," Stephen said, "is a camper, fixed up like yours."

Basil was happy to take the bait. He said he was "right tired of dead Didiers," and would be pleased to help us make our van into a camper. Our joy turned to dejection, however, when we realized the impossibility of such a project that required power tools, for we had no electricity nor any access to it.

"Too bad, too," I said, "when there's electricity all around us . . ."

The maintenance crew at the Collège de France looked up from their lunches, astonished when we drove into the courtyard.

"Why are you driving your vehicle in here?" demanded a gray-haired man in overalls.

"Where else would we outfit it for the expedition?" Stephen retorted.

"What expedition?" the man asked as the rest of the crew stared.

"What expedition?" I asked silently.

Then in the same ringing tone used to call out metro station names, Stephen announced, *"L'expédition à l'Afrique du Nord!"*

The man looked skeptical and the other men laughed.

But Stephen began relating the details of our *"expédition scientifique,"* how we need to collect flowers in Morocco and how outfitting the van for this botanical study was part of the project. Stephen blended gobbledygook with what the New Yorkers had told us about Morocco.

The man threw his cigarette butt on the ground. "I'm sorry but my men cannot help. Union rules absolutely prevent involvement."

"Monsieur!" Stephen cried, "we wouldn't dream of troubling you. We only need to use the electricity here—and some power tools."

The man paused, looking hard at Stephen and me. And in that pause I dared hope he'd play accomplice to honeymooners.

Finally, in a voice low and sly, like beer trickling out of a jug, the man said, "Well then, it's not impossible . . . is it?"

For the next three weeks we spent our mornings in construction. Basil drew a blueprint copying the classic VW camper interior. The crew chatted with us every day and cheered us on. They not only supplied power tools, but gave us steel rods and rollers from the lab to make the couch scoot into a bed. They also told us where to find scraps and army surplus items. While Stephen and Basil built the cabinetry, I bought the supplies and sewed curtains.

Then, each afternoon, when Basil went off to his French class at the Alliance Française, Stephen and I fell in love all over again. With each other and with Paris.

We strolled the Left Bank bookstores, plunging headfirst into

musty books, anticipating delight in finding just the right one—
for each other. We read Baudelaire at twilight in the spooky ruins
of l'Arène de Lutèce, a Roman amphitheater off Rue Monge. We
sipped tea in tulip-shaped glasses in the garden of the Paris mosque,
and every other day crossed the bridge to the Ile St. Louis to bathe
at the municipal baths. In our private washroom, as we splashed
each other with warm water from the copper pail, we were sere-
naded by the soulful tunes of the Muslim men who sang in their
showers. "Mustafaaaa, Mustafaaaaaaaa!" they wailed. Their mel-
lifluous voices washed us in music. Then, damp-haired, we'd stroll
at dusk along the riverbank, our sandals clapping on the cobble-
stones while above us, softly and silently, chestnut leaves fluttered,
like the wings of giant butterflies.

The day our van was finished was also the day Basil ran off to
Toulouse with his French teacher, Jacqueline. It was also the day
before Pompidou was to return and the day the gendarmes told us
to go. "We have to leave all this beauty!" I cried. To cheer me,
Stephen said we'd have a farewell feast in a restaurant. That evening
we climbed up the steep market street, Rue Mouffetard, but found
all the restaurants full. Ambling down an alley we came upon a
Chinese restaurant jammed with boisterous diners at tables no
bigger than record albums.

"Entrez! Entrez!" the diners shouted at us. We were lured
inside and before we understood what was happening, tables got
squeezed together and we were seated with two men plowing
through some inscrutable Chinese dish.

The two were as different as gruyère is from gruel. One was
tall and elegant with dark, wavy hair. An architect, dressed in a chic
suit. The other was short, fat and had a ruddy face. He appeared
to be some sort of factory worker, for he wore the blue working-
class jacket. In minutes we were drinking wine, enjoying mushy
chow mein and listening to the men bemoan how Paris was no fun
anymore as nowadays people were obsessed with making a living.

"What a pity we have forgotten the zany little ways of life!"

the architect wailed, and we all drank a toast to this loss, feeling giddy with joy.

As the evening wore on, I no longer cared that our intimate tête-à-tête had turned into a tête-à-tête-à-tête-à-tête. We drank a lot of wine and laughed like crazy. In fact, the whole restaurant was a boat of merrymakers on the brink of capsizing.

When the lugubrious waiter asked if we'd like dessert, and I declined, the architect appeared offended.

"Do you mean to say, Madame, that you won't even try La Banane du Chef? It is the specialty of the house!"

"I don't have room for it," I answered.

"No room! Nonsense! You will have the room when you taste it!"

"Very true," the ruddy-faced man said. "It tastes like nothing else in the world! Am I not right?" he asked the waiter. The waiter nodded as one might on identifying a body in a morgue.

"Why don't you try it, if it's that good?" Stephen urged, knowing my fondness for sweets.

"I'll have La Banane du Chef!" I said to the waiter.

As conversation and wine flowed, it occurred to me (through a little haze) that this dessert was taking quite a long time. I was about to question the waiter when the lights in the restaurant went out, plunging us into darkness and causing a collective scream from the patrons. Then the kitchen door was flung open and our waiter walked through the black restaurant holding high a tray with a flaming dessert. Somberly, he made his way to our table, guided by the blue-yellow light of the flames. He set the plate in front of me and announced gravely, "Madame, La Banane du Chef!" To my amazement, these words brought a hand-clapping and foot-stomping from the other diners. I looked down.

Banana fritters formed in the shape of a male's private parts.

Every eye in the place was on me, waiting for me to take a bite, but I was giggling so much, I couldn't. At last, when I did take that first bite, loud cries of "Ooh-la-la!" went up and the lights came on. All four of us shared the dessert, which was delicious. After dinner, Stephen took my hand and led me up Rue Mouffetard. Up and up we wound our way along the medieval street. The night was bright with moonlight, which gave the ancient gray houses the look of tarnished silver. We stopped and kissed, our bodies like clasped hands.

"Where are we going?" I whispered.

"You'll see."

For some time, we threaded up and around some side streets until suddenly Paris was spread before us. How beautiful it looked! Exactly like my idea of Paris. Like everyone else's idea of Paris. Vibrant and askew. The gold-lit Eiffel Tower tilted jauntily, and for a beret, wore the moon. The bateaux-mouches were now spaceships floating on a black iridescent ribbon, while at the Place de la Concorde, the obelisk was a rocket taking off. And far at the city's cusp sailed Sacré Coeur—a white ship guided by stars. Yes, that night, it seemed Paris, in sympathy with us, twinkled and trembled, and leaned too in fervent anticipation. An excited city listing toward love. . . .

So if in the day, I recount some delightful French meal, shopping discovery, historical site or museum exhibit, you'll understand if I say that at night, a more passionate nostalgia beckons. At night, when I lie in my husband's arms, I need only whisper "Gucci Hootchie-Kootchie" or *"L'expédition scientifique"* or, if feeling particularly naughty, "La Banane du Chef," to lure us into the realm of memory. Lure us back to that long-ago couple, fearless and fanciful. Back to the quivering nights of a time-distant Paris when the air was dusty with miracles and the stars were hung lower. Closer to our hearts.

Irwin Shaw
(1913–1984)

IRWIN SHAW wrote novels, short fiction, plays, and screenplays including *The Young Lions, Rich Man, Poor Man,* and *Sailor Off the Bremen
and Other Stories*. He contributed frequently to magazines such as *The
New Yorker* and *Esquire*. He also wrote scripts for the popular 1930s
radio shows, "Dick Tracy" and "Andy Gump." Although his novels were
commercially successful and often made into film or television dramas,
critics disdained his books after *The Young Lions*. Today, his critical reputation lies mainly in that novel and in his short stories for which he
received two O. Henry Awards. In the midst of McCarthyism, Shaw
published *The Troubled Air,* which explored the moral complexities surrounding McCarthy's sweeping hunt for Communists. Shortly after its
publication, Shaw moved to Europe and never really returned, although
the stories and the people he continued to write about never stopped
being about Americans.

He never succumbed to what the critics thought or said, but instead,
always kept his readers in mind when he wrote. In a similarly contrarian
manner, he wrote about Paris—not the cliché springtime romance of
Paris, but the harsh, gray, cold, wet Paris that others disavow. In the piece
excerpted here, Shaw laments, "Paris in the winter is for connoisseurs of
melancholy. . . ." Shaw, a true lover of Paris, loved Paris even in winter.

❖ Paris in Winter ❖

from Paris! Paris!

People are always writing about cities to be happy in. Let me be contrary for a moment. Let me write for those who are unhappy and are looking for a city to be unhappy in. Let me write about Paris in the winter.

Paris in the winter is for connoisseurs of melancholy—lovers soon to be parted, merchants on the edge of bankruptcy, poets caught between rhymes and remittance men caught between checks, horse owners whose steeds have just come in last, playwrights who have just had a failure, women whose husbands have left them for younger, prettier, smarter, richer, and all-round *better* girls; Paris in the winter is for deposed kings, discovered spies, leaders of peace movements; for people who owe money to the government—any government; for the editors of little magazines who don't dare go to their office because the printer is waiting there with the bill; for children who don't dare to go home because they have just been given their report cards; Paris in the winter is for brave men who have fought in the wars of this century and who have just read the morning newspaper; for tipplers struggling with the drink; for pregnant unwed girls; for the gentlemen friends of pregnant unwed girls; for movie stars on the way down and movie stars on the way up; for people who get their names in the papers too often and for people who don't get them in often enough; for widows whose husbands have left most of the estate to charity, for disinherited sons, for gamblers who have used up their luck.

Weeks on end the sun is only a pale rumor beyond the slowly moving clouds, and the soft gray sky above the rooftops seems to be about to break into a low, musical sobbing, ready to commiserate with criminals in flight from the police, with middleweights who have been knocked out in the first round. On December afternoons the city extends its stone sympathy to grounded pilots, to sufferers from jealousy, either well- or ill-founded, to newspapermen who have been switched to the night shift, to policemen with sore feet and sopranos with a cough and airplane salesmen who have not sold a jet fighter to Germany in two years. Antique dealers stuck with Louis Quinze commodes that were manufactured at the time of Léon Blum find a reciprocal sorrow in the drizzling streets, and the art collector who has just realized his prize Renoir is a fake discovers the climate of the Seine basin was made for his mood.

Here and there an Englishman can be found happy on brandy in a crowded restaurant, but after London in the wintertime, it is difficult to be unhappy anywhere. And to balance the unchilled Anglo-Saxon there will be the Greek waiter looking out through the misted restaurant window, haunted by the memory of Aegean sunlight, and a native of Mississippi writing his first novel, his imagination inflamed but his blood thinned by his heritage, hunched before a derisively tepid radiator in a hotel off the Place de l'Odéon that should have been condemned at the time of General Boulanger.

Paris in the winter is made to be a background for small disasters and piercing personal disappointments, for the hostess who is called to the telephone at eight-fifteen at night to be told that the dinner for forty people that she is giving that evening will have to do without the guest of honor because he has the grippe or has been arrested. It is the season and the place for mothers whose marriageable daughters have been staying out all night for six months with counts who turn out to have descended from a family of plumbers in Sicily; for American emissaries who come to France with the idea of persuading President de Gaulle to do something he doesn't want to do, or to do anything at all; for representatives of American firms who arrive in Paris for the first time believing everything they have been told back in Chicago about French women; for American women who arrive in Paris for the first time believing everything they have been told back in St. Louis about French men; for tennis players who have just turned pro and believe they can beat Gonzales when they get him on the courts of the Stade Coubertin; for retired generals who have just read what other retired generals have written about them in their memoirs.

Paris in the wintertime is the city of misogynists, misanthropes, and pessimists, for students of history who believe that the whole thing is all one long downhill ride; for all lovers of the human race who are ready to shake their heads at man's ingratitude, to deplore the world's slack forgetfulness, and to weigh the vanity of mortal achievements. Paris is a city studded with monuments, and its streets are named in honor of departed great men, but who knows what General Rochambeau did at the battle of Yorktown that entitles him to wear a bronze sword in front of the Fiat Garage on the Rue de Chaillot; who hums a tune of Ambroise Thomas's as he tries to find a place to park on the street that bears the composer's name; who looks up into the damp sky and sees noble wings and hears the throb of brave primitive engines when he ducks into an espresso bar out of the rain on the Rue Jean Mermoz? Who is cured of anything today on the Rue Dr. V. Hutinel? Does anyone recite *"Sur le printemps de ma jeunesse folle, je ressemblais à l'hirondelle qui vole, puis ça, puis là . . ."* as he gets his hair cut on the Rue Clément Marot? Where are the descendants of Pierre Premier de Serbie? Where is Serbia? Who, going into the Museum of Modern Art on the Avenue du Président Wilson, can honestly say he has lived up to the President's Fourteen Points? These are the January thoughts of Paris.

Paris is constantly being compared to a beautiful woman, and if the comparison is just, in the wintertime Paris is a beautiful woman who has come back two weeks before from a holiday in the sun and who has lost her tan and is now in that unhealthy yellow state that makes the aftermath of vacations look like the onset of jaundice. If Paris is beautiful and feminine in the spring and summer, when the city's two hundred and ninety-five thousand trees put out their leaves, it is the beauty of a fine-boned old lady, with a bright green scarf cunningly thrown around her, making you forget the wrinkles. Winter lays the bones of the city bare, and the old lady shows her age.

[. . .]

In Paris in the winter you notice that there are fewer children on the streets and more ambulances, fewer women and more men, and always too many pigeons, being fed yesterday's bread by insane, antisocial old ladies who give no thought of the damage their feathered clients inflict on the statues of the capital or the millions of hours of sleep they cost the inhabitants of the city with their maddening early-morning cooing and gurgling and throbbing and burbling. If ever a city could use a race of mute and continent birds, it is Paris, and you are led to wonder, if trees and men die in breathing the air of the city, and if there is something in the atmosphere that keeps the human birth rate down, why it is that pigeons can thrive so noisily and propagate with such abandon?

Buildings collapse more frequently in Paris in the winter, jet planes fly lower, the helicopters churning the air above you on their way to and from Brussels and the motorbikes on the avenues flay your nerves with their inescapable mechanical coughing. At the *thés dansants* in the big halls, more of the couples turning gracelessly to the music are composed of girls who are waiting to be victimized by men and who you know will never be satisfied even in this modest ambition. In the evenings, in the restaurants, you are confronted everywhere with the picture of drab marital fidelity, long-married couples eating with their unsanitary dogs on the banquette between them, occasionally addressing a word to the beast and almost never to each other. What Parisians call *les vrais couples d'août* are hard to find. The true couples of August are usually composed of a man whose wife is at the seashore with the children and a pretty girl who is probably in Paris in August because she is modeling the autumn collections. The difference between ordinary winter couples and *les vrais couples d'août* is that the latter help bring a room alive because they have sought each other out, they are dining with each other voluntarily, they take pleasure in each other's company, and they have a great deal to say to each other.

You think of all the literary prizes that are bestowed in Paris, on the average of one a day, which makes about ninety a winter, and instead of sharing the satisfaction of merit rewarded felt by the winners, you ache with the heartburn of the ten thousand writers in the city who have won no prize that season and whose books are in the window of no bookstore that afternoon.

You wince at the cruelty of the city and remember the sentence spoken the night before about a lovely woman of thirty whose face used to be on the cover of all the magazines and who now cannot get a job posing for even the least ambitious of editors—"She's finished," the light voice said gaily, "she overdid it. You know how it is in this town. If they know your name they won't look at you."

In the winter you even feel sorry for news photographers, huddled, blowing on their frozen fingers, in their mass vigils outside the doors of the great hotels from which movie stars or visiting dignitaries may or may not emerge in time for the last edition. Later, when the newsmen are ordered to the Left Bank to cover a student riot, you are even sorrier for them as the police beat them over the head with clubs and break their expensive cameras, since policemen everywhere consider themselves kindly family men and are averse to having easily identified photographs published of themselves whacking young women across the back of the neck with lead-weighted capes.

Extend your sympathy to the owners of famous old restaurants, where nobody ever ate lunch in less than three hours, and who are now bowing to the times and transforming their dining rooms into snack bars. Stand at the sides of these defeated old apostles of joy as they watch their wine cellars being auctioned off, as the Burgundy goes in gross lots, as the names of the great châteaux of the Gironde are called out, as the precious cases are carted away because it is improbable that anyone in the new chromium and plastic café will ever order a La Tâche 1929 with his ham sandwich or a Montrachet with his hamburger.

[. . .]

Winter, like unhappiness, is more biting in Paris than elsewhere. The gayest of cities, it has the farthest to fall in its descent to sorrow. The wittiest of cities, the more noticeable it is there when the joke is flat. The most hospitable of cities, it is the loneliest when the doors are shut. The most openly loving of cities, it is the coldest when the lovers are driven indoors. Here it is impossible to overlook the unheroic fact that not enough people kiss in the rain or at five degrees below zero.

All this is true. And then—

And then the sun comes out.

For two hours, around noon, winter is gone, nobody has ever heard of it. Everybody, somehow, is out and seated at a café table in the open air at chairs and tables that somehow have blossomed there. It is the middle of February, but an amateur botanist can *feel*, in his own blood, the beginning of buds on the trees. Somehow a whole new abundant crop of children between the ages of two and six seems to have been produced overnight, and they are on their way, charmingly dressed and accompanied by the most glorious of young mothers, to the park. Men can be seen hurrying from their offices with tennis rackets in their hands. A sail appears on the Seine. A boy with a beard kisses a girl in blue jeans on a bridge. There is a restaurant that miraculously has a plate of fresh asparagus on the table in the middle of the room. Next to you somebody says he saw the greatest movie of his life the night before and that it was made by a friend of his who is only twenty years old and who borrowed the money to make it from his girlfriend's father. On the other side of you somebody says he is going to Greece for the summer. The boy from Mississippi tells you he has just sold his first short story, and the hat-check girl says she is going to be married in June. The American who is your good friend and who has been paying alimony for seven years calls to tell you that he has just heard that his ex-wife was married the day before in Las Vegas and you must save the afternoon, the evening, and the night to celebrate with him. A jockey you know whispers about a fantastic workout of a two-year-old that morning at Chantilly and you carefully note the date of the two-year-old's next race. The girls parading before your table shake off their scarves and their hair glitters in the sunshine.

Somebody buys a drink for a young man with a mustache because he has just finished his military service and has been promised a job with Air France. Somebody else claps another man on the back because he has just beaten the Austrians in the downhill and the giant slalom and you are pleased to see the young man orders milk instead of Pernod. It turns out that the girl with glasses near the entrance, with her eyes closed and her head tilted back, taking the sun, has just completed the definitive work on Bergson and that she has terrified her professors with her erudition. You overhear someone saying a good word about Americans and you read that President de Gaulle is going to speak that evening, and you are reminded that there is one giant, courageous as Ajax and cunning and merciless as Ulysses, left over from the old great age and that he lives in the heart of Paris.

While the sun shines, you think like a Parisian and know why it is so difficult to get him to live anywhere else. He is at the center of the world here. While London is gray because it is uncertain about whether it can live up to its past and Washington is frantic because it is uncertain about whether it can live up to its future, Paris is glittering because it is triumphantly certain, despite all the overt evidence to the contrary, that it is living up to its present. No success really counts, a Parisian thinks in his secret heart, unless it happens in his city, and no failure is really mortal until it has been ratified here. This concept is the height of egotism and demonstrably untrue, and Parisians live happily by it. No joke is funny if it doesn't make Paris laugh, no woman beautiful if she doesn't make Paris send flowers, no dress worth wearing if Paris hasn't sewn it or had it copied, no play a masterpiece if it hasn't pleased a Paris audience, no man a lady-killer if he hasn't broken Paris hearts, no reputation secure unless the hero's name is known by every Paris concierge.

While the sun shines, you go along with the cliché-makers: Paris *is* a beautiful woman, but so surpassingly so, so vital and self-renewing, that nothing—not the passage of years, not drink or drugs, not bad investments or unworthy loves, not neglect or debauchery—can ruin her.

Not while the sun shines. . . .

Saul Bellow
(1915–   )

THOUGH often associated with Chicago, the beloved city in many of his stories, Saul (born Solomon) Bellow was born in Quebec, Canada. His family didn't move to Chicago until he was nine. He attended the University of Chicago and received a B.S. in sociology and anthropology from Northwestern University. Although he enrolled in graduate studies, he never finished because, as he once wrote, "every time I worked on my thesis, it turned out to be a story." Bellow first went to Paris on a Guggenheim Fellowship in 1948. By then he had already published two novels. He would go on to publish many more novels, short stories, literary criticism, memoirs, and plays including *The Adventures of Augie March* (National Book Award), *Herzog* (National Book Award), *Mr. Sammler's Planet* (National Book Award), *Humboldt's Gift* (Pulitzer Prize), *To Jerusalem and Back: A Personal Account, Him with His Foot in His Mouth, and Other Stories,* and *Ravelstein.* He received the Nobel Prize for Literature in 1976.

In the essay reprinted here from *It All Adds Up,* Bellow contemplates the changes in Paris since years past. The one thing that hasn't changed: for him, Paris is still "the heavenly city of secularists," able to seduce even God.

⚜ My Paris ⚜
(1983)

from It All Adds Up

Changes in Paris? Like all European capitals, the city has under-
gone changes. The most unpleasantly conspicuous are the herds
of tall buildings beyond the ancient gates. Old districts like Passy,
peculiarly gripping in their dinginess, are almost unrecognizable
today with their new apartment houses and office buildings, most
of which would suit a Mediterranean port better than Paris. It's
no easy thing to impose color on the dogged northern gray, the
native Parisian *grisaille*—flinty, foggy,. dripping, and, for most of
the year, devoid of any brightness. The gloom will have its way
with these new *immeubles* too; you may be sure of that. When Ver-
laine wrote that the rain fell into his heart as it did upon the city
(referring to almost any city in the region), he wasn't exaggerating
a bit. As a onetime resident of Paris (I arrived in 1948), I can testify to that. New urban architecture will find itself ultimately pow-
erless against the *grisaille*. Parisian gloom is not simply climatic; it is
a spiritual force that acts not only on building materials, on walls
and rooftops, but also on character, opinion, and judgment. It is a
powerful astringent.

But the changes . . . I wandered about Paris not very long ago
to see how thirty-odd years had altered the place. The new sky-
scraper on the boulevard du Montparnasse is almost an accident,
something that had strayed away from Chicago and come to rest
on a Parisian street corner. In my old haunts between the boulevard du Montparnasse and the Seine, what is most immediately
noticeable is the disappearance of certain cheap conveniences.
High rents have driven out the family bistros that once served
delicious, inexpensive lunches. A certain decrepit loveliness is giv-

ing way to unattractive, overpriced, overdecorated newness. Dense traffic—the small streets make you think of Yeats's "mackerel-crowded seas"—requires an alertness incompatible with absent-minded rambling. Dusty old shops in which you might lose yourself for a few hours are scrubbed up now and sell pocket computers and high-fidelity equipment. Stationers who once carried notebooks with excellent paper now offer a flimsy product that lets the ink through. Very disappointing. Cabinetmakers and other small artisans once common are hard to find.

My neighbor the *emballeur* on the rue de Verneuil disappeared long ago. This cheerful specialist wore a smock and beret, and as he worked in an unheated shop his big face was stung raw. He kept a cold butt end in the corner of his mouth—one seldom sees a *mégot* in this new era of prosperity. A pet three-legged hare, slender in profile, fat in the hindquarters, stirred lopsidedly among the crates. But there is no more demand for hand-hammered crates. Progress has eliminated all such simple trades. It has replaced them with boutiques that sell costume jewelry, embroidered linens, or goose-down bedding. In each block there are three or four *antiquaires*. Who would have thought that Europe contained so much old junk? Or that, the servant class having disappeared, hearts nostalgic for the bourgeois epoch would hunt so eagerly for Empire breakfronts, recamier sofas, and curule chairs?

Inspecting the boulevards, I find curious survivors. On the boulevard Saint-Germain, the dealer in books of military history and memorabilia who was there thirty-five years ago is still going strong. Evidently there is a permanent market for leather sets that chronicle the ancient wars. (If you haven't seen the crowds at the Invalides and the huge, gleaming tomb of Napoleon, if you underestimate the power of glory, you don't know what France is.) Near the rue des Saints-Pères, the pastry shop of Camille Hallu, Aîné, is gone, together with numerous small bookshops, but the dealer in esoteric literature on the next block has kept up with the military history man down the street, as has the umbrella merchant nearby. Her stock is richer than ever, sheaves of umbrellas and canes with parakeet heads and barking dogs in silver. Thanks to tourists, the small hotels thrive—as do the electric Parisian cockroaches who live in them, a swifter and darker breed than their American cousins. There are more winos than in austere postwar days, when you seldom saw *clochards* drinking in doorways.

The ancient gray and yellow walls of Paris have the strength needed to ride out the shock waves of the present century. Invisible electronic forces pierce them, but the substantial gloom of courtyards and kitchens is preserved. Boulevard shop windows, however, show that life is different and that Parisians feel needs they never felt before. In 1949, I struck a deal with my landlady on the rue Vaneau: I installed a gas hot-water heater in the kitchen in exchange for two months' rent. It gave her great joy to play with the faucet and set off a burst of gorgeous flames. Neighbors came in to congratulate her. Paris was then in what Mumford called the Paleotechnic Age. It has caught up now with advancing technology, and French shops display the latest in beautiful kitchens— counters and tables of glowing synthetic alabaster, artistic in form, the last word in technics.

Once every week during the nasty winter of 1950, I used to meet my friend the painter Jesse Reichek in a café on the rue du Bac. As we drank cocoa and played casino, regressing shamelessly to childhood, he would lecture me on Giedion's *Mechanization Takes Command* and on the Bauhaus. Shuffling the cards, I felt that I was simultaneously going backward and forward. We little thought in 1950 that by 1983 so many modern kitchen shops would be open for business in Paris, that the curmudgeonly French would fall in love so passionately with sinks, refrigerators, and microwave ovens. I suppose that the disappearance of the *bonne à tout faire* is behind this transformation. The post-bourgeois era began when your housemaid found better work to do. Hence all these *son et lumière* kitchens and the velvety pulsations of invisible ventilators.

I suppose that this is what "modern" means in Paris now.

It meant something different at the beginning of the century, and it was this other something that so many of us came looking for in 1948. Until 1939, Paris was the center of a great international culture, welcoming Spaniards, Russians, Italians, Romanians, Americans; open to the Picassos, Diaghilevs, Modiglianis, Brancusis, and Pounds at the glowing core of the modernist art movement. It remained to be seen whether the fall of Paris in 1940 had only interrupted this creativity. Would it resume when the defeated Nazis had gone back to Germany? There were those who suspected that the thriving international center had been declining during the thirties, and some believed that it was gone for good.

I was among those who came to investigate, part of the first wave. The blasts of war had no sooner ended than thousands of Americans packed their bags to go abroad. Eager Francophile travelers, poets, painters, and philosophers were vastly outnumbered by the restless young—students of art history, cathedral lovers, refugees from the South and the Midwest, ex-soldiers on the GI Bill, sentimental pilgrims—as well as by people no less imaginative, with schemes for getting rich. A young man I had known in Minnesota came over to open a caramel-corn factory in Florence. Adventurers, black-marketeers, smugglers, would-be *bon vivants*, bargain-hunters, bubbleheads—tens of thousands crossed on old troop ships, seeking business opportunities or sexual opportunities, or just for the hell of it. Damaged London was severely depressed, full of bomb holes and fireweed, whereas Paris was unhurt and about to resume its glorious artistic and intellectual life.

The Guggenheim Foundation had given me a fellowship, and I was prepared to take part in the great revival—when and if it

began. Like the rest of the American contingent, I had brought
my illusions with me, but I like to think that I was also skeptical
(perhaps the most tenacious of my illusions). I was not going to
sit at the feet of Gertrude Stein. I had no notions about the Ritz
Bar. I would not be boxing with Ezra Pound, as Hemingway had
done, or writing in bistros while waiters brought oysters and wine.
Hemingway the writer I admired without limits; Hemingway the
figure was to my mind the quintessential tourist, the one who
believed that he alone was the American whom Europeans took
to their hearts as one of their own. In simple truth, the Jazz Age
Paris of American legend had no charms for me, and I had my
reservations also about the Paris of Henry James—bear in mind
the unnatural squawking of East Side Jews as James described it in
The American Scene. You wouldn't expect a relative of those bar-
barous East Siders to be drawn to the world of Madame de Vion-
net, which had, in any case, vanished long ago.

Life, said Samuel Butler, is like giving a concert on the violin
while learning to play the instrument—that, friends, is real wisdom. (I never tire of quoting it.) I was concertizing and practicing
scales at the same time. I *thought* I understood why I had come to
Paris. Writers like Sherwood Anderson and, oddly enough, John
Cowper Powys had made clear to me what was lacking in American life. "American men are tragic without knowing why they are
tragic," wrote Powys in his *Autobiography.* "They are tragic by reason of the desolate thinness and forlorn narrowness of their sen-
sual mystical contacts. Mysticism and Sensuality are the things that
most of all redeem life." Powys, mind you, was an admirer of
American democracy. I would have had no use for him otherwise.
I believed that only the English-speaking democracies had real
politics. In politics continental Europe was infantile—horrifying.
But what America lacked, for all its political stability, was the
capacity to enjoy intellectual pleasures as though they were sen-
sual pleasures. This was what Europe offered, or was said to offer.

There was, however, a part of me that remained unconvinced

by this formulation, denied that Europe—as advertised—still existed and was still capable of gratifying the American longing for the rich and the rare. True writers from Saint Paul, Saint Louis, and Oak Park, Illinois, had gone to Europe to write their American books, the best work of the twenties. Corporate, industrial America could not give them what they needed. In Paris, they were free to be fully American. It was from abroad that they sent imaginative rays homeward. But was it the European imaginative reason that had released and stirred them? Was it Modern Paris itself or a new universal Modernity working in all countries, an international culture, of which Paris was, or *had* been, the center. I knew what Powys meant by his imaginative redemption from the desolate thinness and forlorn narrowness experienced by Americans, whether or not they were conscious of it. At least I thought I did. But I was aware also of a seldom-mentioned force visible in Europe itself to anyone who had eyes—the force of a nihilism that had destroyed most of its cities and millions of lives in a war of six long years. I could not easily accept the plausible sets: America, the thinning of the life impulses; Europe, the cultivation of the subtler senses still valued, still going on. Indeed, a great European prewar literature had told us what nihilism was, had warned us what to expect. Céline had spelled it out quite plainly in his *Voyage to the End of the Night*. His Paris was still there, more *there* than Sainte-Chapelle or the Louvre. Proletarian Paris, middle-class Paris, not to mention intellectual Paris, which was trying to fill nihilistic emptiness with Marxist doctrine—all transmitted the same message.

Still, I had perfectly legitimate reasons for being here. Arthur Koestler ribbed me one day when he met me in the street with my five-year-old son. He said, "Ah? You're married? Is this your *child?* And you've come to *Paris?*" To be Modern, you see, meant to be detached from tradition and traditional sentiments, from national politics and, of course, from the family. But it was not in order to be Modern that I was living on the rue de Verneuil. My aim was to be free from measures devised and applied by others. I could not agree, to begin with, on any definition. I would be ready for definition when I was ready for an obituary. I had already decided not to let American business society make my life for me, and it was easy for me to shrug off Mr. Koestler's joke. Besides, Paris was not my dwelling place; it was only a stopover. There was no dwelling place.

One of my American friends, a confirmed Francophile, made speeches to me about the City of Man, the City of Light. I took his rhetoric at a considerable discount. I was not, however, devoid of sentiment. To say it in French, I was *aux anges* in Paris, wandering about, sitting in cafés, walking beside the liniment-green, rot-smelling Seine. I can think of visitors who were not greatly impressed by the City of Man. Horace Walpole complained of the stink of its little streets in the eighteenth century. For Rousseau, it was the center of *amour propre*, the most warping of civilized vices. Dostoyevsky loathed it because it was the capital of Western bourgeois vainglory. Americans, however, loved the place. I, too, with characteristic reservations, fell for it. True, I spent lots of time in Paris thinking about Chicago, but I discovered—and the discovery was a very odd one—that in Chicago I had for many years been absorbed in thoughts of Paris. I was a longtime reader of Balzac and of Zola and knew the city of Père Goriot, the Paris at which Rastignac had shaken his fist, swearing to fight it to the finish, the Paris of Zola's drunkards and prostitutes, of Baudelaire's beggars and the children of the poor whose pets were sewer rats. The Parisian pages of Rilke's *The Notebooks of Malte Laurids Brigge* had taken hold of my imagination in the thirties, as had the Paris of Proust, especially those dense, gorgeous, and painful passages of *Time Regained* describing the city as it was in 1915—the German night bombardments, Madame Verdurin reading of battlefields in the morning papers as she sipped her coffee. Curious how the place had moved in on me. I was not at all a Francophile, not at all the unfinished American prepared to submit myself to the great city in the hope that it would round me out or complete me.

In my generation, the children of immigrants *became* Americans. An effort was required. One made oneself, freestyle. To become a Frenchman on top of that would have required a second effort. Was I being invited to turn myself into a Frenchman? Well, no, but it seemed to me that I would not be fully accepted in France unless I had done everything possible to become French. And that was not for me. I was already an American, and I was also a Jew. I had an American outlook, superadded to a Jewish consciousness. France would have to take me as I was.

From Parisian Jews I learned what life had been like under the Nazis, about the roundups and deportations in which French officials had cooperated. I read Céline's *Les Beaux Draps*, a collection of crazy, murderous harangues, seething with Jew-hatred.

A sullen, grumbling, drizzling city still remembered the humiliations of occupation. Dark bread, *pain de seigle*, was rationed. Coal was scarce. None of this inspired American-in-Paris fantasies of gaiety and good times in the Ritz Bar or the Closerie des Lilas. More appropriate now was Baudelaire's Parisian sky weighing the city down like a heavy pot lid, or the Paris of the Communard *pétroleurs* who had set the Tuileries afire and blown out the fortress walls. I saw a barricade going up across the Champs Élysées one morning, but there was no fighting. The violence of the embittered French was for the most part internal.

No, I wasn't devoid of sentiments, but the sentiments were sober. But why did Paris affect me so deeply? Why did this imperial, ceremonious, ornamental mass of structures weaken my American refusal to be impressed, my Jewish skepticism and reticence; why was I such a sucker for its tones of gray, the patchy bark of its sycamores, and its bitter-medicine river under the ancient bridges? The place was, naturally, indifferent to me, a peculiar alien from Chicago. Why did it take hold of my emotions?

For the soul of a civilized, or even partly civilized, man, Paris was one of the permanent settings, a theater, if you like, where the greatest problems of existence might be represented. What future, if any, was there for this theater? It could not tell you what to represent. Could anyone in the twentieth century make use of these unusual opportunities? Americans of my generation crossed the Atlantic to size up the challenge, to look upon this human, warm, noble, beautiful, and also proud, morbid, cynical, and treacherous setting.

Paris inspires young Americans with no such longings and challenges now. The present generations of students, if it reads Diderot, Stendhal, Balzac, Baudelaire, Rimbaud, Proust, does not bring to its reading the desires born of a conviction that American life impulses are thin. We do not look beyond America. It absorbs us completely. No one is stirred to the bowels by Europe of the ancient parapets. A huge force has lost its power over the imagination. This force began to weaken in the fifties, and by the sixties it was entirely gone.

Young M.B.A.'s, management school graduates, gene-splicers, and computerists, their careers well started, will fly to Paris with their wives to shop on the rue de Rivoli and dine at the Tour d'Argent. Not greatly different are the behavioral scientists and members of the learned professions who are well satisfied with what they learned of the Old World while they were getting their B.A.'s. A bit of Marx, of Freud, of Max Weber, an incorrect recollection of André Gide and his gratuitous act, and they had had as much of Europe as any educated American needed.

And I suppose that we *can* do without the drama of Old Europe. Europeans themselves, in considerable numbers, got tired of it some decades ago and turned from art to politics or abstract intellectual games. Foreigners no longer came to Paris to enrich their humanity with modern forms of the marvelous. There was nothing marvelous about the Marxism of Sartre and his followers. Postwar French philosophy, adapted from the German, was less than enchanting. Paris, which had been a center, still *looked* like a center and could not bring itself to concede that it was a center no longer. Stubborn de Gaulle, assisted by Malraux, issued his fiats to a world that badly wanted to agree with him, but when the old man died there was nothing left—nothing but old monuments, old graces. Marxism, Eurocommunism, Existentialism, Structuralism, Deconstructionism, could not restore the potency of French civilization. Sorry about that. A great change, a great loss of ground. The Giacomettis and the Stravinskys, the Brancusis, no longer come. No international art center draws the young to Paris. Arriving instead are terrorists. For them French revolutionary traditions degenerated into confused leftism, and a government that courts the third world made Paris a first-class place to plant bombs and to hold press conferences.

The world's disorders are bound to leave their mark on Paris. Cynosures bruise easily. And why has Paris for centuries now attracted so much notice? Quite simply, because it is the heavenly city of secularists. *"Wie Gott in Frankreich"* was the expression used by the Jews of Eastern Europe to describe perfect happiness. I puzzled over this simile for many years, and I think I can interpret it now. God would be perfectly happy in France because he would not be troubled by prayers, observances, blessings, and demands for the interpretation of difficult dietary questions. Surrounded by unbelievers, He, too, could relax toward evening, just as thousands of Parisians do at their favorite cafés. There are few things more pleasant, more civilized, than a tranquil *terrasse* at dusk.

Food

(How to Eat Like a Parisian)

❦

Ernest Hemingway
(1899–1961)

IN his memoir about Paris, *A Moveable Feast,* Ernest Hemingway wrote, "I decided that I would write one story about each thing that I knew about. I was trying to do this all the time I was writing, and it was good and severe discipline." He wrote about another kind of discipline in the essay reprinted here, "Hunger Was Good Discipline." Hemingway moved to Paris in 1921 with his first wife, Hadley, and their son, John (Mr. Bumby in *A Moveable Feast*). After the First World War, it was cheaper for many Americans to live in Paris than in the United States. The convergence of so many writers, artists, poets, musicians, and bohemians from all over the world made Paris fertile ground for literary and artistic activity in the 1920s.

Hemingway received the Pulitzer Prize in 1953 for *The Old Man and the Sea* and the Nobel Prize for Literature the following year. He began his Paris memoirs in 1957 in Cuba, more than thirty years since his time in Paris. He worked on *A Moveable Feast* for the next three years, dividing his time between Cuba and Ketchum, Idaho. In 1961, Hemingway, plagued by alcoholism, committed suicide in his home in Ketchum.

✢ Hunger Was Good Discipline ✢

from A Moveable Feast

You got very hungry when you did not eat enough in Paris because all the bakery shops had such good things in the windows and people ate outside at tables on the sidewalk so that you saw and smelled the food. When you had given up journalism and were writing nothing that anyone in America would buy, explaining at home that you were lunching out with someone, the best place to go was the Luxembourg gardens where you saw and smelled nothing to eat all the way from the Place de l'Observatoire to the rue de Vaugirard. There you could always go into the Luxembourg museum and all the paintings were sharpened and clearer and more beautiful if you were belly-empty, hollow-hungry. I learned to understand Cézanne much better and to see truly how he made landscapes when I was hungry. I used to wonder if he were hungry too when he painted; but I thought possibly it was only that he had forgotten to eat. It was one of those unsound but illuminating thoughts you have when you have been sleepless or hungry. Later I thought Cézanne was probably hungry in a different way.

After you came out of the Luxembourg you could walk down the narrow rue Férou to the Place St.-Sulpice and there were still no restaurants, only the quiet square with its benches and trees. There was a fountain with lions, and pigeons walked on the pavement and perched on the statues of the bishops. There was the church and there were shops selling religious objects and vestments on the north side of the square.

From this square you could not go further toward the river without passing shops selling fruits, vegetables, wines, or bakery and pastry shops. But by choosing your way carefully you could work to your right around the grey and white stone church and reach the rue de l'Odéon and turn up to your right toward Sylvia Beach's bookshop and on your way you did not pass too many places where things to eat were sold. The rue de l'Odéon was bare of eating places until you reached the square where there were three restaurants.

By the time you reached 12 rue de l'Odéon your hunger was contained but all of your perceptions were heightened again. The photographs looked different and you saw books that you had never seen before.

"You're too thin, Hemingway," Sylvia would say. "Are you eating enough?"

"Sure."

"What did you eat for lunch?"

My stomach would turn over and I would say, "I'm going home for lunch now."

"At three o'clock?"

"I didn't know it was that late."

"Adrienne said the other night she wanted to have you and Hadley for dinner. We'd ask Fargue. You like Fargue, don't you? Or Larbaud. You like him. I know you like him. Or anyone you really like. Will you speak to Hadley?"

"I know she'd love to come."

"I'll send her a *pneu*. Don't you work so hard now that you don't eat properly."

"I won't."

"Get home now before it's too late for lunch."

"They'll save it."

"Don't eat cold food either. Eat a good hot lunch."

"Did I have any mail?"

"I don't think so. But let me look."

She looked and found a note and looked up happily and then opened a closed door in her desk.

"This came while I was out," she said. It was a letter and it felt as though it had money in it. "Wedderkop," Sylvia said.

"It must be from *Der Querschnitt*. Did you see Wedderkop?"

"No. But he was here with George. He'll see you. Don't worry. Perhaps he wanted to pay you first."

"It's six hundred francs. He says there will be more."

"I'm awfully glad you reminded me to look. Dear Mr. Awfully Nice."

"It's damned funny that Germany is the only place I can sell anything. To him and the *Frankfurter Zeitung*."

"Isn't it? But don't you worry ever. You can sell stories to Ford," she teased me.

"Thirty francs a page. Say one story every three months in *the transatlantic*. Story five pages long make one hundred and fifty francs a quarter. Six hundred francs a year."

"But, Hemingway, don't worry about what they bring now. The point is that you can write them."

"I know. I can write them. But nobody will buy them. There is no money coming in since I quit journalism."

"They will sell. Look. You have the money for one right there."

"I'm sorry, Sylvia. Forgive me for speaking about it."

"Forgive you for what? Always talk about it or about anything. Don't you know all writers ever talk about is their troubles? But promise me you won't worry and that you'll eat enough."

"I promise."

"Then get home now and have lunch."

Outside on the rue de l'Odéon I was disgusted with myself for having complained about things. I was doing what I did of my own free will and I was doing it stupidly. I should have bought a large piece of bread and eaten it instead of skipping a meal. I could taste the brown lovely crust. But it is dry in your mouth without something to drink. You God damn complainer. You dirty phony saint and martyr, I said to myself. You quit journalism of your own accord. You have credit and Sylvia would have loaned you money. She has plenty of times. Sure. And then the next thing you would be compromising on something else. Hunger is healthy and the pictures do look better when you are hungry. Eating is wonderful too and do you know where you are going to eat right now?

Lipp's is where you are going to eat and drink too.

It was a quick walk to Lipp's and every place I passed that my stomach noticed as quickly as my eyes or my nose made the walk an added pleasure. There were few people in the *brasserie* and when I sat down on the bench against the wall with the mirror in back and a table in front and the waiter asked if I wanted beer I asked for a *distingué*, the big glass mug that held a liter, and for potato salad.

The beer was very cold and wonderful to drink. The *pommes à l'huile* were firm and marinated and the olive oil delicious. I ground black pepper over the potatoes and moistened the bread in the olive oil. After the first heavy draft of beer I drank and ate very slowly. When the *pommes à l'huile* were gone I ordered another serving and a *cervelas*. This was a sausage like a heavy, wide frankfurter split in two and covered with a special mustard sauce.

I mopped up all the oil and all of the sauce with bread and drank the beer slowly until it began to lose its coldness and then I finished it and ordered a *demi* and watched it drawn. It seemed colder than the *distingué* and I drank half of it.

I had not been worrying, I thought. I knew the stories were good and someone would publish them finally at home. When I stopped doing newspaper work I was sure the stories were going to be published. But every one I sent out came back. What had made me so confident was Edward O'Brien's taking the "My Old Man" story for the *Best Short Stories* book and then dedicating the book for that year to me. Then I laughed and drank some more beer. The story had never been published in a magazine and he had broken all his rules to take it for the book. I laughed again and the waiter glanced at me. It was funny because, after all that, he had spelled the name wrong. It was one of two stories I had left when everything I had written was stolen in Hadley's suitcase that time at the Gare de Lyon when she was bringing the manuscripts down to me to Lausanne as a surprise, so I could work on them on our holidays in the mountains. She had put in the originals, the typescripts and the carbons, all in manila folders. The only reason I had the one story was that Lincoln Steffens had sent it out to some editor who sent it back. It was in the mail while everything else was stolen. The other story that I had was the one called "Up in Michigan" written before Miss Stein had come to our flat. I had never had it copied because she said it was *inaccrochable*. It had been in a drawer somewhere.

So after we had left Lausanne and gone down to Italy I showed the racing story to O'Brien, a gentle, shy man, pale, with pale blue eyes, and straight lanky hair he cut himself, who lived then as a boarder in a monastery up above Rapallo. It was a bad time and I did not think I could write any more then, and I showed the story to him as a curiosity, as you might show, stupidly, the binnacle of a ship you had lost in some incredible way, or as you might pick up your booted foot and make some joke about it if it had been amputated after a crash. Then, when he read the story, I saw he was hurt far more than I was. I had never seen any-one hurt by a thing other than death or unbearable suffering except Hadley when she told me about the things being gone. She had cried and cried and could not tell me. I told her that no matter what the dreadful thing was that had happened nothing could be that bad, and whatever it was, it was all right and not to worry. We would work it out. Then, finally, she told me. I was sure she could not have brought the carbons too and I hired someone to cover for me on my newspaper job. I was making good money then at journalism, and took the train for Paris. It was true all right and I remember what I did in the night after I let myself into the flat and found it was true. That was over now and Chink had taught me never to discuss casualties; so I told O'Brien not to feel so bad. It was probably good for me to lose early work and I told him all that stuff you feed the troops. I was going to start writing stories again I said and, as I said it, only trying to lie so that he would not feel so bad, I knew that it was true.

Then I started to think in Lipp's about when I had first been able to write a story after losing everything. It was up in Cortina d'Ampezzo when I had come back to join Hadley there after the spring skiing which I had to interrupt to go on assignment to the Rhineland and the Ruhr. It was a very simple story called "Out of Season" and I had omitted the real end of it which was that the old man hanged himself. This was omitted on my new theory that you could omit anything if you knew that you omitted and the omitted part would strengthen the story and make people feel something more than they understood.

Well, I thought, now I have them so they do not understand them. There cannot be much doubt about that. There is most certainly no demand for them. But they will understand the same way that they always do in painting. It only takes time and it only needs confidence.

It is necessary to handle yourself better when you have to cut down on food so you will not get too much hunger-thinking. Hunger is good discipline and you learn from it. And as long as they do not understand it you are ahead of them. Oh sure, I thought, I'm so far ahead of them now that I can't afford to eat regularly. It would not be bad if they caught up a little.

I knew I must write a novel. But it seemed an impossible thing to do when I had been trying with great difficulty to write paragraphs that would be the distillation of what made a novel. It was necessary to write longer stories now as you would train for a longer race. When I had written a novel before, the one that had been lost in the bag stolen at the Gare de Lyon, I still had the lyric facility of boyhood that was as perishable and as deceptive as youth was. I knew it was probably a good thing that it was lost, but I knew too that I must write a novel. I would put it off though until I could not help doing it. I was damned if I would write one because it was what I should do if we were to eat regularly. When I had to write it, then it would be the only thing to do and there would be no choice. Let the pressure build. In the meantime I would write a long story about whatever I knew best.

By this time I had paid the check and gone out and turned to the right and crossed the rue de Rennes so that I would not go to

the Deux-Magots for coffee and was walking up the rue Bonaparte on the shortest way home.

What did I know best that I had not written about and lost?
What did I know about truly and care for the most? There was no
choice at all. There was only the choice of streets to take you back
fastest to where you worked. I went up Bonaparte to Guynemer,
then to the rue d'Assas, up the rue Notre-Dame-des-Champs to
the Closerie des Lilas.

I sat in a corner with the afternoon light coming in over my
shoulder and wrote in the notebook. The waiter brought me a *café
crème* and I drank half of it when it cooled and left it on the table
while I wrote. When I stopped writing I did not want to leave the
river where I could see the trout in the pool, its surface pushing
and swelling smooth against the resistance of the log-driven piles
of the bridge. The story was about coming back from the war but
there was no mention of the war in it.

But in the morning the river would be there and I must make
it and the country and all that would happen. There were days
ahead to be doing that each day. No other thing mattered. In my
pocket was the money from Germany so there was no problem.
When that was gone some other money would come in.

All I must do now was stay sound and good in my head until
morning when I would start to work again.

Patric Kuh
(1964–   )

PATRIC KUH immigrated to the United States in 1988, but he was already an American. Born in Madrid, Spain, of an Irish mother and an American father, how does one come to the conclusion that you're an American? For Patric Kuh, it was while working as a foreigner in a Michelin-starred Paris restaurant. Kuh is a Paris-trained chef who has worked in some of the most preeminent restaurants of France, New York, and California. His writing has appeared in numerous publications including *Salon.com, Gourmet, Esquire,* and *Food and Wine.* He wrote the "Burnt-Out Cook" column in *Salon.com* for several years. Currently, he is the restaurant critic for *Los Angeles Magazine.* He is the author of one novel, *An Available Man,* and lives in Los Angeles, California.

⚜ Boulevard des Italiens ⚜

from The Last Days *of* Haute Cuisine

I write about the entrance through the service door because for many years that was how I entered restaurants, as a cook. The last kitchen job I had in France, before coming to the America, was working at an all-night brasserie in Paris on the Boulevard des Italiens. They were so cheap in that restaurant that the first thing they taught me was how to apply butter to the sandwiches they sold at the counter with one movement and then to take it all off as you swept the knife back. My companion, who split the baguettes that

I would then go through the formalities of buttering, called it the "Auvergnat backhand." I didn't yet know the reputation of the natives of the Auvergne region for economy and thrift and I asked him why. "The Auvergnat," he explained, "are our French Jews." I let that one slide. I was trying to pass at the time. Pass as an Auvergnat.

The Auvergne is a poor region in the Massif Central, around the industrial town of Clermont-Ferrand, and the region's inhabitants, when they leave to find work in Paris, often end up owning a café-tabac or a brasserie. The way you get a job in one of these places is to buy their weekly newspaper, *L'Auvergnat de Paris*, in one of the handful of kiosks around the city that sells it, read the help-wanted ads, and then fake some sort of connection to the place. For the French, it is easy. They simply pick out a village name from the listing in the back, gauge its size by whatever information the town fathers have sent in to the newspaper's offices—for example, how many hunting licenses were issued that season—and invent a long-deceased grandmother who came from there. Dishwashers from Mali whose teeth are orange from the betel nuts they chew to give them energy in the draining humidity find it more difficult to fake these credentials. But they know the drill: any connection to the hard workers of the Auvergne will do and so they simply claim to have worked with someone who came from one of the region's hamlets. That is the tack that I took. With my dark, curly hair, the owner took me for a Moroccan come looking for a job. With my American passport, he didn't know what to make of me. But when I told him that I'd worked with someone from the hamlet of Meyrignac-L'Église in Corrèze, (démographie 97:1 décès) I was in.

I'd spent four years in the kitchens of France. I'd cleaned wild ducks in the basement of the Restaurant Guy Savoy when he still had one Michelin star and we'd play rock music stations during the prep and where it was so hot in the tiny kitchen that in the break between the lunch and dinner services, we'd hang our wet jackets over the ranges to dry. I'd worked at a place near Invalides called Chez Françoise, where I'd learned to make huge trays of mackerel in white wine and where the clientele was mostly politicians who would cross over from the French parliament. Here, the rosy-cheeked Breton chef had a screaming fit on the half hour, but every night, before catching the train back to his suburb, he would appear in the kitchen with his acrylic cardigan zipped all the way up to his neck, his wet hair combed across his forehead like a naughty but repentant schoolboy's, and leave us with a meek *"Bon-soir, les gars."* I had gotten to know provincial France, down in Burgundy, at Restaurant Lameloise, just south of Beaune, near the famed wine villages of Meursault and Puligny-Montrachet. At this Michelin three-star, old men in blue overalls would cycle to the backdoor with baskets of sorrel they had cut on nearby riverbanks hanging from their handlebars. In summer, after the dinner service, in a bend in the road that marked the Place d'Armes, the cooks would knock back beers under the Kronenbourg parasols of the local café while the customers we'd just served would sip at their cognacs and *marcs de bourgogne* on the restaurant's terrace.

Now I was back in Paris. I was twenty-two and working the night-to-dawn shift at an all-night brasserie while living in the only place I'd been able to find, a maid's room near Place de la Bastille where the only running water was from a spigot out on the landing. I was looking for a break and that last restaurant provided it.

There was one real Auvergnat working in that kitchen: a young man named Ludovic. He'd arrived in the kitchen delighted to be working in Paris, but he was growing visibly disenchanted by the reality of what a cook's life in Paris was like. He'd been at the onion soup station for months. This meant that every day he had to peel, slice, and sauté the sacks of onions that were required to make the hundreds of portions of this soup that warmed customers all through the day and sobered them up all through the night. His frustration was only augmented by the fact that he was the only true Auvergnat in a kitchen full of people pretending to be and was forced constantly to come to the region's defense.

If anyone in the kitchen said anything particularly stupid, someone else would invariably shout out, "Tell the patron we found another Auvergnat!" with which Ludovic would mutter something about the mishmash of races he found himself among until someone convinced him that it had been meant as a joke. But his patience had its limits. Matters came to a head when one of the Malinese dishwashers somehow got two consecutive days off—an unheard-of treat. Before he left, he did a little imitation Auvergnat clog dance around the kitchen and, egged on by the laughter of the entire kitchen, said he was going down to *le pays*, or the region of France he called home.

Ludovic was slicing his onions on the meat slicer, as he always did, with a pair of motorcycle goggles underneath his toque to keep his eyes from tearing up. "We love pork down in the *pays*," he said, crossing the kitchen and grabbing a slab of pork belly from a cutting board as he went. With that, he shoved it in the dish-washer's face.

Amadou, the dishwasher, was the strictest Muslim who worked there; so strict, in fact, he wouldn't even drink beer. To have raw pork pressed into his face was enough to make him want to kill, and with that clearly in mind, he picked up a cleaver.

This is how I still see it. A group of about ten men forming a monumental sculpture (cooks in white toques, dishwashers in damp T-shirts, the Ceylonese oyster-shuckers who'd run in from outside dressed as Breton fishermen, the waiters, true Parisian *garçons*, in floor-length white aprons) all clamped around Amadou and Ludovic as we tried to keep the strong arm holding the cleaver up in the air. The funniest aspect was that as we lurched out the swinging kitchen doors and slid across the length of the dining room, we all suddenly grew silent and seemed to freeze in our positions thinking that this might just be enough for the customers not to notice us.

Tumbling onto the sidewalk of the Boulevard des Italiens brought us to our senses. Amadou needed his job, he had a large family depending on his paycheck at home. Ludovic was on his own kind of career ladder. Eventually, he would graduate from onion soup, master a limited repertoire of brasserie dishes, and one day, possibly, even be considered for a position as sous-chef. We may not have been Auvergnats but we were French enough to realize that management would not feel that order had been reestablished until dossiers, or reports on what had happened, were filled out.

As soon as we got back into the kitchen someone handed out the blank forms and we started to write, leaning on the clean parts of counters and helping each other with the grammatical points. It was fairly amusing that the only person who knew the kind of French that, if they were to sound official, the reports required was Amadou. "You have to use the *subjonctif*," he offered.

"What's the *subjonctif*?" Ludovic asked sheepishly.

"*Il a fallu que je fasse,*" said Amadou giving an example.

"Ah, that's the *subjonctif*."

We had gotten the correct tense straightened out when Madame, the wife of the patron, stormed into the kitchen. She was furious. "Happy now?" she barked. "You all get to run back in here. Did you notice you knocked the Paris-Brest off the dessert cart? I had to stand out there with *crème pâtissière* all over my shoes."

What was commendable about the French, I thought, was that at no point in the ensuing conversation would the impressions of the customers on the scene they'd just witnessed come up. Epithets had been used, cleavers had been raised, *crème pâtissière* had been spilled, but no one cared about the customers.

"We're filling out the paperwork, Madame," I offered, pointing out that we were following correct procedure and were now well past the cleaver stage of the evening and into the *subjonctif* stage.

"Too perfect," said Madame, glaring at me. "Now I have a *bougnoule* telling me he is filling out the right forms."

Bougnoule is one of the most insulting terms in French, used as an epithet for anyone dark-skinned or of Muslim or African extraction. Anyone who, clearly unlike Madame, could not trace their line all the way back to Clovis, king of the Franks.

"I am not a *bougnoule*, Madame," I said calmly, as if replying to her insult were just a point of order, "I am an American."

This statement, sounding so confident in its identity to others, resounded in my inner ear because of its falsehood. I had probably spent, over several visits, no more than three months in the United States, each time going simply to visit my grandparents, who lived in New York. But no one else knew that. My father had left in 1952, to write poetry in Europe—a picture showed him in a camel hair coat on the deck of a ship leaving from Hoboken. In Spain, he'd met my mother, a traveling Irish girl from County Cork. After their divorce, I'd gone with my sister and mother to live in Ireland, where I'd spent from age eight to eighteen (or what the Irish call "the deformative years"). A year at Trinity College in Dublin spent reading Descartes's ontological argument proving the existence of God had sent me running to Paris to learn something slightly more concrete: cooking. With an entire kitchen looking at me, it was now clearly over. I took off my apron, balled it up loosely, and left it on the counter. "*Au revoir*, Madame," I said and I walked out past her.

I walked that night, feeling at loose ends from the half-worked service, with my knives tipped with wine corks from the restaurant so they wouldn't cut through the paper bag in which I carried them. I joined in with the crowds strolling along the Grands Boulevards in the summer night. They were taking in Paris, but I was saying good-bye. I knew that my next job would not involve the help-wanted pages of *L'Auvergnat de Paris* but rather the use of my American passport. The realization came to me on the steps of the Palais Garnier, looking all the way down the Avenue de l'Opéra. Drouant was only three blocks away and I didn't even know it.

M. F. K. Fisher
(1908–1992)

MARY FRANCES KENNEDY FISHER, better known as M. F. K. Fisher, was a food writer only in the superficial sense. In more than twenty books, such as *Serve It Forth, With Bold Knife and Fork, Consider the Oyster, How to Cook a Wolf,* and *The Art of Eating,* the true subject of Fisher's writing was life. In the foreword to her book *The Gastronomical Me,* she wrote, ". . . when I write of hunger, I am really writing about love and the hunger for it. . . ." She was twenty-one when she first came to France, the country in which, she once wrote, she learned how to truly eat and how to be herself and not what others expected of her. She died of Parkinson's disease at her farm in Glen Ellen, California.

❧ The Measure of My Powers ❧
(1929–1930)

from The Gastronomical Me

Paris was everything that I had dreamed, the late September when we first went there. It should always be seen, the first time, with the eyes of childhood or of love. I was almost twenty-one, but much younger than girls are now, I think. And I was wrapped in a passionate mist.

Al and I stayed on the Quai Voltaire. That was before the trees were cut down, and in the morning I would stand on our balcony and watch him walk slowly along by the bookstalls, and wave to him if he looked up at me. Then I would get into bed again.

The hot chocolate and the rich *croissants* were the most delicious things, there in bed with the Seine flowing past me and pigeons wheeling around the gray Palace mansards, that I had ever eaten. They were really the first thing I had tasted since we were married . . . tasted to remember. They were a part of the warmth and excitement of that hotel room, with Paris waiting.

But Paris was too full of people we knew.

Al's friends, most of them on the "long vac" from English universities, were full of *Lady Chatterley's Lover* and the addresses of quaint little restaurants where everybody spoke in very clipped, often newly acquired British accents and drank sparkling Burgundy.

My friends, most of them middle-aged women living in Paris on allowances from their American husbands "because of the exchange," were expensive, generous, foolish souls who needed several champagne cocktails at the Ritz Bar after their daily shopping, and were improving their French by reading a page a week of Maurois' *Ariel.* Al and I got out as soon as we politely could, or a little sooner, not downcast, because we knew we would come back.

[. . .]

Naomi Barry

NAOMI BARRY is a food and travel writer currently living in Paris, France. Barry says that she once asked a Chinese fortune-teller in Bangkok, "What do you think I do?" The fortune-teller replied, "You show others the way to a place." It was an apt description, because she has contributed numerous travel articles to publications such as *Gourmet* and the *International Herald Tribune*. Barry is also the author of several books including *Paris Personal, Paris at Table, Rome at Table,* and *Food alla Florentine*. Her work can also be found in the anthology, *Sixty Years of Feasting in Gourmet,* and forthcoming anthologies on Morocco, Venice, and southwest France. Barry is currently collaborating with Natale Rusconi, the director of the Cipriani and one of the world's foremost hoteliers since Cesar Ritz, on his memoirs.

❧ Paris's Haute Chocolaterie ❧

In extremis, when nothing else is at hand, there is the baking chocolate. I didn't expect to find fellow weaklings among the All Gauls: slim, sleek deceptive types who look as if they were nourished on a string bean.

Micheline Haardt, the neat-as-a-pin stylist, whispered that Sonia Rykiel, the designer, was also an unbridled fanatic of chocolate.

Generally speaking, chocolate in the French capital is seductive, refined, recherché, noble and expensive. The best part of this town is at the rarefied top. *Haute Couture. Haute Chocolaterie.*

The Paris passion for *haute chocolaterie* is shameless in contrast to my wholesome background of divinity fudge and frosted cupcakes, where chocoholics binged in private and were advised to keep it a dark secret. Parisians, on the other hand, extol a bash of indulgence as a *péché mignon* (an adorable little sin). Just one more proof of Gallic greatness.

For the past few hundred years, the population of Paris has been treating chocolate as a suave, voluptuous and amusing commodity. Back in the eighteenth century a witty Parisian confectioner upped his business by numbering his chocolate truffles from one to ninety. The aristocrats bought big bags full for playing family lottery in their gilded salons. Win or lose, everybody had a consolation prize.

One of the most publicized meals of the 1970s was a lunch at the Élysée Palace prepared by three-star chef Paul Bocuse and a few of his "pan pals" for the then President Valéry Giscard d'Estaing. The crescendo was in chocolate.

The opening bang was an extravagant black truffle soup, all its heady perfume held captive under a dome of puff pastry. Chosen as the climax for the sophisticated menu was a chocolate cake dubbed Le President. It too was a domed masterpiece, smothered under a froufrou of chocolate rufflettes. The cake—created by Maurice Bernachon, the famed Lyons *chocolatier*, and still a leader in his repertory—resembles a saucy dancer dressed for a cancan version of *The Black Swan*. Bernachon, a specialist in the finesse that lifts frivolity to an art, occasionally decorates a cake with chocolate leaves. To obtain them, he paints melted chocolate over a fresh leaf to capture the veined imprint. Once the chocolate hardens the leaf is thrown away.

In Paris the contemporary taste is for a chocolate that is dark, unsweetened and intense. Lovers of The Chocolate Kiss won't like it. They are not yet ready for The True Bite.

Christian Constant's small shop and tearoom at 26 rue du Bac in the stylish seventh arrondissement concentrates on his own artisanal production. Constant is revered as The Chocolate Prince. He is an affable, attractive man, qualities that help quiet the tantrums of exigent hostesses on a day when supplies fall short of the demand.

When professional cooks in Paris make pastries and candies, most of them buy blocks of chocolate from Valrhona, an exacting little factory in Tain l'Hermitage in the Drôme *département* in southeastern France. Constant is such a fanatic that he has Valrhona send him the beans themselves. In the laboratory behind his shop he blends the cocoas from Venezuela, Indonesia and Trinidad to fabricate his own tablets. Part of the result is sold to the public in hundred-gram weights.

Constant's goal is a chocolate stripped of sugar yet still palatable. He crashed through with Bitter Plus, a tablet with only twenty percent sugar. A cult of devotees sprang up immediately. Constant ventured even further to achieve a Pure Pâte Sans Sucre. For straight-out eating, this last is beyond me, but I may come to it yet.

While doing research on chocolate, a doctor at the Hôpital Bichat discovered that in its unadulterated state, chocolate is capable of producing a gentle high. She announced her felicitous findings on a television program with Constant. The immediate reaction was a rash of customers to the rue du Bac shop furtively asking from behind the back of a hand for some Pâte Pure.

"To get the high," says Constant, laughing, "would require more chocolate than anybody could stomach."

Constant serves a *sorbet du chocolat amer* that is a marvel. He wanted no sugar but found that the Pâte Pure didn't work. In the end pure cocoa did. He incorporates raisins that have been soaked in Scotch. The whisky cuts any possible cloying quality from the chocolate's intensity. It is a darkly delicious sherbet with a texture smooth and rich as an ice cream.

Constant is full of praise for America's wine and food but feels the country has not yet grown up to chocolate.

"America looks upon it as a bonbon. France has always regarded it as a jewel."

"*Vive la différence,*" I sighed as I set off to further investigate.

La Maison du Chocolat, 225 Faubourg St.-Honoré, hit Paris in 1981. It didn't take long to become an institution. Something like three weeks. The faces staring in the windows are a study in anticipation. The chocolates are made below the shop in what used to be a wine cellar.

Owner Robert Linxe is less interested in chew than in flavor and melt. Marriages made in heaven are his forte: chocolate and coffee, chocolate and rum, chocolate and orange, an occasional flirt with Kirsch. For a more indissoluble union with the well-defined personality of coffee, Linxe frequently has his coffee and cocoa beans ground up together.

"Good chocolate won't make you sick," he said as he urged us to taste a Romeo, a Bohème, and a Rigoletto. "It won't even make you fat. Look at me and I eat it all day long."

True, he was svelte and active as a live wire and persuasive as a faith healer.

"Bitter chocolate is full of potassium and magnesium."

Convinced that it was so good for me, there was no point in refusing a Bacchus.

"Extraordinary subtlety, this one," said Linxe. "It contains Smyrna raisins that have been macerated in rum and flambéed before going into the chocolate."

La Maison du Chocolat is located near the Salle Pleyel. An enormous amount of energy is expended in the making of good music, which makes it quite right that upper notes of the range with names like Daniel Barenboim, Itzhak Perlman, and Barbara Hendricks should get together as serious clients of La Maison's *chocolat amer.*

"I always know when Zubin Mehta is expected because I get

so many orders to be sent to his hotel. Mehta goes through a kilo of my chocolate in a day and a half," said Linxe proudly.

"Opéra," a flat square or rectangular cake, seemed to be a popular number in quite a few restaurants and pastry shops. The cake, square or rectangular in shape, has alternate fillings of chocolate and coffee and a satin smooth chocolate *couverture*. Some of the *pâtissiers* aver that it was a favorite at the court of Louis XV. Others assume it was invented to coincide with the opening of the present Paris Opera in 1874.

The confusion of the cake's origin is an indication of its settled position in society. Actually, it is a modern classic. In January 1986, Dalloyau—the celebrated *pâtissier* on Faubourg St.-Honoré— held a huge fete for the thirtieth birthday of its famous creation. In a neat twist, it was a party given for a cake instead of a cake produced for a party.

The Dalloyau version of "Opéra" is flecked with twenty-four karat gold supplied by one of the last two artisans of France still working the precious gold leaf. It can be bought in almost any size, from a petit four to a reception piece good for forty generous portions.

"We do not let out the recipe. We often are intimidated, but it is never quite the same. Even we insist on our own daily controls," said Madame Andrée Galavin, *présidente directrice générale* of this temple to gastronomic temptations that has been flourishing at the same address since 1802 and which even offers table service for those in chocolate crisis with time to linger.

"This is *pâtisserie* as I respect it," said Madame Galavin, an impressive woman of the old school. "Rich and with butter. I am antimousse," she said, dismissing the current vogue for cakes that pretend to be lighter than air by using mousse fillings between the layers.

The original Dalloyau opened his catering establishment in

1802, about the time that Paris began to recover its brilliance after the Revolution. Foreign visitors and émigrés were returning. Parties were being given again. Monsieur and Madame Bonaparte, the first consul and his wife, were holding court at the Palais des Tuileries. The year saw new lighting in the Place Vendôme; the Temple of Mars was transformed into the Saint-Louis des Invalides; and the lycée system of secondary education was established. And Monsieur Grimod de la Reynière, the first gastronomic chronicler, with his *Almanach des Gourmands*, praised the confectioner Berthellemot for using as mottoes on his bonbons citations from the work of the most celebrated poets of the "New France."

Questing chocolate in Paris can become a fun foray into social history. The Spanish had first encountered the cocoa bean when the conquistadors brought it back from the New World in their curio bags. In turn, the Spanish princess Anne d'Autriche, who married Louis XIII, made chocolate fashionable in France.

According to Alexandre Dumas who recounted the hegira with his usual gusto, Spain went mad for the new cocoa drink, particularly the women and the monks. The señoras even carried it to church with them, mollifying their reproachful confessors with a proferred cup from time to time. Both sides were absolved from sin by the Reverend Father Escobar who with metaphysical subtlety formally declared that drinking chocolate prepared with water was not to be considered as breaking a fast.

The monks of Spain and France were a sharing community. During the fifteenth century they busily exchanged the sage theories that helped Columbus make his first trip west. Later the Spanish monks sent samples of chocolate as presents to their brethren north of the border.

If the Spanish made chocolate known, the French made it luxurious, packaging it in gift containers of hand-painted silk and delicate porcelain. La Maison du Chocolat's cardboard boxes are as chic as those of Hermès. With good reason, as both come from the same supplier.

One of the first references to chocolate in French literature was made by Madame de Sévigné, whose name now graces two fine chocolate shops in Paris. In February 1671, she recommended chocolate to her daughter Françoise as a cure for insomnia.

The ever-anxious-to-be-modish woman of letters probably overdid the chocolate because she soon complained that although the stuff flattered you for a while, it caused dizziness, palpitations and a burning sensation. Still, she apparently couldn't keep away from it for long because in October of the same year she wrote Françoise that she tried some as an after-dinner digestive and "it acted as it was supposed to."

Brillat-Savarin (1755–1826), the erudite lawyer-gastronome from Belley, took up the torch from Madame de Sévigné and touted chocolate as a stimulant and restorative for night workers, intellectuals suffering from mental blocks and any other soul in torment. His personal recipe for combating old-age lassitude was a cup of strong chocolate well dosed with ambergris (a waxy substance from the sperm whale) and prepared according to the precepts of Madame d'Arestrel, mother superior of Belley's Convent of the Visitation.

A good chocolate drink should, she counseled, be made the day before in an earthenware coffeepot. "The overnight rest provides a velvety concentration which makes it all the better. The Good Lord can't be offended by this little supplement for He Himself is 'all excellence.'"

No doubt it was in deference to the good gourmand sisters of France like Madame d'Arestrel that the *pâtissiers* of Paris created an éclair in the form of a brioche and baptized it "Une Religieuse."

Early in the nineteenth century a clever Parisian pharmacist, Sulpice Debauve, allied himself with a confectioner named Gallais to produce a line of "agreeable medicaments."

Chocolate with an additive of iron salts became the recommended tonic for those whose pallor indicated circulation problems. "Chocolat des Dames," bonbons injected with orange-blossom water, promised relief from migraines and shocks to the morale. Chocolate incorporating almond milk was prescribed for sore throats, gastritis and indispositions resulting from overheated temperaments.

Brillat-Savarin endorsed Debauve & Gallais for their excellent chocolate at moderate prices. The premises, at 26-300 rue des Sts.-Pères, became the rendezvous of chic Paris. The stylish shop with its elegant fan windows and impressive horseshoe-shaped oak counter has been attributed to architects Percier and Fontaine, also responsible for the design of the Arc du Carrousel in the Tuileries. The shop is classed by the Beaux-Arts, a branch of the Ministry of Culture. Although now reduced by half, Percier and Fontaine's original concept is clearly evident when viewed from across the street.

For a taste of Paris Past, Debauve & Gallais is an endearing place to visit. The chocolates are made up to time-honored specifications although the "medical" additions have gone by the boards. Students from the nearby École de Médecine across the way drop in regularly to see Madame Geneviève for a sachet of *orangettes* or the fix of a nougat enrobed in dark chocolate. The *bouchée* is a Paris habit. Generally it refers to a piece of candy bought in a single unit. Somewhat larger than the bonbon and priced at approximately $1, it is a marvelously satisfying pick-me-up for munching en route to the next class or appointment.

The Hédiard shop in the arcade at the Rond-Point des Champs-Elysées has a *truffe au café* that merits serious attention. Jadis et Gourmand, nearby on the Avenue Franklin Roosevelt, is run like a fashion boutique with novelties presented regularly. Preposterously appealing are the "Nattes" and the "Tresses": chocolate that has been braided into long thick plaits studded with mixed nuts or mixed dried fruits.

Not long ago I made a trip to Japan. Advised that the Japanese liked to receive small presents, I had bought a dozen tiny boxes from Jadis et Gourmand. Each contained seventy grams of chocolate coffee beans, which I find one of the most alluring *péchés mignons* on earth. The Japanese, who have their own refinement, averaged three bites to a bean and loved them. My status was saved.

Similar chocolate "Grains de Café" are available at La Maison du Chocolat, the Marquise de Sévigné, Fauchon and other good *confiseurs*. For me they are the perfect *péché mignon*, a dainty little deviltry combining the arm-in-arm flavors of chocolate and coffee in a manner fit for a *petite marquise*.

L'Épicerie is a grocery boutique at 51 rue St.-Louis-en-l'Île with a strong concentration on chocolate specialties. Because a little knowledge is a lot of fun, l'Épicerie provides a genealogy of the beans that go into the various bonbons—an amiable way of becoming knowledgeable about the comparative in the virtues of Venezuela, Trinidad and Indonesia versus Ivory Coast, Madagascar and Ceylon.

I've long been convinced that a touch of Sybaris is therapeutic for everybody. One way to get it without cutting yourself off at the socks is a grand high tea at the Ritz, the most Ritz of all Ritzes. Jean Marie Osmont, the pastry chef, enjoys the elite distinction of having been named a Meilleur Ouvrier de France, and his chocolate desserts on the trolley are sublime.

The hour of tea is a grace note of the day. One of the most sumptuous "tearooms" in the world is the Salon Pompadour of the Hôtel Meurice, which sports gilded *boiseries*, crystal chandeliers, sparkling mirrors, a portrait of the marquise de Pompadour, and a pianist playing in the background for the fortunate few at the marble-topped tables. The pièce de résistance on the trolley is a rich chocolate mousse cake. The discreet and unsuspected retreat is one of the treasures of Paris classed by the Beaux-Arts.

I never pass through the Place de la Concorde without thinking of Madame Defarge with her knitting needles and her folding chair. On the Place de la Concorde is the Hôtel Crillon. Here, on chairs far more comfortable than the folding chairs that are still a fixture in the gardens of the Tuileries, I can forget all about Madame Defarge as I enjoy a beautifully served four-o'clock tea with a few of the Crillon's chocolate caprices.

My self-styled Route du Chocolat led me through a galaxy of restaurants, too. I have long admired the imaginative way such multi-starred chefs of Chiberta, Le Divellec, Gerard Besson, le Petit Bedon, and Tan Dinh handle fish and fowl, vegetables and meat. But they are equally gifted in their uses of chocolate, a theme with myriad variations. Sweetly the chefs gave me the recipes of the desserts that have become the running favorites with their exacting customers.

But for a quintessential interpretation of the rule of opposites, I paid a visit to the sixth-floor Quai Voltaire apartment of Nena Prentice, one of the most gifted young American painters in Paris. Here looking out over the subtly dramatic skies of the Île-de-France, she served me the traditional afternoon *gouter*, or snack, of the French schoolchild: chocolate on good honest bread. It is one of the Great Simplicities.

Grant Rosenberg
(1974–   )

GRANT ROSENBERG currently lives in Paris, France. He is an associate editor and writer at *Gadfly Online* (www.gadflyonline.com), an online culture magazine selected by *UTNE Reader* for Best Culture Coverage in 1999. In addition to covering the City of Light as *Gadfly's* Paris correspondent, Rosenberg also contributes pieces on cinema, music, literature, and art. He graduated from the University of Iowa with a dual B.A. in film and religion in 1996. He is currently at work on several screenplays. More on his writing can be found at his website, www.kolmaravenue.com.

⊰ A Day in the Life of a Parisian Café ⊱

The café-bar is to France what the all-night diner is to the United States. Americans and others have long been romanced by it, with the aid of the writings of Hemingway and the lush black-and-white postwar photographs by Doisneau and others. You cannot walk more than five minutes in Paris without passing one, usually with small tables out front (even when the temperature drops) and chairs facing the same direction—ideal for people watching.

Unlike the United States, it seems that there are no establishments here that do not serve alcohol. There is, to my knowledge, no such thing as an establishment that serves only nonalcoholic beverages. This would seem to be—in the U.S.—akin to a fast-food burger place that didn't have fries (the very fast-food chains that in France, by the way, serve both wine and beer). So all these cafés are really bars, a combination of the neighborhood java stop and pub. But due to some cultural differences, drinking a beer in the middle of the morning is not a habit limited to alcoholics; instead, it is rather commonplace, just as it is to bring in one's dog to a restaurant. This was the very sight I saw a week ago when a 60-plus woman entered a café on an overcast morning and stood at the counter drinking a Kronenbourg while little Toto waited patiently on his leash at her feet. A few minutes later, she downed the last of it and the two of them continued on their stroll.

Of these cafés, some more than others cater to tourists, featuring menus with English translations. Some more than others evoke the belle epoque of Paris. And yet still others are simple, with utilitarian decor and purpose. They have some chairs and tables and a bar without stools, the day's papers nearby. I spent the better part of a morning at a café on rue Beauborg in the arrondissement called La Comédie. It is a modest café, with a capacity of about 30 people, plus six chairs outside. The owner, Jose, a 44-year-old émigré from Portugal, came to Paris in 1970. He is the 9th of 12 children, and followed many of them to France when there wasn't much work where his farming family was trying to make a living. I asked him why France and not Brazil or the United States. At that time, Jose explains, there was work here for immigrants like him. He took different jobs and eventually bought the café, 14 years ago. He and his wife operate it, and they live, along with their 23-year-old daughter, in one of the dozen apartments above it.

Because it is just him and his wife, they do all the work; on the day I was there, they both shared in pouring the beers, making the coffee and hot chocolate, preparing the sandwiches and other uncomplicated foods they offer as well as doing the cleaning and the bookmaking. The clientèle ebbs and flows. For a half hour, after my arrival, there is nobody else in the café, yet moments later, it gradually fills up with some 15 people, half at the bar having a coffee—equivalent here to an espresso Stateside—before getting on with their day. Jose says that the most crowded it gets is between noon and 3 o'clock, but he knows that his place has a different appeal than the other nearby cafés. "There are other places, on these streets nearby," he says, "that are a bit classier, and they are always full of people. It is different. It all depends on the placement of the café."

It is interesting, his clientèle, considering that it is only a minute away on foot from the Pompidou Center, one of the main culture landmarks in Paris, and consequently one that adds to the bustle of the surrounding establishments. Jose's café has its share of regulars, from a shoemaker down the street who comes in every few hours for a couple of minutes each day, never taking off his apron, to the older gentleman, a seller of roasted chestnuts on the street fifty yards away, who may or may not be originally from a Baltic state. It is a working-class joint, to be sure, and the absence of suits and ties or boisterous monoglot tourists are not missed. There is no English heard in this bar and neither he nor his wife speaks it.

As it is in an American diner or bar, the café, with its flux of people in and out, its newspaper headlines laying open waiting to spur an argument, I ask Jose if his place has its share of heated political discussions. I am expecting, in light of the times we are in since September 11, to hear about conspiracy theories, boorish commentaries or Sartre-infused pontifications about the trajectory of world affairs and their philosophical ramifications. But instead, Jose tells me his clientèle mostly talk about soccer. Very little politics. No, it is soccer, they do get hot under the collar about it, and though fights are rare they do happen. And it is Jose (who, despite being Portuguese and not French at all, actually resembles both in looks and not-so-large physique, the late Francois Truffaut), who is the bouncer of his own establishment.

In Europe, by and large, one is never rushed out of a restaurant or a café. I have seen signs in some cafés in Chicago and university towns that politely ask patrons not to hog their booth or table for too long. Here there is never a rush. I ask Jose about this, who tells me that people have been known to use the time allotted to them. "I once had some guys in here from noon until 2 A.M., a full 14 hours. Over the course of that time they ate, drank and played cards. But that was an exceptional case, obviously. Normally, those who stay long, it is just an hour, maybe two, maximum."

He speaks highly of his regulars, those whose names he knows, who are part of his daily routine as well, like the shoemaker or chestnut seller, those who come in for a drink and for food and conversation at the appointed hour each day. "I have clients who have been coming in here for 14 years, since the beginning of my time in this café, for two hours every day, from noon to two, and others, in the evening, at 7, who stay until 9. Every day. For an apéritif, a laugh, some amusement, and to eat. A few days later they pay."

For a while I sit and read and watch the variety of people come in and out of La Comédie. The few who come for lunch, well-dressed, and the rest, a guy with paint on his clothes, a woman with messy hair and a German shepherd and those that enter and are greeted by all, because here, at this time of day, Everybody Knows Your Name. They talk and laugh and at one point we all find ourselves distracted by the sight of some young men trying to push a very large crate into the cargo hold of a truck. They have been at it for about ten minutes, unaware of the peanut gallery inside across the street. They are stumped. Eventually they figure out how to incorporate the power of the lift ramp, along with their own counterweight, to ease it in. This results in laughs and cheers that the workers do not hear. Inside the café, the conversations start up again, business resumes. Jose pours a glass of red wine for a gentleman who just entered while his wife sings as she does the dishes in the back. I slowly eat my sandwich of crude ham and butter and don't leave anytime soon.

The Art of Living

How to Live Like a Parisian

ᖆ

David Sedaris
(1957–   )

DAVID SEDARIS is best known for his collections of autobiographical essays, *Barrel Fever, Naked,* and *Me Talk Pretty One Day*. He is also loved for his work as a commentator for National Public Radio and Public Radio International's "This American Life" with Ira Glass. Many of his essays, short stories, and radio pieces draw from his time growing up in North Carolina and the many odd jobs he held to make ends meet while writing. A humorist with an acerbic wit, he is also know for capturing people, places, and circumstances with great poignancy. He graduated from the School of the Art Institute of Chicago in 1987. He divides his time among New York City, Paris, and Normandy.

⚓ The City of Light in the Dark ⚓

from Me Talk Pretty One Day

When asked to account for the time I've spent in Paris, I reach for my carton of ticket stubs and groan beneath its weight. I've been here for more than a year, and while I haven't seen the Louvre or the Pantheon, I have seen *The Alamo* and *The Bridge on the River Kwai*. I haven't made it to Versailles but did manage to catch *Oklahoma!, Brazil,* and *Nashville*. Aside from an occasional trip to the flea market, my knowledge of Paris is limited to what I learned in *Gigi*.

When visitors come from the United States, I draw up little

itineraries. "If we go to the three o'clock *Operation Petticoat*, that should give us enough time to make it across town for the six o'clock screening of *It Is Necessary to Save the Soldier Ryan*, unless, of course, you'd rather see the four o'clock *Ruggles of Red Gap* and the seven o'clock *Roman Holiday*. Me, I'm pretty flexible, so why don't *you* decide."

My guests' decisions prove that I am a poor judge of my own character. Ayatollahs are flexible. I am not. Given the choice between four perfectly acceptable movies, they invariably opt for a walk through the Picasso museum or a tour of the cathedral, saying, "I didn't come all the way to Paris so I can sit in the dark."

They make it sound so bad. "Yes," I say, "but this is the French dark. It's . . . darker than the dark we have back home." In the end I give them a map and spare set of keys. They see Notre Dame, I see *The Hunchback of Notre Dame*.

I'm often told that it's wasteful to live in Paris and spend all my time watching American movies, that it's like going to Cairo to eat cheeseburgers. "You could do that back home," people say. But they're wrong. I couldn't live like this in the United States. With very few exceptions, video killed the American revival house. If you want to see a Boris Karloff movie, you have to rent it and watch it on a television set. In Paris it costs as much to rent a movie as it does to go to the theater. French people enjoy going out and watching their movies on a big screen. On any given week one has at least 250 pictures to choose from, at least a third of them in English. There are all the recent American releases, along with any old movie you'd ever want to see. On Easter, having learned that *The Greatest Story Ever Told* was sold out, I just crossed the street and saw *Superfly*, the second-greatest story ever told. Unless they're for children, all movies are shown in their original English with French subtitles. Someone might say, "Get your fat ass out of here before I do something I regret," and the screen will read, "Leave."

I sometimes wonder why I even bothered with French class.

"I am truly delighted to make your acquaintance," "I heartily thank you for this succulent meal"—I have yet to use either of these pleasantries. Since moving to Paris my most often used phrase is "One place, please." That's what one says at the box office when ordering a ticket, and I say it quite well. In New York I'd go to the movies three or four times a week. Here I've upped it to six or seven, mainly because I'm too lazy to do anything else. Fortunately, going to the movies seems to suddenly qualify as an intellectual accomplishment, on a par with reading a book or devoting time to serious thought. It's not that the movies have gotten any more strenuous, it's just that a lot of people are as lazy as I am, and together we've agreed to lower the bar.

Circumstances foster my laziness. Within a five-block radius of my apartment there are four first-run multiplexes and a dozen thirty-to-fifty-seat revival houses with rotating programs devoted to obscure and well-known actors, directors, and genres. These are the mom-and-pop theaters, willing to proceed with the two o'clock showing of *The Honeymoon Killers* even if I'm the only one in the house. It's as if someone had outfitted his den with a big screen and comfortable chairs. The woman at the box office sells you a ticket, rips it in half, and hands you the stub. Inside the theater you're warmly greeted by a hostess who examines your stub and tears it just enough to make her presence felt. Somewhere along the line someone decided that this activity is worthy of a tip, so you give the woman some change, though I've never known why. It's a mystery, like those big heads on Easter Island or the popularity of the teeny-weeny knapsack.

I'm so grateful such theaters still exist that I'd gladly tip the projectionist as well. Like the restaurants with only three tables, I wonder how some of these places manage to stay open. In America the theaters make most of their money at the concession stand, but here, at least in the smaller places, you'll find nothing but an ice-cream machine tucked away between the bathroom and the fire exit. The larger theaters offer a bit more, but it's still mainly candy and ice cream sold by a vendor with a tray around his neck. American theaters have begun issuing enormous cardboard trays, and it's only a matter of time before the marquees read TRY OUR BARBECUED RIBS! or COMPLIMENTARY BAKED POTATO WITH EVERY THIRTY-TWO-OUNCE SIRLOIN. When they started selling nachos, I knew that chicken wings couldn't be far behind. Today's hot dogs are only clearing the way for tomorrow's hamburgers, and from there it's only a short leap to the distribution of cutlery.

I've never considered myself an across-the-board apologist for the French, but there's a lot to be said for an entire population that never, under any circumstances, talks during the picture. I've sat through Saturday-night slasher movies with audiences of teenagers and even then nobody has said a word. I can't remember the last time I enjoyed silence in an American theater. It's easy to believe that our audiences spend the day saying nothing, actually saving their voices for the moment the picture begins. At an average New York screening I once tapped the shoulder of the man in front of me, interrupting his spot review to ask if he planned on talking through the entire movie.

"Well . . . yeah. What about it?" He said this with no trace of shame or apology. It was as if I'd asked if he planned to circulate his blood or draw air into his lungs. "Gee, why wouldn't I?" I moved away from the critic and found myself sitting beside a clairvoyant who loudly predicted the fates of the various characters seen moving their lips up on the screen. Next came an elderly couple constantly convinced they were missing something. A stranger would knock on the door, and they'd ask, "Who's he?" I wanted to assure them that all their questions would be answered in due time, but I don't believe in talking during movies, so I moved again, hoping I might be lucky enough to find a seat between two people who had either fallen asleep or died.

At a theater in Chicago I once sat beside a man who watched the movie while listening to a Cubs game on his transistor radio.

When the usher was called, the sports fan announced that this was a free country and that he wanted to listen to the goddamn game. "Is there a law against doing both things at once?" he asked. "Is there a law? Show me the law, and I'll turn off my radio."

Sitting in Paris and watching my American movies, I think of the man with the transistor radio and feel the exact opposite of homesick. The camera glides over the cities of my past, capturing their energetic skylines just before they're destroyed by the terrorist's bomb or advancing alien warship. New York, Chicago, San Francisco: it's like seeing pictures of people I know I could still sleep with if I wanted to. When the high-speed chases and mandatory shoot-outs become too repetitive, I head over to the revival houses and watch gentler movies in which the couples sleep in separate beds and everyone wears a hat. As my ticket is ripped I'll briefly consider all the constructive things I could be doing. I think of the parks and the restaurants, of the pleasantries I'll never use on the friends I am failing to make. I think of the great city teeming on the other side of that curtain, and then the lights go down, and I love Paris.

Sylvia Beach
(1887–1962)

SYLVIA BEACH originally planned to open a French bookstore in New York. It was just after World War I and she had finished serving in the American Red Cross in Serbia. Had it not been for the prohibitive cost of living, even then, in New York, she may never have decided to open a little American bookstore instead in the much more affordable Paris. On November 19, 1919, she opened Shakespeare and Company at 8 rue Dupuytren.

Beach's life and the story of her bookshop are inextricably intertwined with literary history, for Shakespeare and Company became more than a bookstore. It was a subscription library to many writers without means; a meeting place for writers, obscure and celebrated; and famously, a publisher of banned literature. In 1922, she made literary history by publishing James Joyce's *Ulysses*, whose publication was banned in England and the United States. Beach published the book in Paris and arranged to have it smuggled into the United States, several copies at a time. She kept the book in print for several years until the ban on its U.S. publication was finally lifted in 1933 when a New York Federal Court judge declared it "not obscene in the ordinary sense of the word."

In 1941, the Nazis invaded Paris. When threatened with the prospect of her books being confiscated by the Nazis, Beach and several friends took out every book and many of her most valuable papers and put them into hiding. She worked for the French Resistance during the Second World War and was eventually interned at Vittel, a Nazi camp for American women. Many of her papers are now safely kept at Princeton University Library and at the University of Buffalo. The original Shake-

speare and Company never reopened after World War II, but literary pilgrims can see another one named in honor of Beach's bookshop on the
rue de l'Odéon. Beach received the American Red Cross Medal for her
war service and the French Legion of Honor for her services to literature.
She died in Paris.

from

⚜ Shakespeare and Company ⚜

A Bookshop of My Own

I had long wanted a bookshop, and by now it had become an
obsession. I dreamed of a French bookshop but it was to be a
branch of Adrienne's and in New York. I wanted to help the
French writers I admired so much to become more widely known
in my country. I soon realized, however, that my mother's little
savings, which she was willing to risk on my venture, would be
insufficient to cover the cost of a shop in New York. Very regretfully, I had to abandon this fascinating idea.

I thought Adrienne Monnier would be disappointed to hear
of the downfall of our scheme of a French place, a branch of
hers, in my country. On the contrary, she was delighted. And so, in
a minute, was I, as right before our eyes my bookshop turned into
an American one in Paris. My capital would go much further
there. Rents were lower and so was the cost of living in those days.

I saw all these advantages. Moreover, I was extremely fond of
Paris, I must confess, and this was no small inducement to settle
down there and become a Parisian. Then, too, Adrienne had had
four years of experience as a bookseller. She had opened her shop
in the midst of a war and, moreover, kept it going. She promised
to advise me in my first steps; also to send me lots of customers.

The French, as I knew, were very eager to get hold of our new writers, and it seemed to me that a little American bookshop on the Left Bank would be welcome.

The difficulty was to find a vacant shop in Paris. I might have had to wait some time before finding what I wanted if Adrienne hadn't noticed that there was a place for rent in the rue Dupuytren, a little street just around the corner from the rue de l'Odéon. Busy though she was with her library, her publications, and her own writing, she somehow found time to help me with my preparations. We hurried to the rue Dupuytren, where, at No. 8—there were only about ten numbers in this hilly little street—was a shop with the shutters up and a sign saying *"Boutique a louer."* It had once been a laundry, said Adrienne, pointing to the words *"gros"* and *"fin"* on either side of the door, meaning they did up both sheets and fine linen. Adrienne, who was rather plump, placed herself under the *"gros"* and told me to stand under the *"fin."* "That's you and me," she said.

We hunted up the concierge, an old lady in a black lace cap, who lived in a sort of cage between two floors, as concierges do in these old Paris houses, and she showed us the premises. *My* premises, as, without hesitation, I decided they would be. There were two rooms, with a glass door between them, and steps leading into the one at the back. There was a fireplace in the front room; the laundress's stove, with the irons on it, had stood in front of it. The poet Léon-Paul Fargue drew a picture of the stove as it must have looked and to show me how the irons were placed. He seemed familiar with laundries, probably because of the pretty laundresses who ironed the linen. He signed the drawing, "Léon-Paul Fargue," a play on the French word for stove, *"poêle."*

Adrienne, looking at the glass door, remembered something. Yes, she had seen it before. As a child, she had come with her mother to this very laundry one day. While the women were busy, the little girl had swung on the door, and, of course, smashed the glass. She remembered, too, the spanking she had got when they reached home.

These premises—including the dear old concierge, "la Mère Garrouste," as everyone called her, the kitchenette off the back room, and Adrienne's glass door—everything delighted me, not to mention the very low rent, and I went away to think it over. Mère Garrouste was to think me over, too, for a day or two, according to the best French custom.

Shortly, my mother in Princeton got a cable from me, saying simply: "Opening bookshop in Paris. Please send money," and she sent me all her savings.

Setting Up Shop

It was great fun getting my little shop ready for the book business. I took the advice of my friends the Wright-Worthings, who had the antique shop Aladdin's Lamp in the rue des Saints Pères, and covered the rather damp walls with sackcloth. A humpbacked upholsterer did this for me, and was very proud of the fluting with which he finished off the corners. A carpenter put up shelves and made over the windows for the books to be displayed in, and a painter came to do the few feet of shop front. He called it the "façade," and promised it would be as fine when he finished it as that of the Bazar de l'Hôtel de Ville, his latest triumph. Then a "specialist" came and painted the name "Shakespeare and Company" across the front. That name came to me one night as I lay in bed. My "Partner Bill," as my friend Penny O'Leary called him, was always, I felt, well disposed toward my undertaking; and, besides, he was a best seller.

Charles Winzer, a Polish-English friend of Adrienne's, made the signboard, a portrait of Shakespeare, to be hung outside. Adrienne didn't approve of this idea, but I wanted it anyway. The signboard hung from a bar above the door. I took it down at night. Once, I forgot it, and it was stolen. Winzer made another, which also disappeared. Adrienne's sister made a third one, a rather French-looking Shakespeare, which I still have.

Now perhaps some people wouldn't know what a "Bookhop" is. Well, that's what the specialist carefully spelled out above the window at the right, opposite the words "Lending Library." I let "Bookhop" remain for a while. It quite described Shakespeare and Company making its debut in bookselling.

All these artisans, in spite of their interest in the place, were extremely intermittent in their attendance. Sometimes I wondered if they wouldn't still be busy there on the opening day, upholstering, doing carpentry, and painting the place. At least the shop, so full of people, would look bustling.

The "office furniture" in my shop was all antique. A charming mirror and a gate-legged table came from the Wright-Worthings, the rest from the flea market, where you really found bargains in those days.

The books in my lending library, except for the latest, came from the well-stocked English secondhand bookstores in Paris. They, too, were antiques, some of them far too valuable to be circulated; and if the members of my library hadn't been so honest, many, instead of a few, of the volumes would soon have been missing from the shelves. The fascinating bookshop near the Bourse, Boiveau and Chevillet, which has disappeared now, was a field of discovery for excavators who were willing to go down into the cellar, holding a lighted candle provided by dear old Monsieur Chevillet himself—what a risk!—and dig up the treasures buried under layers of stuff.

Cyprian, who was in the United States just then, sent me the latest American books. I went over to London and brought back two trunks full of English books, mostly poetry. Mrs. Alida Monro, who with Harold Monro ran the Poetry Bookshop, a wonderful place, very kindly gave me a great deal of information on the subject of poetry publications and how to procure them. And I went around to see publishers. All of them were most courteous and encouraging about the new bookshop in Paris, and gave me every facility, though, for all they knew, I might be an adventuress. In fact, so I was.

On the way to the boat train, I stopped in Cork Street at the little bookshop of the publisher and bookseller Elkin Mathews to order my Yeats, Joyce, and Pound. He was sitting in a sort of gallery, with books surging around and creeping up almost to his feet. We had a pleasant talk, and he was quite friendly. I mentioned seeing some drawings by William Blake—if only I could have something of Blake's in my shop! Thereupon he produced two beautiful original drawings, which he sold to me for a sum that, according to Blake experts who saw them later, was absurdly small.

Instead of writing down the titles I wanted from Elkin Mathews—indeed, I hadn't time, and anyway we understood each other so well—I gave him a flying order for Yeats, Joyce, and Pound, and for any portraits he might have of them around the shop. A few days later, in Paris, a huge sack arrived from Elkin Mathews. It contained the works I had ordered, and also dozens of what the French call *"rossignols,"* a poetic name for unsalable items. Obviously, it was a good chance to dump these birds on me. Besides the books, the sack contained some enormous portraits: at least half a dozen of Byron, the rest of Nelson, Wellington, and other characters in English history. Judging by their size, they were intended for the walls of official buildings. I sent them back and scolded Elkin Mathews severely. Still, because of the Blakes, I didn't hold it against him; and I have only pleasant memories of the old gentleman.

Another pleasant memory of my time in London was my visit to the Oxford University Press, where Mr. Humphrey Milford

himself showed me the largest Bible in the world, made for
Queen Victoria. It wasn't a book you could read in bed.

Shakespeare and Company Opens Its Doors

Instead of setting a date for the opening of my bookshop, I
decided that I would simply open it as soon as it was ready.

Finally, the day came when all the books I could afford were
on the shelves, and one could walk around the shop without
falling over ladders and buckets of paint. Shakespeare and Company opened its doors. The day was November 19, 1919. It had
taken me since August to reach this point. In the windows were
displayed the works of our Patron, of Chaucer, of T. S. Eliot,
Joyce, and so on. There was also Adrienne's favorite English
book, *Three Men in a Boat.* Inside, a review rack held copies of the
Nation, the *New Republic,* the *Dial,* the *New Masses, Playboy,* the
Chapbook, the *Egoist,* the *New English Review,* and other literary
magazines. On the walls, I had put up my two Blake drawings, and
photographs of Whitman and Poe. Then there were two photographs of Oscar Wilde, in velvet breeches and cloak. They were
framed with some of Wilde's letters that a friend of Cyprian's,
Byron Kuhn, had given me. Also on display were several little
manuscripts of Walt Whitman scribbled on the backs of letters.
These were the gift of the poet to my Aunt Agnes Orbison. Aunt
Agnes, when she was a student at Bryn Mawr, had gone with her
friend Alys Smith to Camden to visit Walt Whitman. (Alys was
afterward married to Bertrand Russell, and her sister Mariechen to
Bernard Berenson; her brother was Logan Pearsall Smith, who
had described some of the doings of this interesting family in his
autobiography, *Forgotten Years.*) Alys's mother, Mrs. Hannah Whitall
Smith, had given Whitman an armchair, and when Alys and Agnes
went to Camden, they didn't find the old man "sitting on a gate,"
but in the armchair. Manuscripts were strewn over the floor, and

some of them, as the shy young Agnes perceived, were in the wastepaper basket. She got up the courage to draw out a few of these scribblings, mostly on the backs of letters addressed to Walt Whitman, Esq., and asked if she might keep them. "Certainly, my dear," he replied. And that's how our family got its Whitman manuscripts.

A good many friends had been waiting for the opening of Shakespeare and Company; and the news soon got around that the time had come. Still, I didn't really expect to see anybody that day. And just as well, I thought. I would need at least twenty-four hours to realize this Shakespeare and Company bookshop. But the shutters in which the little shop went to bed every night were hardly removed (by a waiter from a nearby café) when the first friends began to turn up. From that moment on, for over twenty years, they never gave me time to meditate.

Lending books, just as I had foreseen, was much easier in Paris than selling them. The only cheap editions of English writers were the Tauchnitz and the Conard, and they didn't go much further than Kipling and Hardy in those days. Our moderns, particularly when pounds and dollars were translated into francs, were luxuries the French and my Left Bankers were not able to afford. That is why I was interested in my lending library. So I got everything I liked myself, to share with others in Paris.

My lending library was run on what Adrienne called, though I never knew why, *"le plan américain."* It would have horrified an American librarian, with her catalogues and card indexes and mechanical appliances. It was quite suitable for a library such as mine. There was no catalogue—I preferred to let people find out for themselves how much was lacking; no card index—so unless you could remember, as Adrienne, with her wonderful memory, was able to do, to whom all your books were lent, you had to look through all the members' cards to find out what had become of a volume.

There were, to be sure, the large cards, each bearing the name and address of the member, the date of subscription, the amount of the subscription plus the deposit, and, of course, the title of the book he or she took out. Or books. A member could take one or two volumes, could change them whenever he liked or keep them a fortnight. (Joyce took out dozens, and sometimes kept them for years.) Each member had a small identity card, which he was supposed to produce when claiming the deposit at the expiration of his subscription, or when he was broke. This membership card was as good as a passport, so I was told.

One of the first members of the library was a student at the medical school in the street the rue Dupuytren ran into. This was Thérèse Bertrand, now Dr. Bertrand-Fontaine. I watched her career with excitement. She always passed the exams successfully, went right to the top in her profession, and was appointed *"Médecin des Hôpitaux,"* the first woman to receive that honor. But then, she comes of a family of famous men of science. With all of her work, Thérèse Bertrand found time to read all the new American books in my library, and was a member of it to the day it closed.

The next member (or "bunny," as Holly called them, from the word *abonné:* subscriber) who came along was Gide. I saw Adrienne Monnier coming around the corner from the rue de l'Odéon escorting him. It was just like Gide to hurry up and encourage me in my undertaking. I was always timid in Gide's presence, though Adrienne said, "Pooh!" when I told her; and now, rather overwhelmed by the honor, I wrote on a card: "André Gide: I, Villa Montmorency, Paris XVI; I year; I volume," making a big blot as I did so.

Gide was tall and handsome. He wore a broad-brimmed Stetson, and I saw a resemblance to William S. Hart. He wore either a cape or a sort of Teddy bear coat over his shoulders, and, with his height, he was impressive as he strode along. Gide continued to take an interest in Shakespeare and Company and its proprietor all through the years.

André Maurois was also one of the first to bring me his good wishes. And he brought me a copy of his newly published little masterpiece *Les Silences du Colonel Bramble.*

Anaïs Nin
(1903–1977)

ANAÏS NIN was unique among her American expatriate peers in Paris. She was familiar with European culture as a returning native rather than as a tourist; she was also fluent in French, which allowed her to immerse herself in the French literary tradition in a way impossible for her American peers. Born in Paris, France, to an aristocratic family in 1903, Nin became a naturalized American citizen after her family moved to the United States. Abandoned by their father, Anaïs and her two brothers left Europe for New York with their mother in 1914. Nin was eleven years old. It was during this journey to New York that she began writing her journal, at first in the form of a letter to her father. The writing in her life-long journals eventually became her most famous and controversial literary work. In all, seven volumes of her diary were published, the first in 1966. They were heavily self-edited by Nin. Many friends and family, including her brothers, knew nothing of her incestuous adult affair with her father until after her death when the unexpurgated versions of her journals began to be published.

from

❧ The Early Diary of Anaïs Nin ❧
April 11, 1926

Was struck yesterday by an important discovery. Paris kills my writing. I have been oppressed and belittled and silenced in Paris. As soon as I leave it, I feel free again, vivid, enthusiastic, fervent, creative. Why? Because Paris has a passion for vicious criticism, because Paris is old, envious of youth, an enemy of individualism, an enemy of mysticism, an enemy of energy. I am stifled by the tone of its theatre, by the deadness of its old traditions, by the leering expressions of its crowds, by the decay of its modern literature. I have been spiritually crucified in Paris, and this torment has broken out into all kinds of small irritations, in rebellions against the eternally gray weather. Outside of Paris, I live. I lived in Verneuil, in Tours, in Hendaye, here in Italy. My impulses return, my tongue loosens, I feel my shoulders lighter from the weight of critical, dull, mocking eyes, from the weight of an envious curiosity. Hugh suggests I should take pleasure in this combat, this clash of temperaments. He loves a fight; I don't, at least not now. I had just begun to raise my head when I arrived in Paris, and its superiority passed over me like a violent and unexpected storm, leaving me bewildered and crushed. I must conquer this vulnerability, I must have courage. I act under the glaring eyes of Paris as I do before the cold—I shrink and shiver. While Hugh says always, "Breathe deeply, throw out your chest, fight the cold, and you won't feel it."

Calm days, these. We read, we write letters, we sit in the sun, we dress for dinner and talk softly across the little table on safe philosophical subjects. We fly from the crowd, from the entertainments, even from the walk along the sea which is, as usual, a parade.

I listen with pleasure to the serenade of the wandering musicians, who stand on the long terrace below our balcony. The rain of silver pieces distracts them from their melody, particularly when this rain threatens to roll away into the sea. We write Horace, teasing him about his arguments in favor of sociability, telling him how we live on our balcony and cultivate sauvagerie more than ever. I tease him, too, about his refusal to write me a letter in which he would tell me what he felt on his visit to Florence years ago, an experience which I divined to have been the most important in his spiritual life, and which his adaptation to

Parisian life is slowly effacing. He suspected me of wanting to resuscitate a state of mind which was more in harmony with my own temperament, and as he is always combatting the "spirituality" of this temperament, he chose to remain towards me more the Frenchman than the exalted Italian.

The Legend of Paris. There is a monster in Paris called the Literary Tradition. You come from young America stamped with a respect of it which you have gathered from reading. Professors and those who have traveled and wish to awe you with the importance of what they have seen agree that there are impressive arts in Europe which you must fear and admire. You come to Paris penetrated with Reverence. You read the literary magazines and newspapers. They are celebrating the centenary of some French writer. They are weeping over the loss of a never-known-before genius, essentially French in his virtues, an example of French elegance in style, of French philosophy, of French wit. You are impressed with the opinion of the world (as represented by a French critic) towards another great French writer—they are all great, and they are all French—one thing follows another. You go to the Sorbonne. The voices there are deep and solemn, scholarly and elegant. The sound of it alone and the impeccable intelligence, the impeccable style, are guarantees of intelligence and wisdom. You are again impressed with the awful gravity and awful divinity of French literature.

You wander through French streets, where one café is followed by a library, and a library by a café, and so on. You wander along the quays, and you are again impressed by the perpetual presence of Letters. The Monster swells at every step. It has become immense and fearful. You have become a little mortal of diminutive importance, a speechless worshiper. The whole Nation has agreed to deceive you. The legend arrests the meager flowings of your own pen. It swallows your individuality. At last you can write home to young America and say that you are studying Art in the most artistic city, where the atmosphere is so ideal for growth. Growth of what? Not yourself. Perhaps the growth of Paris and its Legend.

Hugh and I together discover many things. We were talking about my lost battles in Paris. We compared my feelings with those he had in N.Y. towards his work. In N.Y. the Businessman is strong in his success—he is rough, intolerant of weakness, critical of others. It is his field, and he arrogantly crushes the weaker players. Hugh felt weak there. But coming to Paris, where the French are weak in business, he became superior. He felt freer and he worked better. This breathing spell gave him a chance to develop his talents and to gain self-confidence. He was free of criticism and sharpness and was able to grow.

Exactly the reverse happened to me. The French had the authority and the intolerance and the sharpness of the successful man. I had the eyes of the Monster on me, and I had no breathing spell except when I ran away and listened to my own voice. All I need now is a chance to develop in a place where I am allowed to breathe. I have learned enormously, even though I have not worked. I have studied the Monster carefully. I have absorbed everything with great docility. Such rough experiences are salutary if one survives them.

Stanley Karnow
(1925–   )

STANLEY KARNOW has received numerous honors for his work as an Asia journalist. His journalism career didn't start in Asia, however, but in Paris, France. After graduating from Harvard in 1947, Karnow enrolled in the Sorbonne in Paris. He planned to stay only for the summer. He ended up getting a job first as a researcher, then as the Paris correspondent for *Time*. He didn't leave Paris until 1957. He received the Emmy, Polk, Peabody, and Dupont awards for his work on the PBS documentary "*Vietnam: A Television History*." He received the Pulitzer Prize for *In Our Image: America's Empire in the Philippines*. He is also the author of *Mao and China: A Legacy of Turmoil; Vietnam: The War Nobody Won*; and *Paris in the Fifties*. The latter, from which the following reprint comes, covers those early years that he spent in Paris as a student and then as a reporter for *Time*.

✣ The Glass of Fashion ✣

from Paris in the Fifties

The bone-damp chill of winter was lifting, and pale sunlight had begun to etch shadows of the leafless chestnut trees on the cobblestone streets. Children were again playing in the parks, café terraces had started to reopen and lovers could be seen smooching on the banks along the Seine. In the district around the Champs-Élysées, the George V, Prince de Galles and Plaza Athénée lounges were shrill with the shouts of Chicago and Dallas department-store buyers as they cruised from divan to divan, hailing California and Florida dress-chain representatives. At plush restaurants like Lasserre, Ledoyen and Maxim's, stocky, cigar-chomping Seventh Avenue manufacturers in silver ties and white-on-white shirts shared tables with New York designers in jangly bracelets and rhinestone-rimmed glasses. Powder-puff bars were packed with the female editors of women's magazines, photographers, wire service reporters, gossip columnists, press agents, public relations hustlers, titled ladies, rich bourgeois hostesses, stage and screen stars, and the usual celebrities and playboys. This effervescent reunion was a rite of spring—the mystic and sacred moment when the city's top couturiers unveiled to the world the latest variations and dissonances on the theme of the Eternal Feminine.

Though I might drop in on a show once in a while to ogle the mannequins, fashion was not my terrain. In March 1957, however, I was assigned to a mammoth story on the subject. Compared to such industries as food and cars, haute couture contributed little to France's economy. Its income stemmed primarily from serving elite Parisiennes and foreigners, and from exporting designs—especially to America. The thirty or forty *grandes maisons* employed only about seven thousand workers and grossed less than a million dollars a year—in contrast to the four billion dollars' worth of dresses sold annually in the United States. But whatever the balance sheet, Paris fashions swayed the tastes of women everywhere, thereby confirming in the French the conviction that, when it came to producing prestige goods, they were peerless—a belief that, in turn, reinforced their overweening sense of cultural superiority.

Day after day for nearly a month, I crisscrossed the small Right Bank *quartier* where the major fashion houses were clustered. I dutifully viewed the Fath, Balenciaga, Balmain, Castillo, Dessès, Givenchy, Lanvin, Laroche and Patou collections—some of which, for promotional purposes, featured gimmicks like a giraffe-hide coat and a suede bolero lined with alley cat skin. But mainly I focused on Christian Dior, then the preeminent Paris couturier, who was slated to appear on *Time*'s cover.

One morning I took a taxi over to Chez Dior, a baroque granite mansion situated on the Avenue Montaigne, a broad, shaded street between the Rond-Point des Champs-Élysées and the Place de l'Alma. The security reminded me of Fort Knox. Roughly three hundred embossed invitations had been issued to a select list; and, to bar gate-crashers, handsome girls in nondescript black and lockjaw accents guarded the entrance, carefully checking credentials and allocating seats according to a rigid protocol: professional buyers according to their previous purchases, journalists according to the influence of their publications, luminaries according to their current reputations. Punctuality was de rigueur, and absolutely no exceptions. Some months before, the Duchess of Windsor had arrived late, expecting VIP treatment, and she was relegated to a staircase.

The large gold-and-olive salon was a hall of mirrors, the subtle glow of its giant crystal chandeliers overwhelmed by the glare of floodlights. Tucked into alcoves were urns filled with roses, gardenias and carnations whose mélange of fragrances pervaded the chamber. Squeezing into a flimsy gilded chair in the press section, I glanced around. The front rows were crammed with American and European merchandisers cradling pens, notepads and programs. Svelte women in toque hats and pearl chokers leaned forward anxiously; prosperous provincial matrons sat ramrod-upright, clutching stout handbags; a few privileged tourists gazed in awe at the opulence. The mood was as tense and as promising as a Broadway premiere; then the babble subsided as a stereo emitted a medley of waltzes, polkas, ballads and pop tunes—and, in threes and fours, the first of thirteen mannequins glided out from behind a gauze curtain.

Lanky and remote, they seemed to be rapt in an asexual trance as they sashayed up and down the runway in movements and gestures as studiously choreographed as a ballet—hips swiveling, arms akimbo, heads tossing. A woman assistant in basic black, speaking through a microphone, identified their lavish ensembles, tailored sheaths and cocktail casuals in a noncommittal monotone: *"Ariane, trente-trois, zirty-zree," "Chloë, quarante-et-un, fawrty-wan," "Papillon de Printemps, cinquante-cinq, feevty-feeve."* The mannequins would twirl, hover, twirl again, pause, slip off a jacket or a mantle and hand it to an invisible aide, who accepted it silently, like some ancient hetaera. Then yet another pirouette, and they evaporated into the wings. The session lasted three hours, culminating in an array of classic bridal gowns. Most of the audience burst into enthusiastic applause punctuated by cries of *"Magnifique!"* and *"Bravo!"* But, lest the faintest flicker betray their interest in an article to a rival, the pros feigned indifference. Amid it all, a woman reporter for a Fleet Street tabloid nagged me with a torrent of gush: "Isn't that a witty pebble weave?" or "Don't you think that there's a certain je-ne-sais-quoi texture to that velour?"

The frothy pageant was the indispensable prelude to the serious business that began only after the lights had faded. At that juncture, buyers for Henri Bendel, Saks, I. Magnin, Bonwit Teller, Neiman-Marcus and other establishments that catered to the carriage trade huddled with the solemn, black-clad *vendeuses* strategically stationed in the corridors. Every buyer had her personal *vendeuse*, every *vendeuse* her jealously coveted clientele—and, after years of making deals, they trusted each other. Some buyers, enraptured by the models they had just seen, instantly signed contracts, but most of them would shop around and deliberate before deciding. With big bucks at stake, the risks were enormous. An item that glittered in scintillating Paris could bomb in sober Scarsdale.

A spectrum of options was available to wholesalers. I discussed one of them with Sydney Blauner, a chunky man in his fifties whose Manhattan firm turned out a line under the label Suzy Perette. For an ante of two thousand dollars and royalties, he acquired the right to incorporate Dior's notions into dresses that retailed in the United States for fifty or sixty dollars. Thus, on a slim budget, an Atlanta stenographer or a Cleveland nurse could emulate a glamorous Parisienne. As Blauner told me, "If you don't come to Paris, you're missing the boat. There are more ideas in a thimble here than in all of America."

Pirates chronically menaced the couturiers. A case that hit the headlines unfolded in 1948, when a customer complained to Dior that she had paid a whopping sum for an exclusive gown and, at a ritzy nightclub, spotted another woman in exactly the same number. "This is not a joke," she wept, "but a tragedy." Promptly summoned by Dior, the gendarmes launched an investigation that ended six years later in the arrest of a gang of fashion thieves. They had been stealing designs, which they shipped to London, Brussels, Beirut and elsewhere for conversion into cheap facsimiles. Documents compiled by the police divulged their methods. They would bribe a seamstress or a *midinette* to purloin patterns, or coax a mannequin into borrowing a dress for an evening and copy it. Indicted for violating French copyright law, they were convicted and fined. But one couturier, voicing doubts that forgers could ever be stopped, said, "Maybe we ought to take it as a compliment when they rob us."

As I sought to understand fashion, I discovered that it was misty and nebulous—easier described than defined. I reread Proust's passage on Odette Swann: "Attire to her symbolized the delicate and spiritual mechanism of a whole form of civilization." For Jean Cocteau, fertile artist, playwright, filmmaker and aesthetic arbiter, fashion "thrills us briefly with its insolent, enigmatic bouquet—then, like a frail blossom, dies." Cecil Beaton, the chichi English photographer, differed: "Fashions are ephemeral, but fashion is enduring." Over an apéritif at a Saint-Germain-des-Prés café, the sassy Comptesse Louise de Vilmorin discarded all this rhetoric as poppycock: "Fashion is a veneer foisted on naïve women by despots. Give me sincere blue jeans."

Late one afternoon I spent an hour or so with Dior in his green-paneled sanctum above his salon. A plump, balding bachelor of fifty-two whose pink cheeks might have been sculpted from marzipan, he resembled an ambassador or a banker in his charcoal double-breasted suit, the rosette in its lapel denoting his grade as an officer of the Légion d'Honneur. Relaxed after the day's grind, he appreciated the chance to talk. His bland, courteous exterior concealed an inner tension, presumably the result of his dedication to a strenuous, competitive field. When I suggested to him that fashion would wither unless women felt compelled to comply with the latest modes, he peered up his aquiline nose at the ceiling, chuckled and replied, "I'm no philosopher, but it seems to me that women—and men too—instinctively yearn to exhibit themselves. In this machine age, which esteems convention and uniformity, fashion is the ultimate refuge of the human, the personal and the inimitable. Even the most outrageous innovations should be welcomed, if only because they shield us against the shabby and the humdrum. Of course fashion is a transient, egotistical indulgence, yet in an era as somber as ours, luxury must be defended centimeter by centimeter." He resented the charge that dressmakers imposed their will on their clients: "It's a calumny to call us dictators. *Le couturier propose, la femme dispose.*"

The following evening Dior invited me for drinks at his *hôtel particulier* in upscale Passy, near the Château de la Muette. His butler uncorked a vintage Dom Pérignon and, enveloped in magenta upholstered armchairs under a stilted Bernard Buffet portrait of him above the fireplace, we sipped a glass or two. Then, realizing that I was there to gather information for my story, he gave me free rein to poke around. The decor was a ragout of the sublime and the grotesque. Tiers of shelves held sets of leather-bound volumes, odd pieces of bric-a-brac and autographed photos of French and foreign dignitaries, famous writers, composers, opera singers, movie directors, actors and actresses. The vermilion damask walls were a quilt of engravings and aquarelles, Impressionists, Neo-Impressionists, Cubists, Surrealists, Dadaists and kitschy fin de siècle paintings of verdant landscapes and beefy nudes. Ancient Greek amphorae and Roman busts, antique Gallic ceramics and Ming porcelains sat on inlaid medieval Spanish and Italian chests alongside such carnival souvenirs as stuffed animals, plastic *poupées* and plaster statuettes. The boudoir was furnished with a crimson-canopied Empire bed, a purple Louis XIV *prie-dieu*, mauve draperies and a white bearskin rug. Dior frequently switched clothes three or four times a day; and his closets and drawers, I guessed, contained hundreds of suits, pajamas, ties and pairs of socks and shoes. Peeking into the Florentine-tiled bathroom, I noticed a colossal Empire green marble tub lined in zinc and equipped with swan's-head faucets. "My friends tease me for accumulating this stuff," he said, "but valuable or trashy, it inspires me in some way or other. I regard it as my own flea market."

Unlike many of his fellow couturiers, who publicized themselves by mixing with *le tout Paris* at glittering galas, Dior was a hermit and, prizing his privacy, seldom went to the opera, the cinema or the theater. He preferred to dine quietly at home and perhaps play a rubber of bridge with a few intimates. His domestic staff of six included a cook, and, defying his doctor's orders to curb his weight, he was partial to earthy peasant casseroles accompanied by choice wines and liqueurs, among them a fine framboise bottled at his château in the forest of Fontainebleau, near Paris. A devout Catholic, he rarely skipped Sunday mass, but he was deeply superstitious, regularly consulted an astrologer and swore by her communion with the zodiac.

Pursuing our chat, I asked Dior to explain why fashion thrived in France. "First," he responded, "we inherited a tradition of craftsmanship rooted in the anonymous artisans who constructed the cathedrals and expressed their genius in chiseled stone gargoyles and cherubs. Their descendants—skilled automobile mechanics, cabinetmakers, masons, plumbers, handymen—are proud of their métiers. They feel humiliated if they've done a shoddy job. Similarly, my tailors, seamstresses, even novice *midinettes*, constantly strive for perfection. We also benefit, paradoxically, from having a singularly difficult consumer: the Parisienne. At a fitting she behaves like a contortionist. She stands up, sits down, bends and wriggles around; actually she is testing a dress because, she knows, an unhinged strap or a clasp could mean disaster at a fancy soirée. Often she brings along her husband or her lover, and they fidget as well over stitches, seams and buttonholes. They exasperate us, but we cannot afford to ignore their fussing, however petty it may seem. Unless they leave Chez Dior in complete self-confidence, we have blundered and our image will be tarnished as a consequence."

To create his collections, Dior would seclude himself in his château or soak in his bathtub, drafting thousands of spidery sketches on scraps of paper—a kind of hieroglyphic of silhouettes and contours. "Suddenly," he said, "one of them astounds me, as though I have accidentally encountered an acquaintance on a country lane. I embrace it as my motif for the season and give it a name—the A-line, the H-line, the *haricot-vert* line, whatever. Then I refine and color about seven hundred of these *petites gravures*, and they will make up the core of the collection."

Next he conferred with his principal deputies—three female fashion veterans whose opinions he respected. After much debate, they approved about sixty designs, which were then cut into tulle patterns and modeled by mannequins in Dior's spacious atelier. Wearing a white butcher's smock, perched on a high stool and wielding an ivory-tipped bamboo swagger stick, Dior repeatedly reviewed them for weeks. A stickler for detail, he would point his stick at a mannequin and insist on adjusting a pocket, altering a pleat, revising a collar, moving a belt, shifting a bow. Nothing

eluded his sharp eye—purses, necklaces, earrings, stockings, parasols and the myriad other accessories vital to every smart lady's
wardrobe. Particularly troublesome for him were so-called Trafal-
gars, fragile, elaborate ball dresses that easily came unstuck and
had to be stiffened without losing their flossiness. He rehearsed
the mannequins tirelessly, displaying surprising grace as he stepped
onto the floor to demonstrate their routines himself. As the show
approached, he toiled around the clock, pushing his team to the
brink of exhaustion. Spinster *midinettes*, clinging to custom, would
sew a lock of their hair into the hems of the wedding gowns in
hopes of snaring a husband during the year ahead.

"After all the horrors of preparing a collection," Dior con-
fided to me, "I wouldn't think of attending a show." One day,
however, he authorized me to hang out backstage during a presen-
tation, and it was a zoo. Helpers and apprentices raced around,
pushing racks of dresses and bolts of cloth and other paraphernalia.
lia. The mannequins, so cool and distant on the runway, were now
half nude, disheveled and frenetic as fitters brushed their gar-
ments, hairdressers rearranged their coiffures, and cosmeticians
freshened their lipstick, rouge and mascara. Sounding like a railroad conductor, a dispatcher brandishing a watch and a schedule
gently patted their derrieres as he thrust them into the salon under
their pseudonyms: *"Diane, Columbine, Fleur de Lis, Mirabelle . . ."* A
supervisor remarked to me as we stood in a corner, *"C'est de l'anar-
chie, n'est-ce pas, mais ça marche quand même."*

One of four children of a wealthy fertilizer manufacturer, Dior
grew up in an immense, chalky stucco house located on a wind-
swept cliff above the rugged Normandy coast. Exploring its vast
grounds on summer days was a pleasure that he never forgot. He
was pampered by German nannies and coddled by his mother,
from whom he learned to treasure flowers and to decorate the

dinner table when company was coming. Chubby and awkward, he would linger belowstairs, where the maids regaled him with fairy tales and folk songs, and taught him the rudiments of sewing. He delighted in designing costumes and organizing fancy-dress parties for his playmates. After he began school, his teacher scolded him for doodling leggy women in gowns on his exam papers and work sheets. "Despite the reprimands," he told me, "I felt this compulsion to make sketches."

In 1914, when Dior was ten, his parents moved to Paris and bought a house in Passy, where he himself subsequently resided. Many years later, a fortune-teller predicted after reading his palm, "Women will assure your success." He was then contemplating the notion of becoming a couturier, and floated the idea past his father, who laughed and said, "At your age I dreamt of undressing women, not dressing them." Deflated, Dior entered the École des Sciences Politiques, which trained diplomats. He graduated but, instead of enrolling in the civil service, plunged into artsy Paris. Granted a fat allowance by his family, he sported a bowler hat and a fur coat, and mingled with experimental musicians like Satie and Poulenc, and such avant-garde painters as Dalí, Max Jacob, Kandinsky, Klee and Miró. He also rounded up several Braques, Dufys, Chagalls, Matisses and Picassos and, with a partner, opened a gallery. His father agreed to finance him—on condition that the family name never appear on the door.

One day in 1930, Dior was panicked to find a shattered mirror in his room—and justifiably so. Within two months his mother and a brother had died, and shortly afterward the Depression ruined his father. He himself was afflicted with a lung ailment and spent a year recuperating in the Alps. On his return to Paris he was flat broke and had to liquidate the Passy house, his gallery and its canvases. But, during his convalescence, he studied embroidery, which led him to try his hand at designing dresses. To his amazement he sold six sketches to Robert Piguet, a Swiss couturier based in Paris, for twenty francs each. Soon he started to work full-time for Piguet, and was later engaged by Lucien Lelong. "At the age of thirty," he recollected, "I had found my career."

He was inducted into the army on the eve of World War II and put into a labor battalion. Demobilized when France surrendered to Germany, he joined his father and a sister in Provence, where they survived by growing and peddling fruit and vegetables. Dior enjoyed the countryside, but in 1942 he went back to Paris and to a job with Lelong. During the Occupation, women were desperate to preen themselves as a way of boosting their morale; and couturiers, wrestling with shortages of materials, contrived to infuse straw hats, burlap skirts and ersatz leather shoes with a dash of verve. "The styles were incredibly hideous," Dior recalled, "and I couldn't wait to do something better."

His opportunity arose after the Liberation. New York was then threatening to eclipse Paris as the world's fashion center, and France's leading textile tycoon, Marcel Boussac, feared that the decline of French couture would affect his plants. He searched for a designer to rejuvenate the sluggish Paris salons, and considered Dior. Exhilarated by the prospect of managing his own house, Dior envisioned "a venture aimed at serving a few discriminating women." But before long he had qualms about burdening himself with the responsibility, and again turned to a fortune-teller. *"Imaginez! Chez Dior! Acceptez!"* she exhorted him—and he did. Boussac put up a million dollars and, among his initiatives, Dior began to recruit mannequins. He inserted an ad in the newspapers, and a legion of beauties appeared. By coincidence the city authorities had recently closed the brothels, and the girls were shelterless prostitutes who thought that a clandestine bordello had just been inaugurated.

In December 1946 Dior retreated to his house near Paris and, working steadily for three weeks, completed his first collection. "The hardships of the war were finished," he later said. "I revived the ripe bosom, the wasp waist and soft shoulders, and molded them to the natural curves of the feminine body. It was a nostalgic voyage back to elegance." He labeled it the New Look and, the critics ecstatically wrote, made fashion history.

[. . .]

Dior's New Look triggered a storm of controversy. He amplified skirts, tightened waists, brought back petticoats and lowered hems to below the calf—intending through his generous use of material to dramatize the end of austerity. But some mavens cautioned that most women were conservative, and would shun the drastic change. "Again the capitalists are squandering resources while poor children go hungry," thundered *L'Humanité*, while *Combat* blared: *"Aux ciseaux, les citoyennes!"* At the other extreme, Fernand Gregh, a member of the Académie Française, noted: "The more we clothe a woman, the more desirable she becomes." The publicity sent Dior's stock skyrocketing. He was given a six-page layout in *Life*, and American stores anticipated brisk sales.

But, perceiving that haute couture was at best only marginally profitable, Dior quickly expanded his operations. He was the first couturier to develop the boutique, which enabled women to procure *prêt-à-porter* renditions of his premium dresses at relatively modest prices. The outlets also carried a gamut of spin-offs bearing his logo—scarves, handkerchiefs, lingerie, jewelry, sunglasses. In our final talk I returned to the question of what sustained fashion. He countered with a question: "Have you ever seen a woman enter a shop and ask for 'something just like the one I'm wearing'?"

Deborah Baldwin
(1949–   )

DEBORAH BALDWIN is a staff editor at the *New York Times* "House & Home" section. Before joining the *Times*, she lived and worked as a freelance writer in Paris. In the article reprinted here, she examines how the City of Light stays beautiful and keeps urban living civilized. It was informed in part by her curiosity as an American living in Paris during the mid- to late 1990s but also as a resident and beneficiary of Paris's municipal largesse. Baldwin has contributed articles about Paris and France to numerous publications including *Paris Notes*, *France Magazine*, *The Washington Post*, *The Philadelphia Inquirer*, and Discovery Channel Online. She also taught journalism at the Institut d'Études Politiques de Paris, the prestigious school of political science in Paris (nicknamed "Sciences Po" by Parisians). Previously, she was the editor of the award-winning bi-monthly, *Common Cause Magazine*, which covered people and politics in Washington, D.C.

❖ Paying the Way ❖

from Paris Notes

They've been working on our corner—for about five years. First they dug up the sidewalk at the foot of the boulevard de l'Hôpital to fix a sewer line. No sooner was the site paved over than the construction crew was back, this time to make a surgical attack on the curbstones. Soon the intersection had handicap-friendly pedestrian islands, several new traffic lights and the beginnings of a bike path.

It took a little longer to renovate the century-old Pont d'Austerlitz, just a block away. But now it, too, has a bike path and broad sidewalks that make walking over the Seine—which glows under the glittery new Charles de Gaulle bridge—even more pleasant. When the new Météor subway line opened on the far side of the river, piles of construction debris and makeshift offices disappeared. Across the way emerged a manicured vest-pocket park.

Metro workers have sledgehammered and rebuilt the stairs leading into our station twice in the five years we've lived here, if I'm not mistaken, and last year they repositioned the bus stop across the street to bring it a little closer to our apartment. Shrubbery and flowers started appearing a few years ago as part of a city beautification program, and last summer the sidewalk was widened in parts and more new trees went in, making my weekly walk to the supermarket—itself the subject of recent renovations—more aesthetic.

And I can't fail to mention the best little capital improvement since we moved to this block: After years of dodging six lanes of traffic to reach the post office across the street, I awoke recently to find a new traffic light holding back the cars. In case I'd missed it, there was a note, signed by the mayor, in our mailbox. Here's something, I thought, as I cakewalked across the boulevard, I'd never expect to see back home.

This is a story about what happens when public property is treated with the same lavish attention as a wealthy person's private residence. Not that we live in some fancy part of town where the streets are trod by foreign dignitaries, wide-eyed tourists, and well-heeled residents. Indeed, our little patch of the Left Bank, hard by the sprawling Austerlitz train station and bereft of great bakeries and cheese shops, barely qualifies as a neighborhood. It is more like a way station, an area countless people pass through en route to the Bastille, Jardin des Plantes or rue Mouffetard street market. Few are conscious of the myriad improvements, big and small, that contribute to the pleasure of their journey. And that's just the point.

The older you get, the more time and money you have to spend to look good, and Paris is no exception. To maintain its handsome, well-scrubbed self, the city spent 28.6 billion francs in 1999 and the *département* Paris belongs to kicked in another 3.6 billion—all told, the equivalent of $5.3 billion. This doesn't include the billions that will flow out of state coffers and into city services—helping to fund everything from day-care centers and transit systems to parks and gardens, museums and riot police—or the countless billions in private spending that ultimately improve the physical environment.

Americans, said to be enjoying the greatest economic prosperity in history, can only stop and stare at what money can buy. Never mind *grands travaux* like the $1.3 billion Bibliothèque Nationale, or national library, whose immense glass towers rose up two years ago on a formerly forlorn tract beyond Austerlitz station. If urban maintenance is in the details, consider a four-year plan announced by Mayor Jean Tiberi in 1998. If all goes as planned, it will disperse $270 million on such refinements as overhauling the place de la Concorde to make it more pedestrian-friendly; sprucing up twelve kilometers (7.5 miles) of riverside between the Parc André Citroën and the new Parc de Bercy; installing high-tech lighting under various bridges; and constructing a pedestrian *passerelle* (cost: $16 million) that will sail over the Seine between the Bibliothèque Nationale and Bercy Park. These embellishments are separate from the bike paths, off-street parking and other infrastructure projects that are also in the works. It's hard not to wonder what Tiberi would be doing if the economy was booming à l'américaine.

Nowhere is the contrast starker than between the capital of France and Washington, D.C., a city as renowned during the 1980s for its potholes, crime and decaying schools as it was for its cherry blossoms, great museums and bourgeoisie. A three-part CNN series in 1998 comparing the two capitals, *Tale of Two Cities,* dwelled on Washington's murder rate—twenty times that of Paris—and Paris's high-performance high schools, the envy of Washington's elite.

As CNN made clear, money makes a difference, and so does gun control. There are, however, other factors that contribute to Paris's relative well-being. I like to think of the culture gap this way: When the landscape is wanting, Americans pick up and move to greener pastures. Parisians, however, inhabit a city that was once hemmed in by stone walls. The city looks inward, and it invests downtown.

The underclass gets pushed to the edges, to neighborhoods delicately referred to as *quartiers difficiles.* And one hundred years after Napoléon III's urban planner Baron Haussmann rebuilt half of Paris, wiping out countless *quartiers difficiles* in the process, came a second era of sweeping renewal and big-ticket projects.

The edifice complex of the 1970s and 1980s yielded such startling visions as the Parc de la Villette, La Défense, the Louvre's glass pyramid, and the sophisticated Parc André Citroën, culminating with the creation of the hundred-acre spread at Bercy. Today, a mere two thousand years after construction began, Paris is largely "done," leaving only one megaproject still on the drawing board: a twenty-year, 20-billion-franc plan to flesh out the area around the Bibliothèque Nationale.

"We have fewer and fewer *grandes opérations,*" according to Michel Bulté, Mayor Tiberi's *adjoint chargé de l'urbanisme,* who oversaw a Byzantine collection of thirty agencies at the time. "Now it's more like a half acre here and a half acre there." Many of these "human-scale" projects—carried out, he maintained, with 1990s-style neighborhood input—are in the formerly overlooked eastern districts, where a peculiarly French merging of public and private interests is helping to recycle and retrofit historic and abandoned property and the rare vacant lot.

Despite problems associated with speculation and gentrification, "This is not a city just for tourists and the rich," he continued. "Fifty percent of the population is middle class. Twenty percent of the housing is low-income." A concerted effort is being made to lure offices out of apartment dwellings so they can be turned back into housing, and tax policies are designed to keep working-class families in the city and protect mixed-income *quartiers*.

By American standards, the system seems to work. Meanwhile, with its infrastructure largely in place, Paris has the luxury, as city hall elegantly sums it up, of moving "in the direction of the quality of services . . . their diversity, their imagination and their sense of adapting to the evolution of social needs."

Along with refining some social welfare programs (such as a debit card that gives large families entry at city museums and the like), Tiberi is making an "unprecedented environmental push." This translates into money for bigger sidewalks (and not a minute too soon; twenty-eight hundred pedestrians had run-ins with local drivers in 1997) and better controls on three Parisian bugaboos: noise, graffiti, and dog poop.

On the front lines are the platoons of men in green who ply a thousand sidewalks with pressure hoses, tricking me several times a week into thinking it's just rained. Many members of this unusual army come on foot, while others forge a path in fanciful vehicles custom-made to conform to Paris's unique needs: I caught one Dr. Seussian contraption clamping its mechanical arms around the trees on our street and raising the grates at the rootline so that brooms could get under their skirts. Manned *caninettes* the size of Harley-Davidsons (derided as *cacamobiles*, or poop trucks) scurry down the sidewalks, vacuuming up some four tons of dog excrement a day, or about a fifth of what Paris's three hundred thousand pooches leave behind—for ultimate disposal I'm not sure where. Other sanitation vehicles have rotating brushes that work like carpet beaters, and some shoot out hot, soapy water. One person I know insists he saw two green trucks stop in the middle of the sidewalk so *they could scrub off each other.*

Garbage collection and street cleaning consume a stunning 10 percent of the budget, according to *Paris le journal,* an absorbing little magazine distributed free by city hall. The city's obsession with the care and cleaning of pavements goes back a ways—to 1185—when Philippe Auguste introduced those tony granite blocks that look like sugar cubes. It's been build-and-clean ever since.

"Municipal sweeping" began in 1873, and in 1884 the city ordered residents to start using garbage cans. The next milestone, in 1978, was the introduction of those nifty green trash cans on wheels that can be hoisted and emptied mechanically. These days, the city deploys a rolling force of sixteen hundred vehicles, including not only dump trucks, which cart off some three thousand tons of household garbage a day, but two hundred specialized *engins,* nearly half of them *caninettes.* Asked how much the dog-poop control costs taxpayers, a city hall spokeswoman referred vaguely to a private contractor that does the dirty work at some indeterminate fee folded into a nearly $1-billion budget for street, garden and park maintenance. Clearly, it's a lot, and wanton pooches provide much grist for the pages of *le journal'*s letters page ("What a waste!" and so on). Articles politely suggesting that dog owners take advantage of city-sponsored dog-training classes—not to mention eighteen official doggie toilets recently installed in parks around town—haven't had the desired result, so the *cacamobiles* keep rolling.

And so too, night and day, seven days a week, come the ranks of maintenance engineers—seventy-five hundred all told, including forty-five hundred who do nothing but sweep some 10 million square meters of sidewalks and street gutters. Cleanup artists "de-graffiti" some 129,700 square meters of vertical Paris a year and "de-poster" another 284,800; Tiberi announced they would strip every wall in town clean within "a few months." A team of 223 lumberjacks does nothing but trim the city's fifty thousand trees.

When Paris isn't giving its streets what-for, it is giving its parks and gardens the Versailles treatment. The city maintains around nine hundred acres of greenery; spending on green space will rise 34 percent this year, to $190 million, allowing the creation of six new gardens. The city employs one park worker for every fifteen residents, according to two Paris-based producers for CNN, James Bitterman and Patricia Thompson. The city's gardener in chief, Françoise de Panafieu, boasted at a press conference that city greenhouses cultivate 3 million flowers a year. "And five parks escape our supervision," Tiberi chimed in, including such national projects as Luxembourg, the Jardin des Plantes and the Tuileries.

Someone has to pay for all this, of course, and taxes are higher in France than in the United States—by about two-thirds, CNN calculated.

Indeed, there are so many line items on the typical French pay slip I had to be sedated when I was handed my first (the last in a long list on the pay stub: *autres charges patronales*). But you don't have to be on the payroll to help pay Paris's way. Visitors, who number more than 20 million a year, get a taste of the government's *savoir-taxer* at every store, theater, hotel, café or restaurant they walk into because a 20.6 percent VAT, or valued-added tax, is cloaked in the price of nearly all goods and services. In 1998 the VAT brought in $112 billion, according to the Finance Ministry, or twice the amount raised from income taxes.

Less obvious are the miscellaneous taxes on things like *habitation* (read: apartment occupancy), utilities and even TV ownership, all of which, directly or indirectly, help raise money for city services. According to one calculation, municipal taxes come to about $890 per person per year.

Then there's the do-it-yourself law that requires Parisian apartment owners to overhaul their building's facade every ten years, or face fines running as high as $6,600. Last year the owners of some nondescript low-rises near us spent several months scraping and repainting the exterior walls, going so far as to re-create a faded bootmaker's sign inscribed over the alley during some long-ago era. Bitterman says he and Thompson, who co-own a 6th Arrondissement apartment building, coughed up $14,625 toward the *ravalement* of their ten-unit building, only $3,000 of it tax-deductible. Not that it was like throwing money out one of their lovely nineteenth-century windows. "It improves property values," Bitterman says of the *ravalement* requirement. "It improves the city's value. And it improves the way of life."

Not every corner of Paris gets regular facelifts (or even a good sweeping, if the Stalingrad Métro stop is any indication), and the turbulent close-in suburbs suffer from every kind of urban ill. Somewhere in all the municipal spending—handled by a mind-boggling forty thousand city hall employees—are surely examples of waste, fraud and abuse. Moreover, certain aspects of the city's well-being, most notably its low crime rate and competitive schools, cannot be explained in strictly financial terms. But in no other city can a visitor get a better sense of what it means to tax and spend for the common good. Nowhere else can the payoff be so plain.

Live here long enough and you can begin to take it all for granted. Just recently, I got off the Métro at the Pyramides stop and was delighted to find spanking new walls and escalators and floors that shone like glass, part of the new billion-dollar Météor subway line. I felt like an investment banker dropping by her country estate after a long absence and being pleasantly surprised by the new marble floor and wrought-iron gate. Then thinking: "Hey, I'm so well-off that other people take care of all this for me."

Thomas Jefferson
(1743–1826)

THOMAS JEFFERSON, the third U.S. president, was born and educated in Virginia. He came from a well-to-do family of high social standing and received a thorough formal education in the classics. He studied at the College of William and Mary, then law with one of the foremost law teachers of his generation. He lived in Paris from 1784 to 1789, succeeding his friend and compatriot, Benjamin Franklin, as the ambassador to France in 1785. Jefferson wrote in his autobiography: "In what country on earth would you rather live?—Certainly in my own, where are all my friends, my relations, and the earliest & sweetest affections and recollections of my life. Which would be your second choice? France." Jefferson was greatly influenced by his stay in Paris and later advised that no young man's education was complete without having seen the art and architecture of Paris and the civilized manners of its people.

He was hailed even in his day as the "Man of the People" because of his belief that governments should serve the popular interest and will of the common man, hence his sympathies with the French Revolution. Only a few years since the American Revolution, during which France's financial and military support had been invaluable, many Americans including Jefferson took a great interest in the fate of the revolution in France. The excerpt of Jefferson's autobiography shows him following the events preceding the revolution closely while he was in Paris. Surprisingly, Jefferson did not advocate a totally democratic system for the French; he supported a limited monarchy instead, believing that the French were not yet ready for the American variety of self-government. The eventual excesses of the French Revolution disappointed Jefferson, particularly its culmination in Napoleon's dictatorship, which Jefferson also discusses here.

from

☆ The Autobiography ☆

May 18. The pecuniary distresses of France produced this year a measure of which there had been no example for near two centuries, & the consequences of which, good and evil, are not yet calculable. For its remote causes we must go a little back.

Celebrated writers of France and England had already sketched good principles on the subject of government. Yet the American Revolution seems first to have awakened the thinking part of the French nation in general from the sleep of despotism in which they were sunk. The officers too who had been to America, were mostly young men, less shackled by habit and prejudice, and more ready to assent to the suggestions of common sense, and feeling of common rights. They came back with new ideas & impressions. The press, notwithstanding its shackles, began to disseminate them. Conversation assumed new freedoms. Politics became the theme of all societies, male and female, and a very extensive & zealous party was formed which acquired the appellation of the Patriotic party, who, sensible of the abusive government under which they lived, sighed for occasions of reforming it. This party comprehended all the honesty of the kingdom sufficiently at its leisure to think, the men of letters, the easy Bourgeois, the young nobility partly from reflection, partly from mode, for these sentiments became matter of mode, and as such united most of the young women to the party. [...]

On my return from Holland, I had found Paris still in high fermentation as I had left it. Had the Archbishop, on the close of the assembly of Notables, immediately carried into operation the measures contemplated, it was believed they would all have been registered by the parliament, but he was slow, presented his edicts, one after another, & at considerable intervals of time, which gave time for the feelings excited by the proceedings of the Notables to cool off, new claims to be advanced, and a pressure to arise for a fixed constitution, not subject to changes at the will of the King. Nor should we wonder at this pressure when we consider the monstrous abuses of power under which this people were ground to powder, when we pass in review the weight of their taxes, and inequality of their distribution; the oppressions of the tythes, of the tailles, the corvées, the gabelles, the farms & barriers; the shackles on Commerce by monopolies; on Industry by gilds & corporations; on the freedom of conscience, of thought, and of speech; on the Press by the Censure; and of person by lettres de Cachet; the cruelty of the criminal code generally, the atrocities of the Rack, the venality of judges, and their partialities to the rich; the Monopoly of Military honors by the Noblesse; the enormous expenses of the Queen, the princes & the Court; the prodigalities of pensions; & the riches, luxury, indolence & immorality of the clergy. Surely under such a mass of misrule and oppression, a people might justly press for a thoro' reformation, and might even dismount their rough-shod riders, & leave them to walk on their own legs. [. . .]

For, while laboring under the want of money for even ordinary purposes, in a government which required a million of livres a day, and driven to the last ditch by the universal call for liberty, there came on a winter of such severe cold, as was without example in the memory of man, or in the written records of history. The Mercury was at times 50° below the freezing point of Fahrenheit and 22° below that of Reaumur. All out-door labor was suspended, and the poor, without the wages of labor, were of course without either bread or fuel. The government found its necessities aggravated by that of procuring immense quantities of fire-wood, and of keeping great fires at all the cross-streets, around which the people gathered in crowds to avoid perishing with cold. Bread too was to be bought, and distributed daily gratis, until a relaxation of the season should enable the people to work: and the slender stock of bread-stuff had for some time threatened famine, and had raised that article to an enormous price. So great indeed was the scarcity of bread that from the highest to the lowest citizen, the bakers were permitted to deal but a scanty allowance per head, even to those who paid for it; and in cards of invitation to dine in the richest houses, the guest was notified to bring his own bread. To eke out the existence of the people, every person who had the means, was called on for a weekly subscription, which the Curés collected and employed in providing messes for the nourishment of the poor, and vied with each other in devising such economical compositions of food as would subsist the greatest number with the smallest means. This want of bread had been foreseen for some time past and M. de Montmorin had desired me to notify it in America, and that, in addition to the market price, a premium should be given on what should be brought from the U.S. Notice was accordingly given and produced considerable supplies. Subsequent information made the importations from America, during the months of March, April & May, into the Atlantic ports of France, amount to about 21,000 barrels of flour, besides what went to other ports, and in other months, while our supplies to their West-Indian islands relieved them also from that drain. This distress for bread continued till July.

Hitherto no acts of popular violence had been produced by the struggle for political reformation. Little riots, on ordinary incidents, had taken place, as at other times, in different parts of the kingdom, in which some lives, perhaps a dozen or twenty, had been lost, but in the month of April a more serious one occurred in Paris, unconnected indeed with the revolutionary principle, but making part of the history of the day. The Fauxbourg St. Antoine is a quarter of the city inhabited entirely by the class of day-laborers and journeymen in every line. A rumor was spread among them that a great paper manufacturer, of the name of Reveillon, had proposed, on some occasion, that their wages should be lowered to 15 sous a day. Inflamed at once into rage, & without inquiring into its truth, they flew to his house in vast numbers, destroyed everything in it, and in his magazines & work shops, without secreting however a pin's worth to themselves, and were continuing this work of devastation when the regular troops were called in. Admonitions being disregarded, they were of necessity fired on, and a regular action ensued, in which about 100 of them were killed, before the rest would disperse. There had rarely passed a year without such a riot in some part or other of the Kingdom; and this is distinguished only as contemporary with the revolution, altho' not produced by it. [. . .]

The Noblesse were in triumph; the people in consternation. I was quite alarmed at this state of things. The soldiery had not yet indicated which side they should take, and that which they should support would be sure to prevail. I considered a successful reformation of government in France, as ensuring a general reformation thro' Europe, and the resurrection, to a new life, of their people, now ground to dust by the abuses of the governing powers. I was much acquainted with the leading patriots of the assembly. Being from a country which had successfully passed thro' a similar reformation, they were disposed to my acquaintance, and had some confidence in me. I urged most strenuously an immediate compromise; to secure what the government was now ready to yield, and trust to future occasions for what might still be wanting. It was well understood that the King would grant at this time 1. Freedom of the person by Habeas corpus. 2. Freedom of conscience. 3. Freedom of the press. 4. Trial by jury. 5. A representative legislature. 6. Annual meetings. 7. The origination of laws. 8. The exclusive right of taxation and appropriation. And 9. The responsibility of ministers; and with the exercise of these powers they would obtain in future whatever might be further necessary to improve and preserve their constitution. They thought otherwise however, and events have proved their lamentable error. For after 30 years of war, foreign and domestic, the loss of millions of lives, the prostration of private happiness, and foreign subjugation of their own country for a time, they have obtained no more, nor even that securely. They were unconscious of (for who could foresee?) the melancholy sequel of their well-meant perseverance; that their physical force would be usurped by a first tyrant to trample on the independence, and even the existence, of other nations: that this would afford fatal example for the atrocious conspiracy of Kings against their people; would generate their unholy and homicide alliance to make common cause among themselves, and to crush, by the power of the whole, the efforts of any part, to moderate their abuses and oppressions.

When the King passed, the next day, thro' the lane formed from the Chateau to the Hotel des etats, there was a dead silence. He was about an hour in the House delivering his speech & declaration. On his coming out a feeble cry of "Vive le Roy" was raised by some children, but the people remained silent & sullen. [. . .]

These proceedings had thrown the people into violent ferment. It gained the souldiery, first of the French guards, extended to those of every other denomination, except the Swiss, and even to the body guards of the King. They began to quit their barracks, to assemble in squads, to declare they would defend the life of the King, but would not be the murderers of their fellow-citizens. They called themselves the souldiers *of the nation*, and left now no doubt on which side they would be, in case of rupture. Similar accounts came in from the troops in other parts of the kingdom, giving good reason to believe they would side with their fathers and brothers rather than with their officers. The operation of this medicine at Versailles was as sudden as it was powerful. The alarm there was so compleat that in the afternoon of the 27th the King wrote with his own hand letters to the Presidents of the clergy and Nobles, engaging them immediately to join the Tiers. These two bodies were debating & hesitating when notes from the Ct. d'Artois decided their compliance. They went in a body and took their seats with the tiers, and thus rendered the union of the orders in one chamber compleat.

The Assembly now entered on the business of their mission, and first proceeded to arrange the order in which they would take up the heads of their constitution, as follows:

First, and as Preliminary to the whole a general Declaration of the Rights of Man. Then specifically the Principles of the Monarchy; rights of the Nation; rights of the King; rights of the citizens; organization & rights of the National assembly; forms necessary for the enactment of laws; organization & functions of the provincial & municipal assemblies; duties and limits of the Judiciary power; functions & duties of the military power.

A declaration of the rights of man, as the preliminary of their work, was accordingly prepared and proposed by the Marquis de la Fayette.

But the quiet of their march was soon disturbed by information that troops, and particularly the foreign troops, were advancing on Paris from various quarters. The King had been probably advised to this on the pretext of preserving peace in Paris. But his advisers were believed to have other things in contemplation. The Marshal de Broglio was appointed to their command, a high flying aristocrat, cool and capable of everything. Some of the French guards were soon arrested, under other pretexts, but really on account of their dispositions in favor of the National cause. The people of Paris forced their prison, liberated them, and sent a deputation to the Assembly to solicit a pardon. The Assembly recommended peace and order to the people of Paris, the prisoners to the king, and asked from him the removal of the troops. His answer was negative and dry, saying they might remove themselves, if they pleased, to Noyons or Soissons. In the meantime these troops, to the number of twenty or thirty thousand, had arrived and were posted in, and between Paris and Versailles. The bridges and passes were guarded. At three o'clock in the afternoon of the 11th July the Count de la Luzerne was sent to notify

Mr. Neckar of his dismission, and to enjoin him to retire instantly without saying a word of it to anybody. He went home, dined, and proposed to his wife a visit to a friend, but went in fact to his country house at St. Ouen, and at midnight set out for Brussels. This was not known until the next day, 12th when the whole ministry was changed, except Villedeuil, of the Domestic department, and Barenton, Garde des sceaux. [. . .]

The news of this change began to be known at Paris about 1 or 2 o'clock. In the afternoon a body of about 100 German cavalry were advanced and drawn up in the Place Louis XV and about 200 Swiss posted at a little distance in their rear. This drew people to the spot, who thus accidentally found themselves in front of the troops, merely at first as spectators; but as their numbers increased, their indignation rose. They retired a few steps, and posted themselves on and behind large piles of stones, large and small, collected in that Place for a bridge which was to be built adjacent to it. In this position, happening to be in my carriage on a visit, I passed thro' the lane they had formed, without interruption. But the moment after I had passed, the people attacked the cavalry with stones. They charged, but the advantageous position of the people, and the showers of stones obliged the horse to retire, and quit the field altogether, leaving one of their number on the ground, & the Swiss in their rear not moving to their aid. This was the signal for universal insurrection, and this body of cavalry, to avoid being massacred, retired towards Versailles. The people now armed themselves with such weapons as they could find in armorer's shops and private houses, and with bludgeons, and were roaming all night thro' all parts of the city, without any decided object. The next day (13th) the assembly pressed on the king to send away the troops, to permit the Bourgeoisie of Paris to arm for the preservation of order in the city, and offer to send a deputation from their body to tranquillize them; but their propositions were refused. A committee of magistrates and electors of the city are appointed by those bodies to take upon them its government. The people, now openly joined by the French guards, force the prison of St. Lazare, release all the prisoners, and take a great store of corn, which they carry to the Corn-market. Here they get some arms, and the French guards begin to form & train them. The City-committee determined to raise 48,000 Bourgeoise, or rather to restrain their numbers to 48,000. On the 14th they send one of their members (Mons. de Corny) to the Hotel des Invalides, to ask arms for their Garde-Bourgeoise. He was followed by, and he found there a great collection of people. The Governor of the Invalids came out and represented the impossibility of his delivering arms without the orders of those from whom he received them. De Corny advised the people then to retire, and retired himself; but the people took possession of the arms. It was remarkable that not only the Invalids themselves made no opposition, but that a body of 5,000 foreign troops, within 400 yards, never stirred. M. de Corny and five others were then sent to ask arms of M. de Launai, governor of the Bastile. They found a great collection of people already before the place, and they immediately planted a flag of truce, which was answered by a like flag hoisted on the Parapet. The deputation prevailed on the people to fall back a little, advanced themselves to make their demand of the Governor, and in that instant a discharge from the Bastile killed four persons, of those nearest to the deputies. The deputies retired. I happened to be at the house of M. de Corny when he returned to it, and received from him a narrative of these transactions. On the retirement of the deputies, the people rushed forward & almost in an instant were in possession of a fortification defended by 100 men; of infinite strength, which in other times had stood several regular sieges, and had never been taken. How they forced their entrance has never been explained. They took all the arms, discharged the prisoners, and such of the garrison as were not killed in the first moment of fury, carried the Governor and Lt. Governor to the Place de Grève (the place of public execution) cut off their heads, and sent them thro' the city

in triumph to the Palais royal. About the same instant a treacherous correspondence having been discovered in M. de Flesselles,
prevot des marchands, they seized him in the Hotel de Ville where
he was in the execution of his office, and cut off his head. These
events carried imperfectly to Versailles were the subject of two
successive deputations from the assembly to the king, to both of
which he gave dry and hard answers for nobody had as yet been
permitted to inform him truly and fully of what had passed at
Paris. But at night the Duke de Liancourt forced his way into the
king's bed chamber, and obliged him to hear a full and animated
detail of the disasters of the day in Paris. He went to bed fearfully
impressed. The decapitation of de Launai worked powerfully
thro' the night on the whole aristocratic party, insomuch that, in
the morning, those of the greatest influence on the Count d'Artois represented to him the absolute necessity that the king should
give up everything to the Assembly. This according with the dispositions of the king, he went about 11 o'clock, accompanied only
by his brothers, to the Assembly, & there read to them a speech, in
which he asked their interposition to reestablish order. Altho'
couched in terms on some caution, yet the manner in which it was
delivered made it evident that it was meant as a surrender at dis-
cretion. He returned to the Chateau afoot, accompanied by the
assembly. They sent off a deputation to quiet Paris, at the head of
which was the Marquis de la Fayette who had, the same morning,
been named Commandant en chef of the Milice Bourgeoise, and
Mons Bailly, former President of the States General, was called
for as Prevot des marchands. The demolition of the Bastile was
now ordered and begun. A body of the Swiss guards of the regiment of Ventimille, and the city horse guards joined the people.
The alarm at Versailles increased. The foreign troops were
ordered off instantly. Every minister resigned. The king confirmed Bailly as Prevot des Marchands, wrote to Mr. Neckar to
recall him, sent his letter open to the assembly, to be forwarded by
them, and invited them to go with him to Paris the next day, to sat-

isfy the city of his dispositions; and that night, and the next morning the Count D'Artois and M. de Montesson a deputy connected
with him, Madame de Polignac, Madame de Guiche, and the
Count de Vaudreuil, favorites of the queen, the Abbe de Vermont
her confessor, the Prince of Condé and Duke of Bourbon fled.
The king came to Paris, leaving the queen in consternation for his
return. Omitting the less important figures of the procession, the
king's carriage was in the center, on each side of it the assembly, in
two ranks afoot, at their head the M. de la Fayette, as Commander-
in-chief, on horseback, and Bourgeois guards before and behind.
About 60,000 citizens of all forms and conditions, armed with the
muskets of the Bastile and Invalids, as far as they would go, the
rest with pistols, swords, pikes, pruning hooks, scythes &c. lined
all the streets thro' which the procession passed, and with the
crowds of people in the streets, doors, & windows, saluted them
everywhere with cries of "vive la nation," but not a single "vive le
roy" was heard. The King landed at the Hotel de Ville. There M.
Bailly presented and put into his hat the popular cockade, and
addressed him. The King being unprepared, and unable to
answer, Bailly went to him, gathered from him some scraps of
sentences, and made out an answer, which he delivered to the
audience as from the king. On their return the popular cries were
"vive le roy et la nation." He was conducted by a garde bourgeoise
to his palace at Versailles, & thus concluded an amende honorable
as no sovereign ever made, and no people ever received.

And here again was lost another precious occasion of sparing
to France the crimes and cruelties thro' which she has since
passed, and to Europe, & finally America the evils which flowed
on them also from this mortal source. The king was now become
a passive machine in the hands of the National assembly, and had
he been left to himself, he would have willingly acquiesced in
whatever they should devise as best for the nation. A wise constitution would have been formed, hereditary in his line, himself
placed at its head, with powers so large as to enable him to do all

the good of his station, and so limited as to restrain him from its abuse. This he would have faithfully administered, and more than this I do not believe he ever wished. But he had a Queen of absolute sway over his weak mind, and timid virtue; and of a character the reverse of his in all points. This angel, as gaudily painted in the rhapsodies of the Rhetor Burke, with some smartness of fancy, but no sound sense was proud, disdainful of restraint, indignant at all obstacles to her will, eager in the pursuit of pleasure, and firm enough to hold to her desires, or perish in their wreck. Her inordinate gambling and dissipations, with those of the Count d'Artois and others of her clique, had been a sensible item in the exhaustion of the treasury, which called into action the reforming hand of the nation; and her opposition to it her inflexible perverseness, and dauntless spirit, led herself to the Guillotine, & drew the king on with her, and plunged the world into crimes & calamities which will forever stain the pages of modern history. I have ever believed that had there been no queen, there would have been no revolution. No force would have been provoked nor exercised. The king would have gone hand in hand with the wisdom of his sounder counsellors, who, guided by the increased lights of the age, wished only, with the same pace, to advance the principles of their social institution. The deed which closed the mortal course of these sovereigns, I shall neither approve nor condemn. I am not prepared to say that the first magistrate of a nation cannot commit treason against his country, or is unamenable to its punishment: nor yet that where there is no written law, no regulated tribunal, there is not a law in our hearts, and a power in our hands, given for righteous employment in maintaining right, and redressing wrong. Of those who judged the king, many thought him wilfully criminal, many that his existence would keep the nation in perpetual conflict with the horde of kings, who would war against a regeneration which might come home to themselves, and that it were better that one should die than all. I should not have voted with this portion of the legislature. I should have shut up the Queen in a Convent, putting harm out of her power, and placed the king in his station, investing him with limited powers, which I verily believe he would have honestly exercised, according to the measure of his understanding. In this way no void would have been created, courting the usurpation of a military adventurer, nor occasion given for those enormities which demoralized the nations of the world, and destroyed, and is yet to destroy millions and millions of its inhabitants. There are three epochs in history signalized by the total extinction of national morality. The first was of the successors of Alexander, not omitting himself. The next the successors of the first Caesar, the third our own age. This was begun by the partition of Poland, followed by that of the treaty of Pilnitz; next the conflagration of Copenhagen; then the enormities of Bonaparte partitioning the earth at his will, and devastating it with fire and sword; now the conspiracy of kings, the successors of Bonaparte, blasphemously calling themselves the Holy Alliance, and treading in the footsteps of their incarcerated leader, not yet indeed usurping the government of other nations avowedly and in detail, but controuling by their armies the forms in which they will permit them to be governed; and reserving in petto the order and extent of the usurpations further meditated. But I will return from a digression, anticipated too in time, into which I have been led by reflection on the criminal passions which refused to the world a favorable occasion of saving it from the afflictions it has since suffered. [. . .]

Here I discontinue my relation of the French revolution. The minuteness with which I have so far given its details is disproportioned to the general scale of my narrative. But I have thought it justified by the interest which the whole world must take into this revolution. As yet we are but in the first chapter of its history. The appeal to the rights of man, which had been made in the U S. was taken up by France, first of the European nations. From her the spirit has spread over those of the South. The tyrants of the North have allied indeed against it, but it is irresistible. Their opposition will only multiply its millions of human victims; their own satellites will catch it, and the condition of man thro' the civilized world will be finally and greatly ameliorated. This is a wonderful instance of great events from small causes. So inscrutable is the arrangement of causes & consequences in this world that a two-penny duty on tea, unjustly imposed in a sequestered part of it, changes the condition of all its inhabitants. I have been more minute in relating the early transactions of this regeneration because I was in circumstances peculiarly favorable for a knowledge of the truth. Possessing the confidence and intimacy of the leading patriots, & more than all of the Marquis Fayette, their head and Atlas, who had no secrets from me, I learnt with correctness the views & proceedings of that party; while my intercourse with the diplomatic missionaries of Europe at Paris, all of them with the court, and eager in prying into its councils and proceedings, gave me a knolege of these also. My information was always and immediately committed to writing, in letters to Mr. Jay, and often to my friends, and a recurrence to these letters now insures me against errors of memory.

These opportunities of information ceased at this period, with my retirement from this interesting scene of action. I had been more than a year soliciting leave to go home with a view to place my daughters in the society & care of their friends, and to return for a short time to my station at Paris. But the metamorphosis thro' which our government was then passing from its Chrysalid to its Organic form suspended its action in a great degree; and it was not till the last of August that I received the permission I had asked.—And here I cannot leave this great and good country without expressing my sense of its preeminence of character among the nations of the earth. A more benevolent people, I have never known, nor greater warmth & devotedness in their select friendships. Their kindness and accommodation to strangers is unparalleled, and the hospitality of Paris is beyond anything I had conceived to be practicable in a large city. Their eminence too in science, the communicative dispositions of their scientific men, the politeness of the general manners, the ease and vivacity of their conversation, give a charm to their society to be found nowhere else. In a comparison of this with other countries we have the proof of primacy, which was given to Themistocles after the battle of Salamis. Every general voted to himself the first reward of valor, and the second to Themistocles. So ask the travelled inhabitant of any nation, In what country on earth would you rather live?—Certainly in my own, where are all my friends, my relations, and the earliest & sweetest affections and recollections of my life. Which would be your second choice? France.

[. . .]

Gertrude Stein
(1874–1946)

EXPLAINING THE PARISIAN'S habit of living well, Gertrude Stein wrote in her book, *Paris France*, "France could be civilized without having progress on her mind, she could believe in civilization in and for itself." Stein was born in Allegheny, Pennsylvania, but her parents were afflicted with wanderlust and young Gertrude lived the first five years of life traveling through Europe. When the family returned to the United States, five-year-old Gertrude had already tasted Paris, attending school there and speaking French. It was only natural that she would go back.

She received a B.A. from Radcliffe College and went to medical school without finishing her degree. Following her brother Leo to Paris, she set up house on the rue de Fleurus. She shared her Paris apartment with her secretary and lifelong partner, Alice B. Toklas. Their home became a salon for writers and artists of the Lost Generation, a term she coined. She wrote many books but most never reached a large audience because of her experimental prose. When she published *The Autobiography of Alice B. Toklas*, however, it was a critical and financial success. It was Stein's one work using traditional prose sensibilities.

from

❖ Paris France ❖

Paris, France is exciting and peaceful.

I was only four years old when I was first in Paris and talked french there and was photographed there and went to school there, and ate soup for early breakfast and had leg of mutton and spinach for lunch, I always liked spinach, and a black cat jumped on my mother's back. That was more exciting than peaceful. I do not mind cats but I do not like them to jump on my back. There are lots of cats in Paris and in France and they can do what they like, sit on the vegetables or among the groceries, stay in or go out. It is extraordinary that they fight so little among themselves considering how many cats there are. There are two things that french animals do not do, cats do not fight much and do not howl much and chickens do not get flustered running across the road, if they start to cross the road they keep on going which is what french people do too.

Anybody driving a car in Paris must know that. Anybody leaving the sidewalk to go on or walking anywhere goes on at a certain pace and that pace keeps up and nothing startles them nothing frightens them nothing makes them go faster or slower nothing not the most violent or unexpected noise makes them jump, or change their pace or their direction. If anybody jumps back or jumps at all in the streets of Paris you can be sure they are foreign not french. That is peaceful and exciting.

So I was in Paris a year when I was four to five and then I was back in America. A child does not forget but other things happen.

A little later in San Francisco there was more french.

After all everybody, that is, everybody who writes is interested in living inside themselves in order to tell what is inside themselves. That is why writers have to have two countries, the one where they belong and the one in which they live really. The second one is romantic, it is separate from themselves, it is not real but it is really there.

The English Victorians were like that about Italy, the early nineteenth century Americans were like that about Spain, the middle nineteenth century Americans were like that about England, my generation the end of the nineteenth century American generation was like that about France.

Of course sometimes people discover their own country as if

it were the other, a recent instance of that is Louis Bromfield discovering America, there have been a few English like that too, Kipling for instance discovered England but in general that other country that you need to be free in is the other country not the country where you really belong.

In San Francisco it was easy that it should be France. Of course it might have been Spain or China, but really in San Francisco as a child one really knew too much about Spain and China, and France was interesting while Spain and China were familiar, and daily. France was not daily it just came up again and again.

It came up first in such different books, Jules Verne and Alfred de Vigny and it came up in my mother's clothes and the gloves and the sealskin caps and muffs and the boxes they came in.

There was the smell of Paris in that.

And then for quite a long while it was very easy to forget France.

The next thing I remember about France were the Henry Henrys and Sarah Bernhardt, the Panorama of the Battle of Waterloo and Millet's Man With The Hoe.

The Panorama of the Battle of Waterloo.

One of the pleasantest things those of us who write or paint do is to have the daily miracle. It does come.

I was about eight years old and it came with the Panorama of the Battle of Waterloo.

It was painted by a frenchman, I wonder if it would not be interesting to have one now, one of those huge panoramas, where you stood in the center on a platform and all around you on every side of you was an oil painting. You were completely surrounded by an oil painting.

It was then I first realised the difference between a painting and out of doors. I realised that a painting is always a flat surface and out of doors never is, and that out of doors is made up of air and a painting has no air, the air is replaced by a flat surface, and anything in a painting that imitates air is illustration and not art. I seem to have felt all that very intensely standing on the platform and being all surrounded by an oil painting.

And then there was Sarah Bernhardt.

San Francisco had lots of french people in it, and a french theatre and one naturally knew little girls and boys who talked french at home quite naturally. And so when a french actor or actress came to San Francisco they always stayed a long time.

They liked it there and of course when actresses or actors stay anywhere they always act, so naturally there was a great deal of French spoken in the theatre.

It was then that I found out quite naturally, that french is a spoken language and English a written one.

In France whenever anybody writes anything and wants anybody to know what it is like they read it out loud. If it is in English it is natural to pass the manuscript to them and let them read it but if it is in french it is natural to read it out loud.

French is a spoken language English really is not.

Sarah Bernhardt made me see the thin arms of frenchwomen. When I came to Paris and saw the little midinettes and Montmartoises they all had them. It was only many years later when the styles changed, in those days they wore long skirts, that I realised what sturdy legs went with those thin arms. That is what makes the french such good soldiers the sturdy legs, thin arms and sturdy legs, if you see what I mean, peaceful and exciting.

That is what makes all the french able to ride up hill on bicycles the way they do, no hill is so steep but that slowly pedalling up and up they go, men and girls and little children, the sturdy legs and thin arms.

The other thing that was french there in San Francisco were the family of Henry Henrys. That was their name.

There was a father and mother they were known as Monsieur and Madame Henry and there were five children the oldest Henry

Henry played the violin We used to go there in the afternoon and stay to dinner and then we used to dance the Henry children ourselves, to the french music of the violin.

And we always for dinner had a roast of mutton, a gigot they called it, cooked the same way as when I went to school in Paris and potatoes in the butter around it, clean looking potatoes, not so dark as when they were cooked American. But the thing that was most exciting were the knives and forks. The knives had been sharpened so much that the blade was as thin as a dagger with a slight bend on top and the forks so light that when you pressed on them they bent. These knives and forks were the most passionately french things I knew, I might say I ever knew.

Then there was Millet's Man With The Hoe.

I had never really wanted a photograph of a picture before I saw Millet's Man With The Hoe. I was about twelve or thirteen years old, I had read Eugenie Grandet of Balzac, and I did have some feeling about what french country was like but The Man With The Hoe made it different, it made it ground not country, and France has been that to me ever since. France is made of ground, of earth.

When I managed to get a photograph of the picture and took it home my eldest brother looked at it and said what is it and I said it is Millet's Man With The Hoe. It is a hell of a hoe said my eldest brother.

But that is the way french country is, it is ground like that and they work at it just that way with just that kind of a hoe.

All this was all the Paris France I really knew then and then for a very long time I forgot about Paris and about France.

Then one day when I was at college at Radcliffe in Cambridge Massachusetts, I was on a train and sitting next to me was a frenchman. I recognized him as a visiting lecturer and I spoke to him. We talked about American college women. Very wonderful he said and very interesting but and he looked at me earnestly, really not one of them, now you must admit that, not one of them could feel with Alfred de Musset that le seul bien qui me reste au monde c'est d'avoir quelque fois pleuré. I was young then but I knew what he meant that they would not feel like that. That and a certain interest in Zola as a realist but not as much interest as in the Russian realists was all that Paris meant to me until after the medical school when I settled down in Paris France.

Tourism

How You Can't Help Being an American in Paris

❧

Langston Hughes
(1902–1967)

LANGSTON HUGHES wrote poetry, novels, short fiction, stage plays, and two works of autobiography. His works include *The Weary Blues, Fine Clothes to the Jew, Freedom's Plow, One-Way Ticket,* and *Simple Speaks His Mind.* Today, he is considered one of the most important writers of the Harlem Renaissance. Early in his career, however, many black intellectuals criticized him for portraying the lives and street vernacular of working-class blacks. One critic dubbed him the "poet low-rate of Harlem." In his autobiography, *The Big Sea,* Hughes recalled his reaction to criticisms that he should write about a more respectable vision of black life: "I didn't know the upper class Negroes well enough to write much about them," he wrote. "I knew only the people I had grown up with, and they weren't people whose shoes were always shined. . . . But they seemed to me good people, too." Throughout his career, Hughes wrote about life as he saw it, making poetry out of the everyday language of blacks.

from

✧ The Big Sea: An Autobiography ✧

Montmartre

My ticket and the French visa had taken nearly all my money. I got to the Gare du Nord in Paris early one February morning with only seven dollars in my pockets. I didn't know anybody in Paris. I didn't know anybody in the whole of Europe, except the old

Dutch watchman's family in Rotterdam. But I had made up my mind to pass the rest of the winter in Paris.

I checked my bags at the parcel stand, and had some coffee and rolls in the station. I found that my high school French didn't work very well, and that I understood nothing anyone said to me. They talked too fast. But I could read French.

I went outside the station and saw a bus marked *Opéra*. I knew the opera was at the center of Paris, so I got in the bus and rode down there, determined to do a little sight-seeing before I looked for work, or maybe starved to death. When I got to the Opéra, a fine wet snow was falling. People were pouring out of the Métro on their way to work. To the right and left of me stretched the Grands Boulevards. I looked across the street and saw the Café de la Paix. Ahead the Vendôme. I walked down the rue de la Paix, turned, and on until I came out at the Concorde. I recognized the Champs Elysées, and the great Arc de Triomphe in the distance through the snow.

Boy, was I thrilled! I was torn between walking up the Champs Elysées or down along the Seine, past the Tuileries. Finally, I took the river, hoping to see the bookstalls and Notre Dame. But I ended up in the Louvre instead, looking at Venus.

It was warmer in the Louvre than in the street, and the Greek statues were calm and friendly. I said to the statues: "If you can stay in Paris as long as you've been here and still look O.K., I guess I can stay a while with seven dollars and make a go of it." But when I came out of the Louvre, I was tired and hungry. I had no idea where I would sleep that night, or where to go about finding a cheap hotel. So I began to look around for someone I could talk to. To tell the truth, I began to look for a colored person on the streets of Paris.

As luck would have it, I came across an American Negro in a doorman's uniform. He told me most of the American colored people he knew lived in Montmartre, and that they were musicians working in the theaters and night clubs. He directed me to Montmartre. I walked. I passed Notre Dame de Lorette, then on up the hill. I got to Montmartre about four o'clock. Many of the people there were just getting up and having their breakfast at that hour, since they worked all night. I don't think they were in a very good humor, because I went into a little café where I saw some colored musicians sitting, having their coffee. I spoke to them, and said: "I've just come to Paris, and I'm looking for a cheap place to stay and a job."

They scowled at me. Finally one of them said: "Well, what instrument do you play?"

They thought I was musical competition.

I said: "None. I'm just looking for an ordinary job."

Puzzled, another one asked: "Do you tap dance, or what?"

"No," I said, "I've just got off a ship and I want any kind of a job there is."

"You must be crazy, boy," one of them said. "There ain't no 'any kind of a job' here. There're plenty of French people for ordinary work. 'Less you can play jazz or tap dance, you'd just as well go back home."

"He's telling you right," the rest of the fellows at the table agreed, "there's no work here."

But one of them indicated a hotel. "Go over there across the street and see if you can't get a little room cheap."

I went. But it was high for me, almost a dollar a day in American money. However, I had to take the room for that night. Then I ate my first dinner in Paris—*boeuf au gros sel*, and a cream cheese with sugar. Even with the damp and the slush—for the snow had turned into a nasty rain—I began to like Paris a little, and to take it personally.

The next day I went everywhere where people spoke English, looking for a job—the American Library, the Embassy, the American Express, the newspaper offices. Nothing doing. Besides I would have to have a *carte d'identité*. But it would be better to go back home, I was advised, because there were plenty of people out of work in Paris.

"With five dollars, I can't go back home," I said.

People shrugged their shoulders and went on doing whatever they were doing. I tramped the streets. Late afternoon of the second day came. I went back to Montmartre, to that same little café in front of my hotel, where I had no room that night—unless I paid again. And if I did take the same room again, with supper, I'd have scarcely four dollars left!

My bags were still checked at the station, so I had no clean clothes to put on. It was drizzling rain, and I was cold and hungry. I had had only coffee and a roll all day. I felt bad.

I slumped down at a table in the small café and ordered another *café crème* and a *croissant*—the second that day. I ate the croissant (a slender, curved French roll) and wondered what on earth I ought to do. I decided tomorrow to try the French for a job somewhere, maybe the Ritz or some other of the large hotels, or maybe where I had seen them building a big building on one of the boulevards. Perhaps they could use a hodcarrier.

The café had begun to be crowded, as the afternoon darkened into a damp and murky dusk. A tall, young colored fellow came in and sat down at the marble-topped table where I was. He ordered a *fine*, and asked me if I wanted to play dominoes.

I said no, I was looking for a cheap room.

He recommended his hotel, where he lived by the month, but when we figured it out, it was about the same as the place across the street, too high for me. I said I meant a *really* cheap room. I said I didn't care about heat or hot water or carpets on the floor right now, just a place to sleep. He said he didn't know of any hotels like that, as cheap as I needed.

Just then a girl, with reddish-blond hair, sitting on a bench that ran along the wall, spoke up and said: "You say you look at one hotel?"

I said: "Yes."

She said: "I know one, not much dear."

"Where?" I asked her. "And how much?"

"Almost not nothing," she said, "not dear! No! I will show you. Come."

She put on her thin coat and got up. I followed her. She was a short girl, with a round, pale Slavic face and big dark eyes. She had a little rouge on her cheeks. She had on a wine-red hat with a rain-wilted feather. She was pretty, but her slippers were worn at the heels. We walked up the hill in silence, across the Place Blanche and up toward the rue Lepic. Finally I said to her, in French, that I had very little money and the room would have to be very cheap or I would have nothing left to eat on, because I had no *travaille*. No *travaille* and no prospects, and I was not a musician.

She answered that this was the cheapest hotel in Montmartre, where she was taking me. *"Pas de tout cher."* But, as she spoke, I could tell that her French was almost as bad as mine, so we switched back to English, which she spoke passably well.

She said she had not been in Paris long, that she had come from Constantinople with a ballet troupe, and that she was Russian. Beyond that, she volunteered no information. The drizzling February rain wet our faces, the water was soggy in my shoes, and the girl looked none too warm in her thin but rather chic coat. After several turns up and down a narrow, winding street, we came to the hotel, a tall, neat-looking building, with a tiled entrance hall. From a tiny sitting room came a large French woman. And the girl spoke to her about the room, the very least dear, for *m'sieu*.

"Oui," said the woman, "a quite small room, by the week, fifty francs."

"I'll take it," I said, "and pay two weeks." I knew it would leave me almost nothing, but I would have a place to sleep.

I thanked the girl for bringing me to the hotel and I invited her to a cup of coffee with me next time we met at the café. We parted at the Place Blanche, and I went to the station to get my bags, now that I had some place to put them. After paying for the room and the storage of my bags, I had just about enough money left for coffee and rolls for a week—if I ate nothing *but* coffee and one roll a meal.

I was terribly hungry and it took me some time to get to the station by Métro. I got back to the hotel about nine that night, through a chilly drizzle. My key was not hanging on the hallboard, but the landlady pointed up, so I went up. It was a long climb with the bags, and I stopped on each landing to rest. I guess I was weak with hunger, having only eaten those two croissants all day. When I got to my room, I could see a light beneath the door, so I thought maybe I was confused about the number. I hesitated, then knocked. The door opened and there stood the Russian girl.

I said: "Hello!"

I didn't know what else to say.

She said: "I first return me," and smiled.

Her coat was hanging on a nail behind the door and a small bag sat beneath the window. She was barefooted, her wet shoes were beneath the heatless radiator, and her stockings drying on the foot of the bed.

I said: "Are you going to stay here, too?"

She said: "Of course! *Mais oui!* Why you think, I find one room?"

She had her hat off. Her red-blond hair was soft and wavy. She laughed and laughed. I laughed, too, since I didn't know what to say.

"I have no mon-nee nedder," she said.

We sat down on the bed. In broken English, she told me her story. Her name was Sonya. Her dancing troupe had gone to pieces in Nice. She had bought a ticket to Paris. And here we were—in a room that was all bed, just space barely to open the door, that was all, and a few nails in the barren wall, on which to hang clothes. No heat in the radiator. No table, no washstand, no chair, but a deep window seat that could serve as a chair and a place to put things on. It was cold, so cold you could see your breath. But the rent was cheap, so you couldn't ask for much.

We didn't ask for anything.

I put my suitcase under the bed. Sonya hung her clothes on the nails. She said: "If you have some francs I go *chez l'épicerie* and get white cheese and one small bread and one small wine and we have supper. Eat right here. That way are less dear."

I gave her ten francs and she went out shopping for the supper. We spread the food on the bed. It tasted very good and cost little, cheese and crisp, fresh bread and a bottle of wine. But I could see my francs gone in a few days more. Then what would we do? But Sonya said she was looking for a job, and perhaps she would find one soon, then we both could eat.

Not being accustomed to the quick friendship of the dispossessed, I wondered if she meant it. Later, I knew she did. She found a job first. And we both ate.

The day after I took the room, I wrote to my mother in McKeesport, requesting a loan. It was the first time I had ever written home asking for money. I told her that I was stranded in Paris, and would she or Dad please cable me twenty dollars. But I wondered how I would live the ten or twelve days I'd have to wait for the letter to reach America and the answer to come back. I was sure, however, that the money would come if my step-father had it. He was always generous and a good sport, my step-father.

Before I would have written my own father for a penny, I would have died in Paris, because I knew his answer would be: "I told you you should have listened to me, and gone to Switzerland to study, as I asked you!" So I would not write my father, though hunger reduced me to a skeleton, and I died of malnutrition on the steps of the Louvre.

Hunger came, too. Bread and cheese once a day couldn't keep hunger away. Selling your clothes, when you didn't have many, couldn't keep hunger away. Going to bed early and sleeping late couldn't keep hunger away. Looking for a job and always being turned down couldn't keep hunger away. Not sleeping alone couldn't keep hunger away.

Sonya did her stretching exercises on the bed every morning. There wasn't room to do them on the floor, and she wanted to keep in shape in case she got a job dancing. But Montmartre was full of Russian dancers—and no jobs.

She was twenty-four, older than I was. Her father had been on the wrong side in the Russian Revolution and had escaped to Turkey. He died in Roumania. Then Sonya danced in Bucharest, Budapest, Athens and Constantinople, Trieste, and Nice, where the troupe of dancers went to pieces because the manager fell ill, and contracts and working permits ran out. So Sonya, who, like me, had never seen Paris before, had packed up and come north.

Now, her costumes were all in pawn, and her best clothes, too. Still, she didn't look bad when she went out. She walked with her head up. And from the hands of the usurer she had managed to hold back one evening gown of pearl-colored sequins, hanging limp against our wall.

[. . .]

Le Grand Duc

The cook at the Grand Duc's name was Bruce. He was an enormous brownskin fellow, with one eye, stout, and nearing fifty. He wore a white apron, a white cap, and a very fierce frown. He could look at you so fiercely out of his one eye that you would quake in your shoes. His other eye was closed tight. But the one he had looked like three.

Bruce was boss in his own domain, the kitchen. During his hours there, from 11 P.M. to 7 A.M., he would let no one else come in the kitchen, not even the boss or the manager. Only his helper, myself, was permitted. The others called for what they wished at the service window, and woe to the impatient waiter who set foot inside the door. Bruce had once hung a pan of pancake batter over such a waiter's head, and several others had often seen the threat of a raised knife. Bruce was highly respected by the employees of the Grand Duc, and addressed with great gentility.

Because he could fry the best chicken à la Maryland in Paris, with corn fritters and gravy, because he could bake beans the way Boston bakes them, and make a golden brown Virginia corn bread that would melt in your mouth, Bruce had a public all his own, was a distinct asset to the place, and his little vagaries were permitted.

They had to be permitted or he would quit.

It was good, working with Bruce, because he would let no one else give you any orders of any kind, neither the French owners nor the Negro manager. And if any waiter said to me: "Hurry up, boy, and hand me some butter," Bruce would bellow: "If you're in such a rush, why don't you tell *me* to hurry up? I'm in charge of this kitchen."

Not another peep out of the waiter, for Bruce's one big eye would petrify him.

Bruce was no respecter of persons, from the star entertainer, Florence, to the star patrons, such as Belle Livingston and Fannie Ward. If something about his food displeased a customer and it was sent back to the kitchen, Bruce would sometimes leave the kitchen himself, stick his head through the pantry curtains opening on the main room of the club, and glare down with his Cyclops eye on whatever unsuspecting patron had dared return a dish of *his*. If the patron's reasons were satisfactory, however, Bruce would go back to the kitchen and send out as tempting a new plate as mortal ever prepared. But if the patron was rude or drunk, he would get nothing from the hand of Bruce. Then Bruce would turn the order over to me, the dishwasher, without even the benefit of his advice on how to cook what was wanted. In my early days there, I turned out many strange concoctions—so strange that they embarrassed even the waiters.

Bruce did not like Fannie Ward and would never prepare an

order for her table if he knew where the order originated—so I usually did the cooking for Miss Ward. I hope she never suffered indigestion.

A great many celebrities and millionaires came to the Grand Duc in those days, drawn by the fame of Florence Embry—known simply as Florence—the beautiful brownskin girl from Harlem who sang there. Anita Loos and John Emerson, young William Leeds, the Dolly Sisters, Lady Nancy Cunard, various of the McCormicks, the writer, Robert McAlmon, and Belle Livingston with her son and daughter, Fannie Ward, looking not so very young, Prince Tuvalou of Dahomey, Sparrow Robertson of the *Paris Herald*'s sport page, Joe Alix, who became Josephine Baker's dancing partner, the surrealist poet, Louis Aragon, all came—and Florence would notice none of them unless they were very celebrated or very rich.

Part of Florence's reputation was based on snobbishness, no doubt, a professional snobbishness which she deliberately cultivated, because outside the club she was as kind and sociable a person as you would ever wish to find. And those who worked with her, from musicians to waiters, loved her. But to the patrons, she adopted an air of unattainable aloofness. She would sing a requested song with only the most casual glance at the table she was singing for—unless a duke, or a steel magnate, or a world celebrity sat there.

Rich, but lowly, patrons could tip Florence ever so heavily, and she would not even condescend to accept a glass of champagne with them. But the amazing thing was that they would come back and tip her even better for her songs the next time. In the snob world of *de luxe boîte de nuit* society it was considered a mark of distinction for Florence to sit for a moment at your table.

Most of the time when Florence was not singing she would remain at her own table by the orchestra saying: "Tell them, 'No, thank you!'" to the waiters who came with offers of champagne from guests who admired her looks or her singing. These frequent "No, thank you's" greatly infuriated the management, who were too shortsighted to see that that was, no doubt, a part of Florence's spell over her following—because she was by no means a great singer of popular songs. She was no Raquel Meller or Yvette Guilbert. But she was very pretty and brown, and could wear the gowns of the great Paris couturières as few other women could. At that time she went home every morning and got plenty of sleep, and would come to work every night looking as fresh and lovely as a black-eyed susan from some unheard-of Alabama *jardin de luxe*, where sophisticated darkies grow.

In the early part of the evening Florence would often laugh and talk with the waiters and the musicians, or with Bruce and me—but an hour later be as remote as you please to a party of well-to-do tourists from Wisconsin, spending a thousand francs at the front table. It was the first time I had ever seen a colored person deliberately and openly snubbing white people, so it always amused me no end to watch Florence move away from a table of money-spending Americans, who wanted nothing in the world so much as to have her sit down with them.

Her full name was Florence Embry Jones and her husband's name was Palmer Jones. Palmer was a fine piano player, and they frequently sang together. But Palmer at that time was working at the Ambassadeurs, and didn't arrive at the Grand Duc until about three in the morning so, until he came, Florence sang with the orchestra—perhaps a couple of songs an hour between dances, the popular American tunes of the day. Then when Palmer arrived, she would do a group of special numbers with him at the piano, if they felt like it.

Palmer himself knew a great many old blues and folksongs, like "Frankie and Johnnie" and "Henrico." He would occasionally sing one or two of those songs for the guests, inserting off-color lyrics if the crowd was that kind of crowd.

Then when all the other clubs were closed, the best of the musicians and entertainers from various other smart places would often drop into the Grand Duc, and there'd be a jam session until seven or eight in the morning—only in 1924 they had no such name for it. They'd just get together and the music would be on. The cream of the Negro musicians then in France, like Cricket Smith on the trumpet, Louis Jones on the violin, Palmer Jones at the piano, Frank Withers on the clarinet, and Buddy Gilmore at the drums, would weave out music that would almost make your heart stand still at dawn in a Paris nightclub in the rue Pigalle, when most of the guests were gone and you were washing the last pots and pans in a two-by-four kitchen, with the fire in the range dying and the one high window letting the soft dawn in.

Blues in the rue Pigalle. Black and laughing, heartbreaking blues in the Paris dawn, pounding like a pulse-beat, moving like the Mississippi!

> *Lawd, I looked and saw a spider*
> *Goin' up de wall.*
> *I say, I looked and saw a spider*
> *Goin' up de wall.*
> *I said where you goin', Mister Spider?*
> *I'm goin' to get my ashes hauled!*

Through the mist of smoke and champagne, you laughed at the loneliness of a tiny little spider, going up a great big wall to get his ashes hauled. And the blues went on:

> *I did more for my good gal*
> *Than de good Lawd ever done.*
> *Did more for my good gal*
> *Than de good Lawd ever done.*
> *I bought her some hair—*
> *Cause de Lawd ain't give her none.*

Play it, Mister Palmer Jones! Lawd! Lawd! Lawd! Play it, Buddy Gilmore! What you doin' to them drums? Man, you gonna bust your diamond studs in a minute!

> *Is you ever seen a*
> *One-eyed woman cry?*
> *I say, is you ever seen a*
> *One-eyed woman cry?*
> *Jack, she can cry so good*
> *Just out of that one old eye!*

Jennifer Allen
(1961–   )

BORN IN CHICAGO, Jennifer Allen's interest in Paris stems at least partly from family roots: her mother is French-Tunisian, and as a young adult, she regularly visited her French grandmother in Paris. Allen's work has appeared in many publications including *Rolling Stone, The New Republic,* and *The New York Times Magazine.* She is the author of a short-story collection, *Better Get Your Angel On,* and a memoir, *Fifth Quarter: The Scrimmage of a Football Coach's Daughter.* She is currently a writer on the HBO show *Arli$$.* She lives in Los Angeles with her husband and their two sons.

❖ Euro Disney: A Postcard ❖

Past graffitied walls lining the train tracks, past suburban swing sets, past industrial parks, barren trees, silos, farmlands, in a place where nearly 2 million soldiers died in World War I, lies Main Street, U.S.A. This is Euro Disney's main drag. This is where the music begins and never ends, escorting us now and forever. "Tis the Season," "Rudolph the Red-Nosed Reindeer," "Frosty the Snowman." The azaleas are not in bloom. The water fountains reek of chlorine. This is the basse saison. Low season. Cold season. Current temperature: 5 degrees Celsius. The pavement everywhere is wet. The woods are sleeping. Literally. Direct translation of Sleeping Beauty—Chateau de la Belle au Bois Dormant.

"Let's go to the Caribbean!" I shriek, skipping off to Les

Pirouettes du Vieux Moulin, thinking this is the Pirates of the Caribbean. "What are you doing? That's a restaurant!" cries my mother, who is French. "No, it's not!" I scream, running in line, discovering that the structure is in fact a windmill, and that nearby Alice's Curious Labyrinth is closed for winter, and sugared popcorn is for sale everywhere and I am not at the Happiest Place on Earth after all, but at some strange, cruel illusion of it, where there is no Matterhorn, no squeaky, musty, rinky-dink, pre-Hollywood special effects rides, no Country Bear Jamboree.

"The only dommage is the weather," says Serge, a man with his wife and two very small Mickey Mouse–covered children. Serge himself is wearing a Buffalo Bill Show cowboy hat, his favorite attraction so far, he says, explaining it as a show where Père Noël fights for justice in the West. Serge came here with Intel, his company, on discount, adding that a lot of other companies are here today on discounts as well. His wife, Laurence, a Moroccan, says the French have a problem with Euro Disney. "It's because they keep asking themselves, 'Why couldn't we do it?'" she says. "They're just upset they couldn't do it themselves."

Do it themselves? Bilingual drunken pirates? Bilingual crystal ball, Haunted Mansion heads? Seven bilingual dwarfs?

Not needing any translation is the cost of trinkets for any ride you possibly could have ridden or walked past or even missed in your time there. For instance, once you have exited Pirates of the Caribbean there is a shop you have to pass through on your way through Adventureland: swashbuckling swords, 30 ff; captain's hooks, 20 ff; guns, 55 ff.

Three teenage French boys are pulling shotguns off the racks. "Christmas presents?" I ask. "Chouette," one says, meaning "hip," as he holds the barrel up against the temple of his friend's head. The boys are here with their families on a military discount. The boys walk away singing the Pirates theme song, and it isn't long before my mother and I are singing along, too, singing to whatever song currently bombards us as we search through the fake sage, trying to find out just where exactly this music comes from. It is some TV Western theme song that has brought us to this—pawing through plastic leaves—when a security guard named Rahid, with dandruff and sunglasses and an earpiece, asks if he can help us. We're looking for the music, I explain. Rahid is confused. Rahid has worked here since the park opened more than a year ago. Rahid says, "Mais, c'est normal!" meaning it's normal to have a continual sound track blasting wherever you travel, from Frontierland to Adventureland to Fantasyland.

"This smells American," my mother confirms as we enter Le Chalet de la Marionette: a fast-food hall disguised as a ski chalet with a ski lift–length line. The man in front of us is on his fourth visit to Euro Disney. His brother-in-law works here. He gets a price reduction. But he would rather be at Vegas; Caesars, to be exact. "C'est mieux," he tells me, "le vice."

"A lot of the French, they don't get the Disney attitude," says Margie from Missouri. Margie is here with a girlfriend, both of them living in France, both of them getting a discount because a friend works at the park. Margie says the mortician at the Haunted Mansion "almost banged me in the face" hurrying her to get on the ride. "It's a very different service attitude," says Margie. "It's a big problem. You're serving them."

Serving us at L'Échoppe d'Aladdin, is Abdelhaj, a Moroccan craftsman who was brought here from Fez by Disney recruiters. Abdelhaj, 33, engraves brass platters eight hours a day, with a one-hour lunch and a fifteen-minute break, six days a week. Abdelhaj has no problem with the Disney attitude; he says he is happy here.

Outside Abdelhaj's Casbah is a women's rest room, with an arabesque archway entrance, where a man stands with a video camera in hand, awaiting his wife's exit. There is the sense here that everything is worth capturing on camera because never again will you be so happy. Never again will you be surrounded by such clean walls, clean streets, clean, happy workers! It reminds us of Red Square. We finally decide this, my mother and I, while waiting

in line for sugared popcorn, to the blaring music of "Winter Won-
derland." Where is it coming from now, we ask? And at last we
spot the source of all stereophonics: situated among the wrought-
iron baroque-styled lampposts are several large speakers. "Propa-
ganda," my mother says, paying the popcorn man.

"Que le monde est petit!" and "Come a piccolo il mondo!"
and "Es ist eine kleine welt!" and other Fantasyland expressions.
This is the grand finale, my mother's favorite ride: It's a Small
World. Up at the lookout control panel, under an awning, safe
from wind and weather, in a purple cape with a Travolta hair-flip,
sits a young man, clapping his gloved hands, mouthing, "It's a
Small World After All." Everyone really is happy here. There is no
rowdiness. No tipping or rocking of boats. I look back at the faces
in the boat behind us, expecting to see just one bored look, and
everyone's mouth is open, necks stretched, awed.

"It's so beautiful, I'm going to cry," my mother says, and does.

It's late: 17:20 Euro Disney time. How will they get everyone
out? Within seconds, the speakers announce that in ten minutes a
celebration will take place in the Town Square. The celebration
involves watching the lights light up the archways along Main Street.
Everyone stands around gazing. "Look at them," my mother says,
"The French, you see, are cultured, cultured but naive." Immediately after the light show ends, "When You Wish upon a Star"
takes control of us and there is a mad rush to hit the stores for
one last-minute purchase: Euro Disney tennis balls, 45 ff; golf
tees, 60 ff; baseballs, 30 ff. The store is packed, winter coat sleeves
precariously rub up against shelves of porcelain paraphernalia,
while from somewhere above, loudspeakers yell, "Hark the Herald Angels Sing."

At the Disneyland Hotel California Grill, le chef Goofy
comes by our table, his big head nearly clearing away our wine-
glasses, his long plastic tongue caught in the bread basket. Bas-
relief molding, Christolfe cutlery and "Who's Afraid of the Big
Bad Wolf?" all add to our dining experience. "In my country, we

eat with our hands, one plate, five or six people—it's much easier," our waiter, Gufed Jama Dirir of Somalia, tells us. "What's the most common question you get asked around here?" I ask. "If I like my job," Jama says. "And I say, 'Yes,' with a smile."

We eat. Or, as my mother says, being American, we feed. Sleeping Beauty's castle is turned off. We wait for our check. "These are Americans, you can tell, look at them, walking in like they own the place," my mother says, directing my attention to three men striding past our table. "Feet spread, arms swinging, big rears," my mother goes on. And she was right. They were.

Benjamin Franklin
(1706–1790)

BORN IN BOSTON, Massachusetts, Benjamin Franklin was the son of a candle maker and soap boiler. He received only two years of formal schooling but was an avid reader all his life. He was a self-taught scientist, inventor, diplomat, successful businessman, newspaper man, best-selling author, leader of civic affairs, postmaster general, and the first American ambassador to France. His accomplishments are too many to cite in full. His letters, some of which are reprinted here, were written during his residence in Paris from 1776 to 1785. Franklin was welcomed by Parisian society, both high and low. To the Parisians, Franklin's fur cap and wigless attire represented the rugged, independent spirit of America they imagined.

Few knew of his secret mission in Paris—to raise badly needed money for the American war against England and to persuade France and Spain to enter the war against the British. In 1778, Franklin was elected the sole ambassador to France. Though he offered several times to resign, citing age and health problems, his resignations were always declined, pending peace. During his post, Franklin raised more than 24 million livres, or sterling pounds, from the French government. (The loans were never fully repaid.) At the age of 79, Franklin was finally allowed to resign. His colleague and friend, Thomas Jefferson, succeeded him as ambassador to France.

from

✣ The Papers of Benjamin Franklin ✣

To Mary Hewson

ALS: Yale University Library

Paris, Jan. 12. 1777

My dear dear Polley

Figure to yourself an old Man with grey Hair appearing under a Martin Fur Cap, among the Powder'd Heads of Paris. It is this odd Figure that salutes you; with Handfuls of Blessings on you and your dear little ones.

On my Arrival here, Mlle. Biheron gave me great Pleasure in the Perusal of a Letter from you to her. It acquainted me that you and yours were well in August last. I have with me here my young Grandson Benja Franklin Bache, a special good Boy. I give him a little French Language and Address, and then send him over to pay his Respects to Miss Hewson.

My Love to all that love you, particularly to dear Dolly. I am ever, my dear Friend, Your affectionate

BF.

Temple who attends me here presents his Respects. I must contrive to get you to America. I want all my Friends out of that wicked Country. I have just read in s[ome?] Newspapers 7 Paragraphs about me, of which 6 were Lies.

To Mary Hewson

AL: Yale University Library

Paris, Jan. 26[–27]. 1777

Dear Polley

I wrote a few Lines to you by Dr. B. and have since seen your Letter to Jona, by which I have the great Pleasure of learning that you and yours were well on the 17th.

What is become of my and your dear Dolly? Have you parted? for you mention nothing of her. I know your Friendship continues; but perhaps she is with one of her Brothers. How do they all do?

I have not yet receiv'd a Line from my dear old Friend your Mother. Pray tell me where she is, and how it is with her. Jonathan, who is now at Nantes, told me that she had a Lodging in Northumberland Court. I doubt her being comfortably accommodated there.

Is Miss Barwell a little more at rest; or as busy as ever? Is she well? And how fares it with our good Friends of the Henckel Family?

But principally I want to know how it is with you. I hear you have not yet quite settled with those People. I hope, however, that you have a sufficient Income, and live at your Ease; and that your Money is safe out of the Funds. Does my Godson remember anything of his Doctor Papa? I suppose not. Kiss the dear little Fellow for me, not forgetting the others. I long to see them and you.

What became of the Lottery Tickit I left with your good Mother, which was to produce the Diamond Earings for you? Did you get them? If not, Fortune has wrong'd you! For you *ought* to have had them. I am, my dear Friend, ever yours, with sincere Esteem and Affection.

If you write to me, direct for me thus *A Monsr. Monsieur François*, chez M. de Chaumont à Passy, près de Paris.

P.S. 27th Jany. They tell me that in writing to a Lady from Paris, one should always say something about the Fashions. Temple observes them more than I do. He took Notice that at the Ball in Nantes, there were no Heads less than 5, and a few were 7 Lengths of the Face, above the Top of the Forehead. You know that those who have practis'd Drawing, as he has, attend more to Proportions, than People in common do. Yesterday we din'd at the Duke de Rochefocault's, where there were three Dutchesses and a Countess, and no Head higher than a Face and a half. So it seems the farther from Court the more extravagant the Mode.

NOTATION: Paris Jan. 26. 77

To Jan Ingenhousz

ALS: Henry Huntington Library

Passy, near Paris, April 26. 1777

My dear Friend,

I find by your Favour of the 2d Inst. that my Letter to you had been stopt in the Post Office. I am sorry I omitted Payment of the Postage; it was thro' Ignorance. As you mention having order'd your Banker to forward it, I hope you have it before this time. I shall take care of this.

It is probable that I shall remain here still some Months, so that if you resolve to call at Paris in your Way to England, I shall once more enjoy the very great Pleasure of seeing you in this World.

As to the Peace you so much desire between America and England, there is at present no Appearance of its soon taking Place. The several States having separately, during Years past, and the Congress for the whole, sent Petitions, Remonstrances, and humble Addresses without Number: to the King and Parliament, which were all treated with Contempt, and answered only by additional Injuries, no farther Proposition is to be expected from them, especially since they have settled their new Government, after being compelled to relinquish and renounce their Connection with Great Britain. And I imagine Britain is yet too proud to make any reasonable Propositions on her Part, and has not yet suffer'd enough by the War; which I therefore [*think?*] is likely to continue a long time, as we on our part are every Year in a better Condition to support it.

Here is nothing new in the philosophical Way, or I should have a Pleasure in communicating it to you. The Emperor is arriv'd, and very industrious in seeing every thing worth a Sovereign's Notice: The French appear to be much pleased with him.

I hear sometimes of our Friend Sir John, by means of M. Le Roy: but my Regard for him prevents my writing to him directly, as his having any Correspondence with me would if known be certainly made use of against him by his Enemies, and hurt him with the King; &c. I am ever, my dear Friend, Yours most affectionately

B FRANKLIN

To Francis Hopkinson

AL (DRAFT): Library of Congress

Passy, Sept. 13. 1781

Dear Sir,

I have received your kind Letter of July 17 with its Dupli-
cate, enclosing those for Messrs Brandlight and Sons,
which I have forwarded. I am sorry for the Loss of the
Squibs. Every thing of yours gives me Pleasure.

As to the Friends and Enemies you just mention, I
have hitherto, Thanks to God, had Plenty of the former
kind; they have been my Treasure. And it has perhaps
been of no Disadvantage to me that I have had a few of
the latter. They serve to put us upon correcting the Faults
we have, and avoiding those we are in danger of having.
They counteract the Mischief Flattery might do us, and
their Malicious Attacks make our Friends more zealous in
serving us and promoting our Interest. At present I do
not know of more than two such Enemies that I enjoy,
viz. Lee & Izard. I deserved the Enmity of the latter,
because I might have avoided it by paying him a Compliment, which I neglected. That of the former I owe to
the People of France, who happen'd to respect me too
much & him too little; which I could bear and he couldn't.
They are unhappy that they cannot make every body hate
me as much as they do; and I Should be so if my Friends
did not love me much more than those Gentlemen can
possibly love one another.

Enough of this Subject. Let me know if you are in
Possession of my Gimcrack Instruments, and if you have
made any new Experiments. I lent many years ago a large
Glass Globe mounted to Mr Coombe, and an electric
Battery of Bottles which I remember; perhaps there were

some other things: He may have had them so long as to think them his own. Pray ask him for them, and keep them for me together with the rest.

You have a new Crop of Prose Writers. I see in your Papers many of their fictitious Names; but nobody tells me the real. You will oblige me by a little of your literary History.—Adieu, my dear Friend, and believe me ever, Yours most affectionately.

F. HOPKINSON ESQR

John Adams
(1735–1826)

JOHN ADAMS, the second president of the United States, was born in Braintree (now Quincy), Massachusetts. Adams spent one year in Paris (1778 to 1779) as a joint commissioner to France with Benjamin Franklin, until Congress appointed Franklin the official American ambassador to France. These early letters reveal Adams's initial delight in Paris: though a New England Puritan at heart, he can't help being charmed and seduced. The excerpt of his autobiography shows his growing Puritan distrust of Parisian life as embodied by Franklin. In his rejection of the Parisian habit of sensuality, luxury, and intellectual pleasures of all sorts, he is harshest with his fellow American. To Adams, Franklin appeared to have wholeheartedly adopted the French way at the expense of fulfilling his duties. He could not see that Franklin's many dinners and social engagements were an essential part of diplomacy, one which Adams himself did not enjoy. In a way, they made an ideal team. To his credit, Adams did carry out the bulk of the business correspondence, organizing of papers, and settling of the commission's accounts—in short, most of the "Drudgery," as Adams called it.

During his presidency, Adams delayed releasing information about the XYZ Affair in which Talleyrand, the foreign minister of France, tried to extort a bribe before diplomatic negotiations. Adams was rightly concerned that word of it would escalate an unofficial naval war with France. Adams was called anti-French and pro-England. He was, in fact, suspicious of all European nations as he was of European manners in general. The United States and France never declared war; instead, Adams and Bonaparte negotiated a peace treaty, in which the United States was finally released from its revolutionary alliance with France.

Adams died on July 4, 1826, the fiftieth anniversary of the Declara-

tion of Independence, the same day that Thomas Jefferson died. A life-
long friend and political rival of Jefferson, Adams's final words were to
have been, "Thomas Jefferson still lives."

Passy April 12, 1778

My dearest Friend[1]

I am so sensible of the Difficulty of conveying Letters
safe, to you, That I am afraid to write, any Thing more
than to tell you that after all the Fatigues and Dangers of
my Voyage, and journey, I am here in Health. . . .

The Reception I have met, in this Kingdom, has been
as friendly, as polite, and as respectfull as was possible. It
is the universal Opinion of the People here, of all Ranks,
that a Friendship between France and America, is the
Interest of both Countries, and the late Alliance, so happily
formed, is universally popular: so much so that I have been
told by Persons of good judgment, that the Government
here, would have been under a Sort of Necessity of agree-
ing to it even if it had not been agreable to themselves.

The Delights of France are innumerable. The Politeness, the Elegance, the Softness, the Delicacy, is extreme.

In short stern and hauty Republican as I am, I cannot
help loving these People, for their earnest Desire, and
Assiduity to please.

It would be futile to attempt Descriptions of this
Country especially of Paris and Versailles. The public
Buildings and Gardens, the Paintings, Sculpture, Architec-
ture, Musick, &c. of these Cities have already filled many
Volumes. The Richness, the Magnificence, and Splendor,
is beyond all Description.

This Magnificence is not confined to public Build-

---

[1]The "Friend" whom he addresses in both letters is his wife, Abigail.

ings such as Churches, Hospitals, Schools &c., but extends to private Houses, to Furniture, Equipage, Dress, and especially to Entertainments.—But what is all this to me? I receive but little Pleasure in beholding all these Things, because I cannot but consider them as Bagatelles, introduced, by Time and Luxury in Exchange for the great Qualities and hardy manly Virtues of the human Heart. I cannot help suspecting that the more Elegance, the less Virtue in all Times and Countries.—Yet I fear that even my own dear Country wants the Power and Opportunity more than the Inclination, to be elegant, soft, and luxurious.

All the Luxury I desire in this World is the Company of my dearest Friend, and my Children, and such Friends as they delight in, which I have sanguine Hopes, I shall, after a few Years enjoy in Peace.—I am with inexpressible Affection Yours, yours,

JOHN ADAMS

Passi[2] *April 25, 1778*

My dearest Friend

Monsieur Chaumont has just informed me of a Vessell bound to Boston: but I am reduced to such a Moment of Time, that I can only inform you that I am well, and inclose a few Lines from Johnny, to let you know that he is so. I have ordered the Things you desired, to be sent you, but I will not yet say by what Conveyance, for fear of Accidents.

If human Nature could be made happy by any Thing that can please the Eye, the Ear, the Taste or any other

---

[2]Passy, or Passi: a small suburb just outside of Paris. The spelling variation is Adams's.

sense, or Passion or Fancy, this Country would be the Region for Happiness:——But, if my Country were at Peace, I should be happier, among the Rocks and shades of Pens hill: and would chearfully exchange, all the Elegance, Magnificence and sublimity of Europe, for the Simplicity of Braintree and Weymouth.

To tell you the Truth, I admire the Ladies here. Dont be jealous. They are handsome, and very well educated. Their Accomplishments are exceedingly brilliant. And their Knowledge of Letters and Arts, exceeds that of the English Ladies much, I believe.

Tell Mrs. W[arren] that I shall write her a Letter, as she desired, and let her know some of my Reflections in this Country.

My venerable Colleague[3] enjoys a Priviledge here, that is much to be envyd. Being seventy Years of Age, the Ladies not only allow him to ~~buss[4] them as often as he p~~ [crossed out] embrace them as often as he pleases, but they are perpetually embracing him.[5]——I told him Yesterday, I would write this to America.

---

[3]Benjamin Franklin.

[4]kiss.

[5]Not without a sense of humor, and missing her husband terribly, Abigail Adams wrote back: ". . . you must console me in your absence by a Recital of all your adventures, tho methinks I would not have them in all respects too similar to those related of your venerable Colleigue. . . ."

from

⚜ The Autobiography ⚜

I found that the Business of our Commission would never be done, unless I did it. My two Colleagues[6] would agree in nothing. The Life of Dr. Franklin was a Scene of continual discipation. I could never obtain the favour of his Company in a Morning before Breakfast which would have been the most convenient time to read over the Letters and papers, deliberate on their contents, and decide upon the Substance of the Answers. It was late when he breakfasted, and as soon as Breakfast was over, a crowd of Carriges came to his Levee or if you like the term better to his Lodgings, with all Sorts of People; some Phylosophers, Accademicians and Economists; some of his small tribe of humble friends in the litterary Way whom he employed to translate some of his ancient Compositions, such as his Bonhomme Richard and for what I know his Polly Baker &c.; but by far the greater part were Women and Children, come to have the honour to see the great Franklin, and to have the pleasure of telling Stories about his Simplicity, his bald head and scattering strait hairs, among their Acquaintances. These Visitors occupied all the time, commonly, till it was time to dress to go to Dinner. He was invited to dine abroad every day and never declined unless when We had invited Company to dine with Us. I was always invited with him, till I found it necessary to send Apologies, that I might have some time to study the french Language and do the Business of the mission. Mr. Franklin kept a horn book always in his Pockett in which he minuted all his invitations to dinner, and Mr. Lee said it was the only thing in which he was punctual. It was the Custom in France to dine between one and two O Clock: so that when the time came to dress, it was time for the Voiture to be ready to carry him to

---

[6]Arthur Lee, who eventually left the commission, and Franklin.

dinner. Mr. Lee came daily to my Appartment to attend to Business, but we could rarely obtain the Company of Dr. Franklin for a few minutes, and often when I had drawn the Papers and had them fairly copied for Signature, and Mr. Lee and I had signed them, I was frequently obliged to wait several days, before I could procure the Signature of Dr. Franklin to them. He went according to his Invitation to his Dinner and after that went sometimes to the Play, sometimes to the Philosophers but most commonly to visit those Ladies who were complaisant enough to depart from the custom of France so far as to procure Setts of Tea Geer as it is called and make Tea for him. Some of these Ladies I knew as Madam Hellvetius, Madam Brillon, Madam Chaumont, Madam Le Roy[7] &c. and others whom I never knew and never enquired for. After Tea the Evening was spent, in hearing the Ladies sing and play upon their Piano Fortes and other instruments of Musick, and in various Games as Cards, Chess, Backgammon, &c. &c. Mr. Franklin I believe however never play'd at any Thing but Chess or Checquers. In these Agreable and important Occupations and Amusements, The Afternoon and Evening was spent, and he came home at all hours from Nine to twelve O Clock at night. This Course of Life contributed to his Pleasure and I believe to his health and Longevity. He was now between Seventy and Eighty and I had so much respect and compassion for his Age, that I should have been happy to have done all the Business or rather all the Drudgery, if I could have been favoured with a few moments in a day to receive his Advice concerning the manner in which it ought to be done. But this condescention was not attainable. All that could be had was his Signature, after it was done, and this it is true he very rarely refused though he sometimes delayed.

---

[7]For a wonderfully readable account of Franklin's friendships with these and other French society ladies, see *Mon Cher Papa: Franklin and the Ladies of Paris* by Claude-Anne Lopez (Yale University Press).

Mark Twain

(1835–1910)

BORN SAMUEL L. CLEMENS in Florida, Missouri, Twain was a novelist, humorist, satirist, essayist, and a popular lecturer. Mark Twain is the enduring pen name among many of his lesser-known pseudonyms including Quentin Curtius Snodgrass, Thomas Jefferson Snodgrass, and Sieur Louis de Conte. His career was just as varied as his pen names. He was forced to leave school to work at the age of twelve when his father died. Twain worked as a printer's apprentice and typesetter, a riverboat pilot, a gold miner, a newspaper reporter, and even briefly as a soldier in the Confederate Army during the Civil War. Many of his experiences became the basis for his books: life on a Mississippi riverboat became *The Adventures of Tom Sawyer* and *The Adventures of Huckleberry Finn;* mining and living in the frontier West became *Roughing It;* and going on a worldwide tour of Europe and the Middle East became *The Innocents Abroad.*

This last book, from which the Paris chapter is excerpted here, was published under the pen name Mark Twain. The book brought him commercial and critical success. *The Innocents Abroad* is Twain's collected dispatches as a reporter for the *Alta California.* True to form, he had convinced his editors to finance the five-month cruise aboard the "Quaker City," bound for Europe and the Middle East. His humorous articles about his cruise members and their adventures appeared in the *Alta California* and the *New York Tribune.* Samuel Clemens died April 21, 1910, in Redding, Connecticut.

from

☆ The Innocents Abroad ☆

But I forgot. I am in elegant France now, and not skurrying through the great South Pass and the Wind River Mountains, among antelopes and buffaloes and painted Indians on the warpath. It is not meet that I should make too disparaging comparisons between humdrum travel on a railway and that royal summer flight across a continent in a stagecoach. I meant in the beginning to say that railway journeying is tedious and tiresome, and so it is—though at the time I was thinking particularly of a dismal fifty-hour pilgrimage between New York and St. Louis. Of course our trip through France was not really tedious because all its scenes and experiences were new and strange; but as Dan says, it had its "discrepancies."

The cars are built in compartments that hold eight persons each. Each compartment is partially subdivided, and so there are two tolerably distinct parties of four in it. Four face the other four. The seats and backs are thickly padded and cushioned and are very comfortable; you can smoke if you wish; there are no bothersome peddlers; you are saved the infliction of a multitude of disagreeable fellow passengers. So far, so well. But then the conductor locks you in when the train starts; there is no water to drink in the car; there is no heating apparatus for night travel; if a drunken rowdy should get in, you could not remove a matter of twenty seats from him or enter another car; but above all, if you are worn out and must sleep, you must sit up and do it in naps, with cramped legs and in a torturing misery that leaves you withered and lifeless the next day—for behold they have not that culmination of all charity and human kindness, a sleeping car, in all France. I prefer the American system. It has not so many grievous "discrepancies."

In France, all is clockwork, all is order. They make no mis-

takes. Every third man wears a uniform, and whether he be a marshal of the empire or a brakeman, he is ready and perfectly willing
to answer all your questions with tireless politeness, ready to tell
you which car to take, yea, and ready to go and put you into it to
make sure that you shall not go astray. You cannot pass into the
waiting room of the depot till you have secured your ticket, and
you cannot pass from its only exit till the train is at its threshold
to receive you. Once on board, the train will not start till your
ticket has been examined—till every passenger's ticket has been
inspected. This is chiefly for your own good. If by any possibility
you have managed to take the wrong train, you will be handed
over to a polite official who will take you whither you belong
and bestow you with many an affable bow. Your ticket will be
inspected every now and then along the route, and when it is time
to change cars you will know it. You are in the hands of officials
who zealously study your welfare and your interest, instead of
turning their talents to the invention of new methods of discom-
moding and snubbing you, as is very often the main employment
of that exceedingly self-satisfied monarch, the railroad conductor
of America.

But the happiest regulation in French railway government
is—thirty minutes to dinner! No five-minute boltings of flabby
rolls, muddy coffee, questionable eggs, gutta-percha beef, and pies
whose conception and execution are a dark and bloody mystery to
all save the cook that created them! No, we sat calmly down—it
was in old Dijon, which is so easy to spell and so impossible to
pronounce except when you civilize it and call it Demijohn—and
poured out rich Burgundian wines and munched calmly through a
long table d'hôte bill of fare, snail patties, delicious fruits and all,
then paid the trifle it cost and stepped happily aboard the train
again, without once cursing the railroad company. A rare experience and one to be treasured forever.

They say they do not have accidents on these French roads,
and I think it must be true. If I remember rightly, we passed high

above wagon roads or through tunnels under them, but never crossed them on their own level. About every quarter of a mile, it seemed to me, a man came out and held up a club till the train went by, to signify that everything was safe ahead. Switches were changed a mile in advance by pulling a wire rope that passed along the ground by the rail from station to station. Signals for the day and signals for the night gave constant and timely notice of the position of switches.

No, they have no railroad accidents to speak of in France. But why? Because when one occurs, *somebody* has to hang for it![1] Not hang, maybe, but be punished at least with such vigor of emphasis as to make negligence a thing to be shuddered at by railroad officials for many a day thereafter. "No blame attached to the officers"—that lying and disaster-breeding verdict so common to our softhearted juries is seldom rendered in France. If the trouble occurred in the conductor's department, that officer must suffer if his subordinate cannot be proven guilty; if in the engineer's department and the case be similar, the engineer must answer.

The Old Travelers—those delightful parrots who have "been here before" and know more about the country than Louis Napoleon knows now or ever will know—tell us these things, and we believe them because they are pleasant things to believe and because they are plausible and savor of the rigid subjection to law and order which we behold about us everywhere.

But we love the Old Travelers. We love to hear them prate and drivel and lie. We can tell them the moment we see them. They always throw out a few feelers; they never cast themselves adrift till they have sounded every individual and know that he has not traveled. Then they open their throttle valves, and how they do brag, and sneer, and swell, and soar, and blaspheme the sacred name of Truth! Their central idea, their grand aim, is to subjugate

---

[1] They go on the principle that it is better that one innocent man should suffer than five hundred. [Twain's note.]

you, keep you down, make you feel insignificant and humble in
the blaze of their cosmopolitan glory! They will not let you know
anything. They sneer at your most inoffensive suggestions; they
laugh unfeelingly at your treasured dreams of foreign lands; they
brand the statements of your traveled aunts and uncles as the stu-
pidest absurdities; they deride your most trusted authors and
demolish the fair images they have set up for your willing worship
with the pitiless ferocity of the fanatic iconoclast! But still I love
the Old Travelers. I love them for their witless platitudes, for their
supernatural ability to bore, for their delightful asinine vanity, for
their luxuriant fertility of imagination, for their startling, their
brilliant, their overwhelming mendacity!

By Lyons and the Saône (where we saw the lady of Lyons and
thought little of her comeliness), by Villa Franca, Tonnere, venerable Sens, Melun, Fontainebleau, and scores of other beautiful
cities, we swept, always noting the absence of hog wallows, broken fences, cow lots; unpainted houses, and mud, and always noting, as well, the presence of cleanliness, grace, taste in adorning
and beautifying, even to the disposition of a tree or the turning of
a hedge, the marvel of roads in perfect repair, void of ruts and
guiltless of even an inequality of surface—we bowled along, hour
after hour, that brilliant summer day, and as nightfall approached
we entered a wilderness of odorous flowers and shrubbery, sped
through it, and then, excited, delighted, and half persuaded that
we were only the sport of a beautiful dream, lo, we stood in magnificent Paris!

What excellent order they kept about that vast depot! There
was no frantic crowding and jostling, no shouting and swearing,
and no swaggering intrusion of services by rowdy hackmen. These
latter gentry stood outside—stood quietly by their long line of
vehicles and said never a word. A kind of hackman general seemed
to have the whole matter of transportation in his hands. He
politely received the passengers and ushered them to the kind of
conveyance they wanted, and told the driver where to deliver

them. There was no "talking back," no dissatisfaction about over-charging, no grumbling about anything. In a little while we were speeding through the streets of Paris and delightfully recognizing certain names and places with which books had long ago made us familiar. It was like meeting an old friend when we read "Rue de Rivoli" on the street corner; we knew the genuine vast palace of the Louvre as well as we knew its picture; when we passed by the Column of July we needed no one to tell us what it was or to remind us that on its site once stood the grim Bastile, that grave of human hopes and happiness, that dismal prison house within whose dungeons so many young faces put on the wrinkles of age, so many proud spirits grew humble, so many brave hearts broke.

We secured rooms at the hotel, or rather, we had three beds put into one room, so that we might be together, and then we went out to a restaurant, just after lamplighting, and ate a comfortable, satisfactory, lingering dinner. It was a pleasure to eat where everything was so tidy, the food so well cooked, the waiters so polite, and the coming and departing company so moustached, so frisky; so affable, so fearfully and wonderfully Frenchy! All the surroundings were gay and enlivening. Two hundred people sat at little tables on the sidewalk, sipping wine and coffee; the streets were thronged with light vehicles and with joyous pleasure-seekers; there was music in the air, life and action all about us, and a conflagration of gaslight everywhere!

After dinner we felt like seeing such Parisian specialties as we might see without distressing exertion, and so we sauntered through the brilliant streets and looked at the dainty trifles in variety stores and jewelry shops. Occasionally, merely for the pleasure of being cruel, we put unoffending Frenchmen on the rack with questions framed in the incomprehensible jargon of their native language, and while they writhed we impaled them, we peppered them, we scarified them, with their own vile verbs and participles.

We noticed that in the jewelry stores they had some of the articles marked "gold" and some labeled "imitation." We wondered at this extravagance of honesty and inquired into the matter. We were informed that inasmuch as most people are not able to tell false gold from the genuine article, the government compels jewelers to have their gold work assayed and stamped officially according to its fineness and their imitation work duly labeled with the sign of its falsity. They told us the jewelers would not dare to violate this law, and that whatever a stranger bought in one of their stores might be depended upon as being strictly what it was represented to be. Verily, a wonderful land is France!

Then we hunted for a barbershop. From earliest infancy it had been a cherished ambition of mine to be shaved some day in a palatial barbershop in Paris. I wished to recline at full length in a cushioned invalid chair, with pictures about me and sumptuous furniture; with frescoed walls and gilded arches above me and vistas of Corinthian columns stretching far before me; with perfumes of Araby to intoxicate my senses and the slumbrous drone of distant noises to soothe me to sleep. At the end of an hour I would wake up regretfully and find my face as smooth and as soft as an infant's. Departing, I would lift my hands above that barber's head and say, "Heaven bless you, my son!"

So we searched high and low, for a matter of two hours, but never a barbershop could we see. We saw only wigmaking establishments, with shocks of dead and repulsive hair bound upon the heads of painted waxen brigands who stared out from glass boxes upon the passerby with their stony eyes and scared him with the ghostly white of their countenances. We shunned these signs for a time, but finally we concluded that the wigmakers must of necessity be the barbers as well, since we could find no single legitimate representative of the fraternity. We entered and asked, and found that it was even so.

I said I wanted to be shaved. The barber inquired where my room was. I said never mind where my room was, I wanted to be shaved—there, on the spot. The doctor said he would be shaved also. Then there was an excitement among those two barbers!

There was a wild consultation, and afterwards a hurrying to and fro and a feverish gathering up of razors from obscure places and a ransacking for soap. Next they took us into a little mean, shabby back room; they got two ordinary sitting-room chairs and placed us in them with our coats on. My old, old dream of bliss vanished into thin air!

I sat bolt upright, silent, sad, and solemn. One of the wig-making villains lathered my face for ten terrible minutes and finished by plastering a mass of suds into my mouth. I expelled the nasty stuff with a strong English expletive and said, "Foreigner, beware!" Then this outlaw strapped his razor on his boot, hovered over me ominously for six fearful seconds, and then swooped down upon me like the genius of destruction. The first rake of his razor loosened the very hide from my face and lifted me out of the chair. I stormed and raved, and the other boys enjoyed it. Their beards are not strong and thick. Let us draw the curtain over this harrowing scene. Suffice it that I submitted and went through with the cruel infliction of a shave by a French barber; tears of exquisite agony coursed down my cheeks now and then, but I survived. Then the incipient assassin held a basin of water under my chin and slopped its contents over my face, and into my bosom, and down the back of my neck, with a mean pretense of washing away the soap and blood. He dried my features with a towel and was going to comb my hair, but I asked to be excused. I said, with withering irony, that it was sufficient to be skinned—I declined to be scalped.

I went away from there with my handkerchief about my face, and never, never, never desired to dream of palatial Parisian barbershops, anymore. The truth is, as I believe I have since found out, that they have no barbershops worthy of the name in Paris— and no barbers, either, for that matter. The impostor who does duty as a barber brings his pans and napkins and implements of torture to your residence and deliberately skins you in your private apartments. Ah, I have suffered, suffered, suffered, here in Paris, but never mind—the time is coming when I shall have a dark and bloody revenge. Someday a Parisian barber will come to my room to skin me, and from that day forth that barber will never be heard of more.

At eleven o'clock we alighted upon a sign which manifestly referred to billiards. Joy! We had played billiards in the Azores with balls that were not round and on an ancient table that was very little smoother than a brick pavement—one of those wretched old things with dead cushions, and with patches in the faded cloth and invisible obstructions that made the balls describe the most astonishing and unsuspected angles and perform feats in the way of unlooked-for and almost impossible "scratches" that were perfectly bewildering. We had played at Gibraltar with balls the size of a walnut on a table like a public square—and in both instances we achieved far more aggravation than amusement. We expected to fare better here, but we were mistaken. The cushions were a good deal higher than the balls, and as the balls had a fashion of always stopping under the cushions, we accomplished very little in the way of caroms. The cushions were hard and unelastic, and the cues were so crooked that in making a shot you had to allow for the curve or you would infallibly put the "English" on the wrong side of the ball. Dan was to mark while the doctor and I played. At the end of an hour neither of us had made a count, and so Dan was tired of keeping tally with nothing to tally, and we were heated and angry and disgusted. We paid the heavy bill—about six cents—and said we would call around sometime when we had a week to spend, and finish the game.

We adjourned to one of those pretty cafés and took supper and tested the wines of the country, as we had been instructed to do, and found them harmless and unexciting. They might have been exciting, however, if we had chosen to drink a sufficiency of them.

To close our first day in Paris cheerfully and pleasantly, we now sought our grand room in the Grand Hotel du Louvre and climbed into our sumptuous bed to read and smoke—but alas!

It was pitiful,
In a whole city-full,
  Gas we had none.

No gas to read by—nothing but dismal candles. It was a shame. We tried to map out excursions for the morrow; we puzzled over French "guides to Paris"; we talked disjointedly in a vain endeavor to make head or tail of the wild chaos of the day's sights and experiences; we subsided to indolent smoking; we gaped and yawned and stretched—then feebly wondered if we were really and truly in renowned Paris, and drifted drowsily away into that vast mysterious void which men call sleep.

The next morning we were up and dressed at ten o'clock. We went to the *commissionaire* of the hotel—I don't know what a *commissionaire* is, but that is the man we went to—and told him we wanted a guide. He said the great International Exposition had drawn such multitudes of Englishmen and Americans to Paris that it would be next to impossible to find a good guide unemployed. He said he usually kept a dozen or two on hand, but he only had three now. He called them. One looked so like a very pirate that we let him go at once. The next one spoke with a simpering precision of pronunciation that was irritating and said:

"If ze zhentlemans will to me make ze grande honneur to me rattain in hees serveece, I shall show to him everysing zat is magnifique to look upon in ze beautiful Parree. I speaky ze Angleesh pairfaitemaw."

He would have done well to have stopped there, because he had that much by heart and said it right off without making a mistake. But his self-complacency seduced him into attempting a flight into regions of unexplored English, and the reckless experiment was his ruin. Within ten seconds he was so tangled up in a maze of mutilated verbs and torn and bleeding forms of speech that no human ingenuity could ever have gotten him out of it with credit. It was plain enough that he could not "speaky" the English quite as "pairfaitemaw" as he had pretended he could.

The third man captured us. He was plainly dressed, but he had a noticeable air of neatness about him. He wore a high silk hat which was a little old, but had been carefully brushed. He wore secondhand kid gloves, in good repair, and carried a small rattan cane with a curved handle—a female leg—of ivory. He stepped as gently and as daintily as a cat crossing a muddy street; and oh, he was urbanity; he was quiet, unobtrusive self-possession; he was deference itself! He spoke softly and guardedly; and when he was about to make a statement on his sole responsibility or offer a suggestion, he weighed it by drachms and scruples first, with the crook of his little stick placed meditatively to his teeth. His opening speech was perfect. It was perfect in construction, in phraseology, in grammar, in emphasis, in pronunciation—everything. He spoke little and guardedly after that. We were charmed. We were more than charmed—we were overjoyed. We hired him at once. We never even asked him his price. This man—our lackey, our servant, our unquestioning slave though he was—was still a gentleman—we could see that—while of the other two one was coarse and awkward and the other was a born pirate. We asked our man Friday's name. He drew from his pocketbook a snowy little card and passed it to us with a profound bow:

A. BILLFINGER
Guide to Paris, France, Germany,
Spain, &c., &c.
Grande Hotel du Louvre

"Billfinger! Oh, carry me home to die!"

That was an "aside" from Dan. The atrocious name grated harshly on my ear, too. The most of us can learn to forgive, and even to like, a countenance that strikes us unpleasantly at first, but few of us, I fancy, become reconciled to a jarring name so easily. I was almost sorry we had hired this man, his name was so unbearable. However, no matter. We were impatient to start. Billfinger stepped to the door to call a carriage, and then the doctor said:

"Well, the guide goes with the barbershop, with the billiard table, with the gasless room, and maybe with many another pretty romance of Paris. I expected to have a guide named Henri de Montmorency or Armand de la Chartreuse or something that would sound grand in letters to the villagers at home, but to think of a Frenchman by the name of Billfinger! Oh! This is absurd, you know. This will never do. We can't say Billfinger; it is nauseating. Name him over again; what had we better call him? Alexis du Caulaincourt?"

"Alphonse Henri Gustave de Hauteville," I suggested.

"Call him Ferguson," said Dan.

That was practical, unromantic good sense. Without debate, we expunged Billfinger *as* Billfinger and called him Ferguson.

The carriage—an open barouche—was ready. Ferguson mounted beside the driver, and we whirled away to breakfast. As was proper, Mr. Ferguson stood by to transmit our orders and answer questions. By and by, he mentioned casually—the artful adventurer—that he would go and get his breakfast as soon as we had finished ours. He knew we could not get along without him and that we would not want to loiter about and wait for him. We asked him to sit down and eat with us. He begged, with many a bow, to be excused. It was not proper, he said; he would sit at another table. We ordered him peremptorily to sit down with us.

Here endeth the first lesson. It was a mistake.

As long as we had that fellow after that, he was always hungry;

he was always thirsty. He came early; he stayed late; he could not pass a restaurant; he looked with a lecherous eye upon every wineshop. Suggestions to stop, excuses to eat and to drink, were forever on his lips. We tried all we could to fill him so full that he would have no room to spare for a fortnight, but it was a failure. He did not hold enough to smother the cravings of his superhuman appetite.

He had another "discrepancy" about him. He was always wanting us to buy things. On the shallowest pretenses he would inveigle us into shirt stores, boot stores, tailor shops, glove shops—anywhere under the broad sweep of the heavens that there seemed a chance of our buying anything. Anyone could have guessed that the shopkeepers paid him a percentage on the sales, but in our blessed innocence we didn't until this feature of his conduct grew unbearably prominent. One day Dan happened to mention that he thought of buying three or four silk dress patterns for presents. Ferguson's hungry eye was upon him in an instant. In the course of twenty minutes the carriage stopped.

"What's this?"

"Zis is ze finest silk *magasin* in Paris—ze most celebrate."

"What did you come here for? We told you to take us to the palace of the Louvre."

"I suppose ze gentleman say he wish to buy some silk."

"You are not required to 'suppose' things for the party, Ferguson. We do not wish to tax your energies too much. We will bear some of the burden and heat of the day ourselves. We will endeavor to do such 'supposing' as is really necessary to be done. Drive on." So spake the doctor.

Within fifteen minutes the carriage halted again, and before another silk store. The doctor said:

"Ah, the palace of the Louvre—beautiful, beautiful edifice! Does the Emperor Napoleon live here now, Ferguson?"

"Ah, Doctor! You do jest; zis is not ze palace; we come there

directly. But since we pass right by zis store, where is such beautiful silk——"

"Ah! I see, I see. I meant to have told you that we did not wish
to purchase any silks today, but in my absentmindedness I forgot
it. I also meant to tell you we wished to go directly to the Louvre,
but I forgot that also. However, we will go there now. Pardon my
seeming carelessness, Ferguson. Drive on."

Within the half hour we stopped again—in front of another
silk store. We were angry; but the doctor was always serene, always
smooth-voiced. He said:

"At last! How imposing the Louvre is, and yet how small!
How exquisitely fashioned! How charmingly situated! Venerable,
venerable pile——"

"Pairdon, Doctor, zis is not ze Louvre—it is——"

"*What* is it?"

"I have ze idea—it come to me in a moment—zat ze silk in
zis *magasin*——"

"Ferguson, how heedless I am. I fully intended to tell you that
we did not wish to buy any silks today, and I also intended to
tell you that we yearned to go immediately to the palace of the
Louvre, but enjoying the happiness of seeing you devour four
breakfasts this morning has so filled me with pleasurable emotions that I neglect the commonest interests of the time. However, we will proceed now to the Louvre, Ferguson."

"But, Doctor" (excitedly), "it will take not a minute—not but
one small minute! Ze gentleman need not to buy if he not wish
to—but only *look* at ze silk—*look* at ze beautiful fabric. [Then
pleadingly.] *Sair*—just only one *leetle* moment!"

Dan said, "Confound the idiot! I don't want to see any silks
today, and I *won't* look at them. Drive on."

And the doctor: "We need no silks now, Ferguson. Our hearts
yearn for the Louvre. Let us journey on—let us journey on."

"But, *Doctor!* It is only one moment—one leetle moment.

And ze time will be save—entirely save! Because zere is nothing to see now—it is too late. It want ten minute to four and ze Louvre close at four—*only* one leetle moment, Doctor!"

The treacherous miscreant! After four breakfasts and a gallon of champagne, to serve us such a scurvy trick. We got no sight of the countless treasures of art in the Louvre galleries that day, and our only poor little satisfaction was in the reflection that Ferguson sold not a solitary silk dress pattern.

I am writing this chapter partly for the satisfaction of abusing that accomplished knave Billfinger, and partly to show whosoever shall read this how Americans fare at the hands of the Paris guides and what sort of people Paris guides are. It need not be supposed that we were a stupider or an easier prey than our countrymen generally are, for we were not. The guides deceive and defraud every American who goes to Paris for the first time and sees its sights alone or in company with others as little experienced as himself. I shall visit Paris again someday, and then let the guides beware! I shall go in my war paint—I shall carry my tomahawk along.

I think we have lost but little time in Paris. We have gone to bed every night tired out. Of course we visited the renowned International Exposition. All the world did that. We went there on our third day in Paris—and we stayed there *nearly two hours*. That was our first and last visit. To tell the truth, we saw at a glance that one would have to spend weeks—yea, even months—in that monstrous establishment to get an intelligible idea of it. It was a wonderful show, but the moving masses of people of all nations we saw there were a still more wonderful show. I discovered that if I were to stay there a month, I should still find myself looking at the people instead of the inanimate objects on exhibition.

[. . .]

We went to see the Cathedral of Notre Dame. We had heard of it before. It surprises me sometimes to think how much we *do* know and how intelligent we are. We recognized the brown old Gothic pile in a moment; it was like the pictures. We stood at a little distance and changed from one point of observation to another and gazed long at its lofty square towers and its rich front, clustered thick with stony, mutilated saints who had been looking calmly down from their perches for ages. The Patriarch of Jerusalem stood under them in the old days of chivalry and romance, and preached the third Crusade, more than six hundred years ago; and since that day they have stood there and looked quietly down upon the most thrilling scenes, the grandest pageants, the most extraordinary spectacles that have grieved or delighted Paris. These battered and broken-nosed old fellows saw many and many a cavalcade of mail-clad knights come marching home from Holy Land; they heard the bells above them toll the signal for the St. Bartholomew's Massacre, and they saw the slaughter that followed; later they saw the Reign of Terror, the carnage of the Revolution, the overthrow of a king, the coronation of two Napoleons, the christening of the young prince that lords it over a regiment of servants in the Tuileries today—and they may possibly continue to stand there until they see the Napoleon dynasty swept away and the banners of a great republic floating above its ruins. I wish these old parties could speak. They could tell a tale worth the listening to.

[. . .]

One night we went to the celebrated Jardin Mabille, but only stayed a little while. We wanted to see some of this kind of Paris life, however, and therefore the next night we went to a similar place of entertainment in a great garden in the suburb of Asnières. We went to the railroad depot toward evening, and Ferguson got tickets for a second-class carriage. Such a perfect jam of people I have not often seen—but there was no noise, no disorder, no rowdyism. Some of the women and young girls that entered the train we knew to be of the demimonde, but others we were not at all sure about.

The girls and women in our carriage behaved themselves modestly and becomingly all the way out, except that they smoked. When we arrived at the garden in Asnières, we paid a franc or two admission and entered a place which had flower beds in it, and grass plots, and long, curving rows of ornamental shrubbery, with here and there a secluded bower convenient for eating ice cream in. We moved along the sinuous gravel walks, with the great concourse of girls and young men, and suddenly a domed and filigreed white temple, starred over and over and over again with brilliant gas jets, burst upon us like a fallen sun. Nearby was a large, handsome house with its ample front illuminated in the same way, and above its roof floated the Star-Spangled Banner of America.

"Well!" I said. "How is this?" It nearly took my breath away.

Ferguson said an American—a New Yorker—kept the place, and was carrying on quite a stirring opposition to the Jardin Mabille.

Crowds composed of both sexes and nearly all ages were frisking about the garden or sitting in the open air in front of the flagstaff and the temple, drinking wine and coffee or smoking. The dancing had not begun yet. Ferguson said there was to be an exhibition. The famous Blondin was going to perform on a tightrope in another part of the garden. We went thither. Here the light was dim, and the masses of people were pretty closely packed together. And now I made a mistake which any donkey might make, but a sensible man never. I committed an error which I find myself repeating every day of my life. Standing right before a young lady, I said:

"Dan, just look at this girl, how beautiful she is!"

"I thank you more for the evident sincerity of the compliment, sir, than for the extraordinary publicity you have given to it!" This in good, pure English.

We took a walk, but my spirits were very, very sadly dampened. I did not feel right comfortable for some time afterward. Why *will* people be so stupid as to suppose themselves the only foreigners among a crowd of ten thousand persons?

But Blondin came out shortly. He appeared on a stretched cable, far away above the sea of tossing hats and handkerchiefs, and in the glare of the hundreds of rockets that whizzed heavenward by him he looked like a wee insect. He balanced his pole and walked the length of his rope—two or three hundred feet; he came back and got a man and carried him across; he returned to the center and danced a jig; next he performed some gymnastic and balancing feats too perilous to afford a pleasant spectacle; and he finished by fastening to his person a thousand Roman candles, Catherine wheels, serpents and rockets of all manner of brilliant colors, setting them on fire all at once and walking and waltzing across his rope again in a blinding blaze of glory that lit up the garden and the people's faces like a great conflagration at midnight.

The dance had begun, and we adjourned to the temple. Within it was a drinking saloon, and all around it was a broad circular platform for the dancers. I backed up against the wall of the temple and waited. Twenty sets formed, the music struck up, and then—I placed my hands before my face for very shame. But I looked through my fingers. They were dancing the renowned "Cancan." A handsome girl in the set before me tripped forward lightly to meet the opposite gentleman, tripped back again, grasped her dresses vigorously on both sides with her hands, raised them pretty high, danced an extraordinary jig that had more activity and exposure about it than any jig I ever saw before, and then, drawing her clothes still higher, she advanced gaily to the center and launched a vicious kick full at her *vis-à-vis* that must infallibly have removed his nose if he had been seven feet high. It was a mercy he was only six.

That is the cancan. The idea of it is to dance as wildly, as noisily, as furiously as you can; expose yourself as much as possible if you are a woman; and kick as high as you can, no matter which sex you belong to. There is no word of exaggeration in this. Any of the staid, respectable, aged people who were there that night can testify to the truth of that statement. There were a good many such people present. I suppose French morality is not of that straight-laced description which is shocked at trifles.

I moved aside and took a general view of the cancan. Shouts, laughter, furious music, a bewildering chaos of darting and inter-mingling forms, stormy jerking and snatching of gay dresses, bob-bing heads, flying arms, lightning flashes of white-stockinged calves and dainty slippers in the air, and then a grand final rush, riot, a terrific hubbub, and a wild stampede! Heavens! Nothing like it has been seen on earth since trembling Tam O'Shanter saw the devil and the witches at their orgies that stormy night in "Alloway's auld haunted kirk."

We visited the Louvre, at a time when we had no silk pur-chases in view, and looked at its miles of paintings by the old mas-ters. Some of them were beautiful, but at the same time they carried such evidences about them of the cringing spirit of those great men that we found small pleasure in examining them. Their nauseous adulation of princely patrons was more prominent to me and chained my attention more surely than the charms of color and expression which are claimed to be in the pictures. Grat-itude for kindnesses is well, but it seems to me that some of those artists carried it so far that it ceased to be gratitude and became worship. If there is a plausible excuse for the worship of men, then by all means let us forgive Rubens and his brethren.

But I will drop the subject, lest I say something about the old masters that might as well be left unsaid.

Of course we drove in the Bois de Boulogne, that limitless park, with its forests, its lakes, its cascades, and its broad avenues. There were thousands upon thousands of vehicles abroad, and the scene was full of life and gaiety. There were very common hacks, with father and mother and all the children in them; conspicuous little open carriages with celebrated ladies of questionable reputation in them; there were dukes and duchesses abroad, with gorgeous footmen perched behind, and equally gorgeous outriders perched on each of the six horses; there were blue and silver, and green and gold, and pink and black, and all sorts and descriptions of stunning and startling liveries out, and I almost yearned to be a flunky myself, for the sake of the fine clothes.

But presently the Emperor came along and he outshone them all. He was preceded by a bodyguard of gentlemen on horseback in showy uniforms, his carriage horses (there appeared to be somewhere in the remote neighborhood of a thousand of them) were bestridden by gallant-looking fellows, also in stylish uniforms, and after the carriage followed another detachment of bodyguards. Everybody got out of the way; everybody bowed to the Emperor and his friend the Sultan; and they went by on a swinging trot and disappeared.

I will not describe the Bois de Boulogne. I cannot do it. It is simply a beautiful, cultivated, endless, wonderful wilderness. It is an enchanting place. It is in Paris now, one may say, but a crumbling old cross in one portion of it reminds one that it was not always so. The cross marks the spot where a celebrated troubadour was waylaid and murdered in the fourteenth century. It was in this park that that fellow with an unpronounceable name made the attempt upon the Russian czar's life last spring with a pistol. The bullet struck a tree. Ferguson showed us the place. Now in America that interesting tree would be chopped down or forgotten within the next five years, but it will be treasured here. The guides will point it out to visitors for the next eight hundred years, and when it decays and falls down they will put up another there and go on with the same old story just the same. [. . .]

Enough of Paris for the present. We have done our whole duty by it. We have seen the Tuileries, the Napoleon Column, the Madeleine, that wonder of wonders the tomb of Napoleon, all the great churches and museums, libraries, imperial palaces, and sculpture and picture galleries, the Panthéon, Jardin des Plantes, the opera, the circus, the legislative body, the billiard rooms, the barbers, the grisettes—

Ah, the grisettes! I had almost forgotten. They are another romantic fraud. They were (if you let the books of travel tell it) always so beautiful—so neat and trim, so graceful—so naïve and trusting—so gentle, so winning—so faithful to their shop duties, so irresistible to buyers in their prattling importunity—so devoted to their poverty-stricken students of the Latin Quarter—so light-hearted and happy on their Sunday picnics in the suburbs—and oh, so charmingly, so delightfully immoral!

Stuff! For three or four days I was constantly saying:

"Quick, Ferguson! Is that a grisette?"

And he always said, "No."

He comprehended at last that I wanted to see a grisette. Then he showed me dozens of them. They were like nearly all the Frenchwomen I ever saw—homely. They had large hands, large feet, large mouths; they had pug noses as a general thing, and moustaches that not even good breeding could overlook; they combed their hair straight back without parting; they were ill-shaped, they were not winning, they were not graceful; I knew by their looks that they ate garlic and onions; and lastly and finally, to my thinking it would be base flattery to call them immoral.

Aroint thee, wench! I sorrow for the vagabond student of the Latin Quarter now, even more than formerly I envied him. Thus topples to earth another idol of my infancy.

We have seen everything, and tomorrow we go to Versailles. We shall see Paris only for a little while as we come back to take up our line of march for the ship, and so I may as well bid the beautiful city a regretful farewell. We shall travel many thousands of miles after we leave here and visit many great cities, but we shall find none so enchanting as this.

Some of our party have gone to England, intending to take a

roundabout course and rejoin the vessel at Leghorn or Naples several weeks hence. We came near going to Geneva, but have concluded to return to Marseilles and go up through Italy from Genoa.

I will conclude this chapter with a remark that I am sincerely proud to be able to make—and glad, as well, that my comrades cordially endorse it, to wit: by far the handsomest women we have seen in France were born and reared in America.

I feel now like a man who has redeemed a failing reputation and shed luster upon a dimmed escutcheon by a single just deed done at the eleventh hour.

Let the curtain fall, to slow music.

Dave Barry
(1947–   )

COLUMNIST DAVE BARRY is also the bestselling author of *Dave Barry Turns Forty, Bad Habits: A 100% Fact-Free Book, Dave Barry Slept Here: A Sort of History of the United States,* and many other books. His *Miami Herald* column is syndicated in more than 150 newspapers, and his humorous observations about the lives of ordinary Americans won him the Pulitzer Prize in 1988. He encamps himself firmly with the middle-class Americans about whom he writes, making fun of himself as much as others. What funny writers does a humor columnist read? Barry lists Robert Benchley, P. J. O'Rourke, Roy Blount, and Art Buchwald. But, it is in the tradition of Ernest Hemingway, Henry Miller, and F. Scott Fitzgerald (and Mark Twain, though he goes unnamed) that Barry goes to Paris in the two-part article reprinted here.

from

✢ Dave Barry Is Not Taking This Sitting Down ✢

Parlez-Vous Français?

This summer, for my vacation, I went to Paris, France. I went there to follow in the footsteps of such great writers as Ernest Hemingway, Henry Miller, and "F." Scott Fitzgerald, all of whom, for the record, are currently dead.

I blame the Parisian drivers. Paris has only one vacant parking space, which is currently under heavy police guard in the Louvre museum. This means that thousands of frustrated motorists have been driving around the city since the reign of King Maurice XVII looking for a space, and the way they relieve their frustrations is by aiming at pedestrians, whom they will follow onto the sidewalk if necessary. Often the only way to escape them is to duck into one of Paris's historic cathedrals, which fortunately are located about every 25 feet (or 83.13 liters).

Nevertheless it's very pleasant to walk around Paris and feel—as so many Americans feel when they're in that incredibly beautiful city—fat. Because the fact is that we Americans look like enormous sneaker-wearing beef cattle compared to the Parisians, who tend to be very slim, with an average body weight of 38 pounds (7.83 meters). It's odd that the French appear to be in such good shape, because the major activity in Paris, aside from trying to run over pedestrians, is sitting around in cafés for days at a time looking French.

Sometimes we Americans try to blend in to the café scene, but the French immediately spot us as impostors, because we cannot pronounce the Secret French Code letter, which is "r." They have learned to say "r" in a certain secret way that sounds as though they are trying to dislodge a live eel from their esophagus. It is virtually impossible for a non-French person to make this sound; this is how the Parisian café waiters figure out that you are an American, even if you are attempting to pass as French:

WAITER: *Bonjour. Je suspect que vous êtes American.*
          ("Good day. I suspect that you are American.")
YOU: *Mais je ne portes pas les Nikes!*
          ("But I am not wearing the sneakers!")
WAITER: *Au quais, monsieur pantalons intelligents, prononcez le mot "Rouen."*
          ("OK, Mr. Smarty Pants, pronounce the word 'Rouen.'")

YOU: *Woon.*
         ("Woon.")
WAITER: *Si vous êtes français, je suis l'Homme de la Batte.*
         ("If you are French, I am Batman.")

The other surefire way to tell the difference between French people and Americans in a café is that the French are all smoking, whereas the Americans are all trying to figure out how much to tip. The tourist guidebooks are vague about tipping: They tell you that a service charge is USUALLY included in your bill, but it is not ALWAYS included, and even if it IS included, it is not necessarily TOTALLY included. On top of that, to convert from French money to American, you have to divide by six, and I have yet to meet anybody who can do this.

And so while the French are lounging and smoking and writing novels, we Americans spend our café time darting nervous glances at the bill, which is often just a piece of paper with a lone, mysterious, not-divisible-by-six number scrawled on it such as "83." We almost always end up overtipping, because we're afraid that otherwise the waiter will make us say another "R" word. I frankly don't know how the French handle tipping, because in my two weeks in Paris I never saw a French person actually leave a café.

Not that I am being critical. As a professional journalist, I like the idea of a society where it is considered an acceptable occupation to basically sit around and drink. In fact, I liked almost everything about Paris. The city is gorgeous, the food is wonderful, and they have these really swoopy high-tech public pay toilets on the streets that look as though, if you went into one, you might get beamed up to the Mother Ship. Also Paris has a terrific subway system, Le Metro (literally, "The Metro"). I always felt safe and comfortable in the Metro, although one time, when I was waiting for a train, the loudspeaker made an announcement in French, which was repeated in English, and I swear this was the whole thing: "Ladies and gentlemen, your attention please. Robbers are in the station. Thank you." None of the Parisians seemed the least bit alarmed, and nobody robbed me, which was a good thing, because I would have had no idea how much to tip.

I have run out of space here, but in next week's column I will tell you about some of the famous tourist attractions of Paris, such as the L'Arc D. Triomphe, Notre Dame, the Leaning Tower of Pisa, etc. So until next week, as the French say, *"Au revoir"* (Literally, "Woon.")

An Aesthetically Challenged American in Paris (Part II)

Today I'll be concluding my two-part series on Paris, France. In writing this series, my goal, as a journalist, is to provide you with enough information about this beautiful and culturally important city so that I can claim my summer vacation trip there as a tax deduction.

My topic in Part II is the historic tourist attractions of Paris. The Parisians have been building historic attractions for more than 1,500 years as part of a coordinated effort to kill whatever tourists manage to escape the drivers. The key is stairs. Most tourist attractions, such as L'Arc de Triomphe (literally, "The Lark of Triumph") and the Hunchback of Notre Dame Cathedral, have some kind of lookout point at the top that you, the tourist, are encouraged to climb to via a dark and scary medieval stone staircase containing at least 5,789 steps and the skeletons of previous tourists (you can tell which skeletons are American, because they're wearing sneakers). If you make it to the top, you are rewarded with a sweeping panoramic view of dark spots before your eyes caused by lack of oxygen. Meanwhile, down at street level, the Parisians are smoking cigarettes and remarking, in French, "Some of them are still alive! We must build more medieval steps!"

Of course the tallest monument in Paris is the Eiffel Tower, named for the visionary engineer who designed it, Fred Tower. The good news is, there are elevators to the top. The bad news is, pretty much the entire tourist population of Europe is up there taking flash pictures of itself. There are so many people crowded into the smallish observation area that you get the feeling, crazy as it seems, that the whole darned Eiffel Tower is going to topple over. Ha ha! In fact this has happened only twice since 1991.

Paris also has many excellent art museums, the most famous being the Louvre (pronounced "Woon"). If you plan to visit it, you should allow yourself plenty of time to see everything—say, four years—because the Louvre is the size of Connecticut, only with more stairs. The museum contains 30,000 pieces of painting and sculpture, and as you walk past these incredible works of art, depicting humanity through the centuries, you cannot help but be struck, as millions of people have been struck before you, by the fact that for a whole lot of those centuries, humanity was stark naked. To judge from the Louvre, until about 1900, everybody on Earth—men, women, children, gods, goddesses, horses—basically just stood around all the time without a stitch of clothing on. There's one gigantic painting of a bunch of warriors getting ready to go into battle, and all they're wearing is swords. You expect to see a comics-style speech balloon coming out of the lead warrior's mouth, saying, "Fight hard, men! If we win the war, we can afford pants!"

I think the reason why the *Mona Lisa* is so famous is that she's just about the only artistic subject in the Louvre who's wearing clothes. On any given day, every tourist in Europe who is not on top of the Eiffel Tower is gathered in front of the *Mona Lisa*, who gazes out at the crowd with the enigmatic expression of a person who is pondering the timeless question: "How come they keep taking flash photographs, even though the signs specifically prohibit this?"

I enjoyed the art museums, but for me the most moving cultural experience I had in Paris was—and you may call me a big fat stupid low-rent American pig if you wish—visiting a gourmet food store called Fauchon (pronounced "Woon"), which contains two-thirds of the world's calorie supply. In the great art museums, I eventually reached a saturation point and found myself walking right past brilliant masterpiece paintings by van Gogh, Renoir, Matisse, LeRoy Neiman, etc., without even glancing at them; whereas after a lengthy period of browsing in Fauchon, I was still enthusiastically remarking, with genuine artistic appreciation: "Whoa! Check out THESE éclairs!"

In conclusion, I would say that Paris is the most beautiful city in the world, and its inhabitants have an amazing sense of *"savoir-faire,"* which means, literally, "knowing how to extinguish a fire." I say this because one Sunday afternoon I was in a crowded café when smoke started billowing from a cabinet into which waiters had been stuffing trash. It was a semi-scary situation; I stood up and gestured toward the smoke in an alarmed American manner, but the French diners paid no attention. In a moment, a waiter appeared carrying some food; he noted the smoke, served the food, went away, then returned to douse the fire with, I swear, a bottle of mineral water. And you just know it was the correct *kind* of mineral water for that kind of fire. So the meal ended up being very pleasant. It was also—I state this for the benefit of the Internal Revenue Service—quite expensive.

T. S. Eliot

(1888–1965)

BORN September 26, 1888, in St. Louis, Missouri, Thomas Stearns Eliot, or T. S. Eliot, wrote poetry, literary criticism, essays, and dramas. He received the Nobel Prize for Literature in 1948. Eliot once commented on his literary reputation: "One seems to become a myth, a fabulous creature that doesn't exist. . . . It isn't that you get bigger to fit the world, the world gets smaller to fit you. You remain exactly the same." Eliot, a naturalized British citizen, died in his adopted home of England.

His 1911 letter to his niece is printed here. He was twenty-two when he wrote it and had recently graduated from Harvard. Still looking for his poetic voice, he was studying for a year at the Sorbonne in Paris. He had not yet written "The Love Song of J. Alfred Prufrock," (1915) or "The Waste Land" (1922). Readers will glimpse a young Eliot, charmed by Paris, who hasn't yet entered the pantheon of modern literature. His observations of Parisian schoolchildren and the Luxembourg Gardens are spontaneous and descriptive for a young niece's imagination. The second letter, to the American poet, Robert McAlmon, in 1921, reveals an Eliot who has found his voice. Here, readers can glimpse the deep erudition and strong opinions for which Eliot, the critic, would become famous, in the way he susses up the Paris expatriate literati scene, Ezra Pound, and James Joyce.

from

❧ The Letters of T. S. Eliot ❧

To Theodora Eliot Smith

[late February? 1911]   Paris

My Dear Theodora

Thank you very much for the nice letter that you sent me, and the Valentine of Puss in Boots. Have you the puss in the green boots still, and do you remember the story about him?

You must have been studying hard in order to be able to write so nicely. I have been studying too. But I often go out and walk in the Luxembourg Gardens, which is a sort of park like the Boston Public Gardens, or the park back down the hill from your home in Brookline, where you used to go. There is a pond there too, and the children play boats when it is not too cold. There are lots of boats and they sail right across the pond and right through the fountain and never upset. They spin tops and roll hoops. You would like the French children. I don't think they have as many playthings as the American children, but they seem quite happy. I see lots of them in the Champs Elysées (which is a long wide street) on Sunday afternoon, riding in little carts behind goats. But it is hard to talk to the little ones, because they don't talk French very well yet, and I don't either.

When they are older and go to school you see them walking out two by two, very quiet and proper, in a long line, with their teachers. They all wear black capes, and carry their schoolbooks on their backs underneath the capes, so that they all look as if they had big bumps on

their backs. And they wear black pinafores, and have their
legs bare all winter. But it is never very cold in Paris. It has
not snowed here all winter, and the little steamboats go
up and down the river like black flies: "fly-boats", they
call them.

Just about now you are having supper in America,
and here, it is my bed time. Isn't that funny?

—With love to mother and father and all the dolls

YOUR

UNCLE

TOM

To Robert McAlmon

2 May 1921
9 Clarence Gate Gardens,
London N.W.1

Dear Bob,

I was glad to hear from you. I will go through your poems
at leisure if I may, and write you about them in due
course. I'm glad to hear that you like Paris; the right way
of course is to take it as a place and a tradition, rather
than as a congeries of people who are mostly futile and
timewasting, except when you want to pass an evening
agreeably in a café. The chief danger about Paris is that it
is such a strong stimulus, and like most stimulants incites
to rushing about and produces a pleasant illusion of great
mental activity rather than the solid results of hard work.
When I was living there years ago I had only the genuine
stimulus of the place, and not the artificial stimulus of
the people, as I knew no one whatever, in the literary
and artistic world, as a companion—knew them rather as

spectacles, listened to, at rare occasions, but never spoken to. I am sure Julien Benda is worth knowing and possibly Paul Valéry. But Paris is still alive. What is wonderful about French literature is its solidarity: you don't know one part of it, even the most contemporary, unless you know the seventeenth and eighteenth centuries, and more too, in a way in which Pound and [Clive] Bell don't— Pound because he has never taken the trouble, and Bell because he couldn't. Bell is a most agreeable person, if you don't take him seriously, but a great waster of time if you do, or if you expect to get any profound knowledge or original thought out of him, and his Paris is a useless one. If I came to live in Paris the first thing to do would be to cut myself off from it, and not depend upon it. Joyce I admire as a person who seems to be independent of outside stimulus, and who therefore is likely to go on producing first-rate work until he dies.

I should not worry at all about what Thayer says. I thought his witticisms in the May number very tasteless and pointless. Why do our compatriots try so hard to be clever? Furthermore, his language is so opaque, through his cleverness, that it is unintelligible gibberish. Cummings has the same exasperating vice.

But Joyce has form—immensely careful. And as for literary—one of the last things he sent me contains a marvellous parody of nearly every style in English prose from 1600 to the *Daily Mail*. One needs a pretty considerable knowledge of English literature to understand it. No! you can't generalize, in the end it is a question of whether a man has genius and can do what he sets out to do. Small formulas support small people. Aren't the arty aesthetes you mention simply the people without brains?

Write to me again soon, yours,

TOM

Janet Flanner
(1892–1978)

JANET FLANNER is better known as Genet, the pen name with which she wrote the "Letter from Paris" column from 1925 to 1939 for *The New Yorker*. The late *New York Review of Books* critic Virgil Thomson compared Flanner to the English writer and diarist Samuel Pepys, "who could go on and on about London and still make us wish for more." Flanner's own observations of Paris have the same effect. In her "letters," Flanner covered the current day's trends and culture in literature, entertainment, sports, art, theater, music, people and fashions, and the local city politics of Paris. She cast her view wide to cover anything that would give her American readers a real, unglamorized, and local view of Paris. With the German occupation of the city and World War II, she returned to New York in 1939, determined to go back as soon as possible. With the liberation of Paris in 1944, she returned and stayed until 1975. She published many books about Paris including *An American in Paris, Paris Was Yesterday,* and *Paris Journal* (volumes 1 and 2) for which she won a National Book Award for the first volume. She received the French Legion of Honor for her work in "Letter from Paris." She died in New York City.

❖ Tourist ❖

from An American in Paris

The late Jean De Koven was an average American tourist in Paris but for two exceptions. She never set foot in the Opéra, and she was murdered. In the first four July days of her initial visit to the capital of France, her routine had been classic: she had settled in a quaint little Left Bank hotel near the Place Saint-Germain-des-Prés, she had seen the boulevards by night, had attended the Folies-Bergère, admired the Louvre, and bought a ticket, ironically enough, for Dukas' *Ariadne and Bluebeard*. But when the opera's red-and-gold curtain rose, her seat was empty—for she was dead and probably already buried under the front porch of a cottage in Saint-Cloud.

The relation of the murdered and the murderer is the base of any assassination. The relations between Jean De Koven, professional dancer from Brooklyn, and Eugen Weidmann, practiced criminal from Frankfurt am Main, were merely social. Sociability with strangers was her personal weakness and his professional stock in trade. Urbanity (until it was interrupted by her strangulation) marked both their brief meetings—the first at the Hôtel Ambassador, when Weidmann, presenting himself with what Miss De Koven's aunt, Miss Ida Sackheim, afterward described as the most gracious smile she ever saw, offered to interpret for the two ladies, who were with difficulty trying to locate a friend in the building. "I have just met a charming German of keen intelligence who calls himself Siegfried," Miss De Koven wrote that day to an American friend (though to the aunt, anyhow, he had called himself plain Bobby). "Perhaps I am going to another Wagnerian role—who knows? I am going to visit him tomorrow at his villa in a beautiful place near a famous mansion that Napoleon gave Josephine."

While Miss De Koven must have been disappointed historically in the villa—French house agents' standard euphemism for three rooms without bath—the Bonapartian and Wagnerian talk probably satisfied. Her Siegfried was well read, having been prison librarian at Saarbrücken while serving five years for robbery. He loved *The Ring*, and in the weeks after she had gone used to leave his house (over her buried corpse) to go to his next-door neighbor's and listen to Wagner on the radio. In the brief hour spent with him before Miss De Koven went to her new operatic role, sheer sociality reigned; they smoked, she took pictures of him with her nice new camera, he kindly refreshed her with a glass of milk. When, five months later, his unfortunate guest was disinterred, she still summed up (except for the murderous cord tight around her throat and the awful action of time) the sartorial elements of the sociable summer tourist. She was still wearing her cute brown sports hat, her gloves, her blue dress with its red Scotch plaid top, her new patent-leather shoes—still had with her her white handbag (empty of $430 in American Express checks and about 300 francs cash), still had at her side her nice new camera containing snapshots of her murderer.

The De Koven case started the next morning, Saturday, July 23, 1937, when her aunt received a telegram stating that all was well and not to worry (which she had done all night). That evening a letter came, mentioning "Chikago" gangster methods but assuring her that the girl was sound and safe, kidnaped, and held for ransom $500, the Teutonic phrasing and spelling being illustrated by the Gothic shaped j's, the triangular t's, and the general Nordic slant of the handwriting. Miss Sackheim went immediately to the American Consulate and the police. But the case didn't get seriously under way, owing to the constabulary's cynical laughter. One of the rare gaieties of the Sûreté Nationale in Paris is provided by the missing Americans and English who later turn up, abashed, repentant, or still dazed after their first foolish fling in gay Paree. Furthermore, as the police pointed out, Miss De Koven was twenty-two years old; she was (the aunt had shown the police an overflattering press photo of the dancer) beautiful; she had departed voluntarily with a man whom the aunt described as handsome and Swiss; her disappearance was probably a publicity scheme; the kidnaping was an American *truc* that couldn't happen in France, and anyhow Saint-Cloud (if she'd really gone there, which she probably hadn't, since her aunt had heard her say she would) was lovely in summer *pour un beau couple d'amoureux.*

Still smirking, the police nevertheless kept an official eye on the contact messages which the aunt, at the kidnaper's request, was running in English in the agony column of the Paris edition of the *New York Herald Tribune:* "Jean, please come back." "Jean, everything ready. Why did you not answer?" "Jean, do not understand your way of acting. Want proposition immediately." The police also had their eye on the two rendezvous mentioned in notes from the kidnaper. One was the Luxembourg Gardens, where the password was to be "Jean," spoken three times; the other was in Saint-Sulpice Church, where the word was to be simply "Baby." Indeed, the police kept such an obvious gaze fixed on these places that the kidnaper never turned up, sending instead a final, angry, ungrammatical post card. "Remind," he said on it (though he meant "remember"), "the least sign we have of the police and we don't send nobody to get the money."

It was money that finally sobered the French Sûreté, for the girl's $10 American Express checks began coming in, execrably forged. Honest voyagers like you and me may have difficulties in cashing our modest traveler's checks, aided by our proper passports, our unimpeachable calligraphy, our respectable faces, and the backing of bourgeois friends. With perfect ease, $240 worth of Miss De Koven's checks had been cashed by what, judging by various cashiers' descriptions, was a motley pair of men, one big and maybe Austrian, one little and French, and, apparently, two local women, one blonde, one dark. These four had among them one passport—Miss De Koven's. The most respectable Parisian houses were accepting the forged paper—Guerlain's perfumery, two French banks, Lancel's leather shop on the Place de l'Opéra, and the French Bureau de Tourisme. When the Trocadéro gateman of the Paris Exposition turned in a forged De Koven check, the police changed their tactics and the De Koven "kidnaping" (the sarcastic quotation marks are the Paris *Herald Tribune*'s) was for the first time made public on August 7, fifteen days after the American girl's "disappearance."

The reaction was immediate and twofold. No more checks were cashed, and Jean De Koven, once her photograph was published, was reported as being seen all over France. A sharp-eyed M. Poo, headwaiter at the roguish Réserve at Saint-Cloud, saw her lunching on his terrace *en flirt* with a handsome French athlete; a taxi driver said she had screamed, in his taxi, to be taken to the American Embassy but that her two gentlemen escorts had preferred he deposit them all at the Closerie-des-Lilas café in Montparnasse; a fortune-teller in Nancy saw her in a trance, by the ocean somewhere; a cruel M. Tarashkoff telephoned five times in one afternoon to the aunt's hotel to give his name and announce "in a frightful voice" that the girl was dead; some crooks offered to sell clues to her whereabouts for $600. On August 16, Henry De Koven, brother of the girl, arrived in Paris, made a touching, dignified statement that "in our modest family my sister is considered a serious-minded girl, incapable of the acts which have been insinuated, either any escapade or publicity stunts," and offered in the name of his father, Abraham De Koven, a 10,000-franc reward. The brother was convinced that his sister was dead and so were the police.

The faithful aunt, "Sacky," as the niece always called her (the kidnaper's first telegram had been oddly addressed to "Secky," which had convinced her that the criminal was that smiling Swiss "Bobby" she had met), was too loving to believe the girl had been done away with, too sensible not to know that tragedy of some sort seemed affirmed though it could not be defined. Despairing, she and the brother sailed for home on September 18. By the Sûreté Nationale of Paris, by the French Police de l'État, by the American Embassy, by the American Consulate in Paris, by Secretary Cordell Hull, who had been appealed to for G-men's aid, by Governor Lehman of New York, by all on both sides of the

Atlantic who had by this time been drawn into the unprofitable search, the De Koven case was considered closed, unsolved.

As a matter of fact it was just beginning to open. Unfortunately, it needed five more murders to be complete. On September 7, a Parisian chauffeur named Couffy was found dead, robbed of 2,500 francs and his car, and with a bullet in the nape of his neck, in a forest near Tours. He was driver-owner of a luxurious limousine, ordinarily stationed for hire near the Opéra, and had started in it for Cannes with a client who was Anglo-Saxon, or at any rate spoke English fluently. He was a cool client. When a passing Touraine peasant named Blé saw, just after lunch, a rotund recumbent figure on the grass with a newspaper over its face, he called to the stranger sitting nearby and whistling, "Aren't you afraid you'll wake your friend?" and received the reply, "No danger. He's sleeping soundly." This was true. Beneath the newspaper covering his bloody face, Couffy was sleeping the sleep of the dead.

On October 3, though the police did not then know it, a Strasbourg cook, Mme Jeanine Keller, came to Paris in response to a help-wanted ad, had been killed in the Fontainebleau Forest by a bullet in the nape of her neck, and robbed of 1,400 francs and a pitiful little diamond ring. On October 16, opposite the cemetery of Neuilly, a parked car was discovered to contain the corpse of M. Roger Leblond, who had been shot, robbed of 5,000 francs, and then wrapped in a green-and-brown curtain, laundry-marked M.B. Leblond's latest mistress said he was a press agent, that he had gone to meet a business-advertisement correspondent named Pradier about a new cinema agency. The seven hundred Pradier families of France were vainly questioned by the police, and three hundred Parisian laundries were vainly consulted about the M.B. tag. On November 22, though again the police were not then aware of it, a German-Jewish youth, Frommer, who for his anti-Hitlerian political views had once been incarcerated in the prison at Saarbrücken, was robbed of 300 francs, murdered by a bullet in the nape of the neck, and buried in the basement of a villa near the famous mansion which Napoleon gave Josephine at Saint-Cloud. On November 27, only five days later and also at Saint-Cloud, a house agent, Monsieur Lesobre, was robbed of 5,000 francs and murdered by a shot in the nape of the neck by the pal of a client with a foreign accent to whom Lesobre was showing a three-room villa more than usually euphemistically called Mon Plaisir.

It was at this point that what began and ended as the De Koven case entered into the peripheries of a master detective story, transferred, for once, from the folly of fiction into grim, real life. It was at this moment that an unusually intelligent and lucky criminal began to be tracked by an unusually intelligent and lucky detective. Into the hands of a Commissaire Primborgne, detective *sous-chef* of the State Police at Versailles, county seat of the Saint-Cloud district, fell a bloody visiting card found beside Lesobre's body. The card was that of Arthur Schott, traveling salesman of the Rue Parc-Impérial of Nice. From Nice the detective traced Schott to Strasbourg and summoned him to Versailles, only to learn that the cards had been distributed to thousands, including, among six other recent recipients, Schott's nephew Frommer, the young anti-Nazi.

Primborgne's search for Miss De Koven now began by his hunting a man he'd never heard of alive and didn't know was dead. All that Frommer's meager Idéal Hôtel in the Rue Saint-Sébastien knew was that Frommer had walked out on November 22, leaving his belongings and no explanation. The municipal registration offices for furnished rooms, for prisons, for hospitals, and for foreigners knew even less. However, in the Île de la Cité's *carte d'identité* files the detective discovered that Frommer's application blank gave, as resident reference, one Hugh Weber, 58 Rue de Clichy. Weber had moved, leaving no new address. Through the neighborhood police, the detective discovered he now lived somewhere in the Rue Véron, and there he found Herr Weber—and found, too, that Herr Weber spoke nearly no French. However, the patient Primborgne gleaned that Weber was another of Frommer's uncles and was worried because the youth had failed to appear for the usual family Sunday dinner. He was even more perturbed at his nephew's occasional luncheons with a criminal compatriot apparently named Sauerbrei, whom Frommer had known in Saarbrücken Prison. Sauerbrei lived, Weber thought, under the name of Karrer in the woods around Saint-Cloud.

Primborgne knew that, wherever Leblond had been murdered by that bullet in the back of the neck, it was near trees, for their leaves were on the soles of the dead man's shoes; he knew also that Lesobre had been killed by the same sort of shot, and, *parbleu*, near trees, since he had been murdered at Saint-Cloud. He was sure that Jean De Koven had also disappeared in Saint-Cloud. The detective was by now nearly sure of certain things but didn't know where in Saint-Cloud to set about searching for them. Inquiring always through house agents and garages (Weber said Frommer said Sauerbrei said he had a car), Primborgne at last located Karrer's landlady, Mme Marie Binder. Though she didn't yet know that her best green-and-brown curtain, laundry-tagged M.B., was gone from Karrer's cottage, she had another complaint: for all his charming smile, good manners, intelligent air, and excellent neighborhood reputation, Karrer had been late with his October rent—hadn't, indeed, paid it till November 29. On November 27, Lesobre had been robbed of 5,000 francs.

Nobody being at home in the Karrer villa, the methodical Primborgne set off to telephone the villa's house agent for further details, leaving two men to watch the house. Within five minutes of his departure, Siegfried-Bobby-Sauerbrei-Karrer-Pradier-Weidmann walked through his front gate, playing with a neighbor's dog. The watchers, interrogated, said they were tax collectors; were politely requested to show their proofs and showed their police cards instead. Weidmann's last courtesy consisted in begging them to precede him into his house. Thinking of the backs of their necks, they refused. Weidmann entered first, but once over the threshold wheeled on them and fired three times, wounding them both. Being economically unarmed, as are all French State Police unless they choose to buy guns at their own expense, the men fell on him with their bare hands. One of them, tumbling in their struggle upon a little hammer (Weidmann had been doing some small household repairs), knocked their host unconscious. By the time he came to, in the police station, Couffy's automobile and Lesobre's had been found, neatly parked, and with a light covering of December snow, in the villa's back yard. The day had been unlucky for two lucky men. The lucky murderer had finally been caught, and the lucky detective had not been present when the capture was made.

The next morning, with a cigarette which the police put into his manacled hands and a brazier which they put at his feet (the French Sûreté believe comfort brings better results than American brutality in grilling), Weidmann started on his orderly confession. Saying that there was one thing he couldn't say, but could write, he wrote down the name Jean De Koven. For her he then shed his only repentant tears. "She was gentle and unsuspecting," he said. "I enjoyed speaking English to her, which I learned in Canada. When I reached out for her throat, she went down like a doll."

Eugen Weidmann was born in Frankfurt, February 15, 1908, of respectable parents—his father is still agent for a small exporting business at Frankfurt, where his son went through grade school. At the age of sixteen, he served time for his first theft and was afterwards imprisoned for robbery in both Canada and Germany. He was a model prisoner, a favorite with German wardens, who considered him remarkably intellectual and well read; they have said since that they can hardly believe he killed five times. He spoke, besides German, fluent English, French, and some Portuguese. After his final arrest, in France, he spent his time in his cell reading *Aventures de Télémaque*, by Fénelon, and writing his memoirs; indeed, he had so little time for working at the regular paid prison labor, brushmaking, that he lacked the money to pay the prison barber for a shave. Before the investigating magistrates, his uncouth appearance humiliated him, especially the fact that, having caught cold in a chill cell, he had need of a handkerchief, denied him lest he hang himself with it.

Weidmann was an exceptionally handsome male in the medieval manner; his features were those of an etching by Holbein of some German *moyen âge* merchant, with an alert, inquiring, virile, hungry eye, with a well-cartilaged nose terminating in a cold, curious ball like that on the end of a thermometer, and a large, amply delineated classical mouth with adequate lips. The hair rolled free from the forehead in tidy artistic profusion. He looked and acted like a man who, if he hadn't had in his make-up the criminal compartment, would have made a good Gothic citizen.

He was scrupulously veracious with the police. "I never lie," he truthfully told them in relating the murder of Leblond, which, on his terms, they could hardly believe. "Here is the proof," he said, and flipped open his coat to show Leblond's suspenders, which he was wearing. He had also saved the press agent's incriminating cigarette lighter, watch, and gold pencil, the baldish Mme Keller's blonde wigs, and Lesobre's useless small shoes, which he neatly preserved on shoe trees. He was also obligingly helpful to the authorities, who otherwise certainly never would have been able to find the grave of Mme Keller in a subterranean grotto in the Fontainebleau Forest, though he never explained why on earth his photograph came to be found by her side. Because she was also discovered without her shoes on, the theory of an erotic fetishism was raised, principally in a brilliant article by Mme Colette in *Le Journal*. Certain of the official investigators were at first also inclined to a belief that his emotional nature must be peculiar, largely because, outside of his terrible crimes, he seemed so sensible. The court interpretess assigned to him—he had fits of saying in German that he had forgotten all his French, and usually

consulted with his French lawyer only in English—bluntly said
she thought, in his collecting instinct, that he was less erotic than
plain practical. To Mme Tricot, mistress of his assistant, a novice
French gangster named Million, Weidmann gave Mme Keller's
imitation fur coat and one of her wigs. They were useful when a
disguise was needed for check cashing.

Contrary to his name, Million's part of the four months'
swag—including his reward for having practiced up on murder
for the first time by killing Lesobre under Weidmann's tutelage
with what Weidmann called "the shot in the back of the neck that
never fails"—netted him only a fourth of the paltry 22,000 francs
which the six murders brought in from July through November.
For there was a fourth in the Weidmann combine—clown-faced
Monsieur Jean Blanc, of good middle-class family and with a private income from a doting widowed mother. The previous summer Blanc backed Weidmann with 13,000 francs, apparently just
for the thrill of being in on big crime. He and Million had already
been arrested in Germany for some trifling illicit reichsmark
transactions and had indeed first met Weidmann in prison, where
sure enough they all met again.

Probably the most esoteric feature of the whole case was that
while hundreds of officials were searching for what they thought
was Jean De Koven's coy hiding place, seven people knew she was
dead, and where the body was, and never told. Outside of the
murderer, the six others were Million, Million's father, Million's
father's café boss, and his boss's wife, Million's mistress, Mme Tricot, and her innocent cuckolded husband, M. Tricot, to whom she
told all. Jean Blanc was evidently such a bourgeois boob that he
was told little and allowed to pay the big bills. It should be noted
that Weidmann gave away none of these accomplices to the
police—categorically denied, at first, that anybody had helped
him. He admitted they existed only after the police caught them.
As the police said, he was chic.

The Weidmann case was the biggest murder trial in France

since Landru, whose cell at Saint-Pierre Prison the German occupied. Like the other so-called Bluebeard, the new mass murderer was tried in Versailles. His chief defense lawyer was Maître Henri Géraud, who failed to save the neck of Gorguloff, the assassin of President Doumer of France, and Moro-Giufferi, who failed to save Landru; assistant counsel was a lady lawyer, Maître Renée Jardin, assigned to the case by the court. The granddaughter of George Sand, the novelist, was the defense's handwriting expert in the affair. Together it was not thought they would be able to save Weidmann's head. The French are still a rational-minded race and their law courts show it. In France there's little legal nonsense such as pleading insanity for a man who had an exceptionally high I.Q., as Weidmann showed.

His trial turned out to be not only one of the most important and popular, but also proved to be, psychologically, the strangest *procès* recorded in French criminal history. That he would escape the death sentence was expected by no one, not even Weidmann, who in one of his two sensational Rousseaulike confessions said to his judge, "I am guilty, terribly guilty. I offer all I can offer—my life." He also offered a truthfulness so impressive and solicitous that he, the criminal, gradually assumed the role of a judge and became the arbiter in the desperate conflicts among the three other prisoners, the regiment of bibbed lawyers, and the crowd of weeping, bereaved, black-swathed relatives, all of whom (whenever it was useful to them) accepted the murderer's "Yes" and "No," or even the taciturn nod of his head, as gospel. "Give me the final consolation of believing in the sincerity of my sentiments," begged Weidmann of the court during one of the dramatic moments, when his devotion to veracity led him to declare that while he had murdered five times, Million, his petty-gangster confederate, had made the sixth kill. As a futile Faustian character whose power of speculation on good and evil was profoundly revealed—if a little tardily—in the prisoner's dock, Weidmann appropriately inspired some of the best newspaper literature Paris had seen since the trial, in the same courtroom, of Landru. *Le Journal*'s, and France's star crime reporter, Geo London, and *L'Œuvre*'s crack man, Pierre Bénard, both turned out pages of that mixture of malice, insight, libel, philosophy, and inaccurate reporting that constitutes the genius of the fourth estate here. And as a special reporter for *Paris-Soir,* Mme Colette, in a brilliant appreciative essay on the murderer's spiritual capacity for truth, honored Weidmann with fine writing such as she has hitherto bestowed only on nature and animals.

It is indicative of the rational attitude of the French, during the particular moment of acute nationalistic tension, that Weidmann's being a German was not considered an additional crime.

Indeed, as a Gothic cruel criminal, the French more than gave him the benefit of their curious international-minded sympathy. Million, like Weidmann, was condemned to death but was later pardoned by the President of France and permitted to look forward to life imprisonment. That the murderous Frenchman was allowed to keep his head while the even more murderous German lost his was a source of acute dissatisfaction to the average Paris man in the street. "It didn't look right," he said. "It had an air of giving the Boche the worst of it."

Weidmann's decapitation was more important than he could have dreamed. Ever since Dr. Joseph Guillotin, Parisian professor of anatomy, imposed his instrument "for decollation" in 1792, executions, as part of the murderer's awful punishment, have taken place in a public place in France. Weidmann will go down in modern French judicial history as the last to lose his head while morbid crowds gaped at dawn—at a criminal whose popularity was so great that it changed the law. Within a fortnight of Weidmann's death the French Minister of Justice passed a new decree, ordaining that in the future French executions would take place privately behind prison walls. The *kermesse* scenes in Versailles the night before Weidmann's punishment were considered too scandalous; cafés were given an all-night license extension, wine flowed, around the little prison blared jazz on radios whose previous announcement of his approaching death the prisoner had already overheard. Desfourneaux, the new Monsieur de Paris, or high executioner, nervous at only his third performance, insisted, against the Procuror of the Republic, that Greenwich rather than summertime dawn should be the official hour. Weidmann was, contrary to custom, thus executed—and clumsily to boot—in broad daylight. He met his end bravely. That is to say he shut his eyes when he saw the guillotine and walked to his death like a somnambulist.

Only a typical Frenchman like Million, accustomed to the old apprentice system and his country's gerontocratic policy, by which the young always work (and at low pay) for their elders, would have participated in such a poor proposition as the Weidmann murders. Only a typical postwar German like Weidmann, unfamiliar with the value of money as the rest of the freer world knows it, would have killed so many people for so little. And only a typical American, like poor Miss De Koven, would have been so sociable, so confidential, and could have seemed so rich. The De Koven case was a small and sinister European entanglement.

Bricktop
(1894–1984)

ADA SMITH was known simply as "Bricktop." The nickname was a term of endearment given by friends to describe her red hair, but it stuck to her professionally as well. Born in poverty in West Virginia, she started her career in Harlem in the 1920s as a singer and a chorus girl. She took a ship to Paris as the replacement chanteuse at Le Grand Duc. Though not an instant sensation in Paris, Bricktop eventually earned a following, most notably that of Cole Porter. Porter wrote the song "Miss Otis Regrets" for her. Nightlife in Paris was vibrant and vital during the 1920s. Bricktop describes some of that scene in the excerpt of her autobiography here. As a nightclub entertainer, she met all the Americans in Paris of her day: a young Langston Hughes (who worked in the kitchen at Le Grand Duc), Zelda and F. Scott Fitzgerald, Duke Ellington, Josephine Baker, the heiress Doris Duke, the Gershwins, Vernon and Irene Castle, Hemingway, and many others. She went on to open her own nightclub in Paris, and when the Second World War broke out, she returned to the United States. After the war, she opened two more nightclubs, in Mexico City and Rome.

❖ Cole Porter . . . and
Josephine Baker ❖

from Bricktop

(cowritten with James Haskins)

One morning in the late fall or early winter of 1925 a slight, immaculately dressed man came in, sat down at one of the tables, and ordered a plate of corned-beef hash with a poached egg on top and a bottle of wine. By morning I mean between three a.m. and six a.m.—we stayed open after the other clubs closed and got quite a few customers during those hours. We only served three things at that time of day—corned-beef hash with a poached egg, creamed chicken on toast, or a club sandwich—but we served them courtesy of the house.

I got up to sing and could sense that the man was watching and listening with more than ordinary interest. He applauded when I finished the set. I bowed and took up my usual position at the door. He finished eating and got up to leave. Just then Buddy Gilmore came through the door. Buddy was a drummer who'd come to Paris with Vernon and Irene Castle and stayed to form his own group. He grabbed the stranger and started hugging him.

"Who was that?" I asked Buddy later.

"That was Cole Porter," he said.

"Oh, my God!" I said. "I've just been singing one of his songs!"

The normally unexcitable me was suddenly shaken. It's one thing to take someone like Fannie Ward in stride. It's quite another to find out you've just performed in front of a giant-sized talent like Cole Porter—and performed one of his own songs! Everyone in Paris knew that Cole was funny about people singing his songs. If a singer didn't do it just right, Cole wouldn't embarrass him or her, but he'd leave quickly—and that would be the most embarrassing situation imaginable for the singer. I was worrying about what I'd done to "I'm in Love Again," the Porter song I'd been singing, when it occurred to me that he *hadn't* left. In fact, he'd applauded. I was to find out that he was interested in me for other reasons.

Cole came back the very next night. I was excited. It meant he liked me. I was also nervous, because now I knew who he was. I didn't chance singing another one of his songs.

Pretty soon he sent for me. I thought he was going to ask me to sing something, but he'd heard me sing. What he wanted to know was, could I dance? I couldn't believe it when he asked, "Can you dance the Charleston?"

The Charleston hadn't been introduced to Europe yet. Songs and dances didn't travel as fast then as they do today. They also lived a lot longer. I'd learned the Charleston in New York, and I said, "Sure can." I launched into a quick rendition.

When I finished, Cole thanked me and told me I had "talking feet and legs." I laughed. He laughed, too, and said he would see me again.

A couple of nights later he came back, this time with Elsa Maxwell and four or five other people. Again he sent for me and asked me to dance the Charleston. Elsa loved it. She clapped and shrieked. That's the way she was. If anything pleased her, her enthusiasm was boundless. She was just as intense about her dislikes. Luckily, I was on the right side of Elsa's enthusiasm. Me and the Charleston were something new for her to play with. I was in.

Once I had Elsa's stamp of approval, Cole got around to telling me why he was so interested. "I'm going to give Charleston cocktail parties at my house two or three times a week, and you're going to teach everyone how to dance the Charleston."

I didn't have to think twice. I accepted right away. I didn't know how much I was going to be paid or who I was going to teach. It didn't matter. If Cole Porter had asked me, I would have taught all of Paris to do the Charleston for nothing.

At the agreed-upon time on the agreed-upon date, I arrived at Cole's house at 13 Rue Monsieur. The house itself was already a legend. It didn't look like much from the outside—in fact, it looked as if it might come tumbling down any minute—but inside it was spectacular. Cole's wife, Linda, was the decorator. There were zebra skins on the floors and on some of the walls. The chairs were painted red and upholstered in white kid. There was even a room with platinum wallpaper.

The house contained all the *objets d'art* that the Porters had collected. The chandeliers were magnificent. The whole place was like a palace, and it took my breath away. Later on I learned that there was one small room, close to the front door, that didn't look at all as if it belonged in a palace. It looked more like a monk's cell. That was where Cole did most of his composing.

I was prepared to find that the Porters were living in a palace. I wasn't prepared to find royalty there. However, there was the Aga Khan, eager to learn the Charleston, along with Elsa, of course, and about fifty other VIPs. I was about to become the dance teacher to the most elegant members of the international set.

I have to give the Charleston the credit it deserves for launching me on my career as a saloonkeeper. It was a great dance. You could do it by yourself. You were never embarrassed about having to keep up with a partner. All you had to do was to keep time, and if you couldn't, who knew the difference? It wasn't so different from the dances that were popular before the disco craze. And it was a fast dance. It appealed to people who led fast lives. It caught on and I caught on, Cole Porter standing right there behind me and never leaving me until I became Bricktop, the one and only.

That afternoon of Cole's first Charleston party, I must have been a success, because people started coming to Le Grand Duc to see more Charleston. A lot of people were too shy to dance with the group at Cole's. I started teaching them at the club, but some were too shy even for that. They asked me to give private lessons. They sent their cars for me. I charged ten dollars a lesson. Sometimes I gave three or four lessons a day.

The shyest would-be Charleston dancer was the Aga Khan, and who wouldn't be, at over three hundred pounds? He was a delightful man with a very dry wit. Every time one of his horses won the English Derby, he'd tell the English, "I know you hate to see this nigger win the Derby, but I have the best horses." And he did, right up until Nijinsky. He didn't drink because of his religion, but he entertained lavishly his friends who did. He also hit all the night spots. He'd come into Le Grand Duc and bow very low and kiss my hand. "How does it feel to have royalty kiss this little freckled hand of yours?" he'd ask. I had a stock answer: "I don't feel anything. Royalty? They're only people." That always tickled him.

He never managed to ask me personally for Charleston lessons. The Marquise de Polignac was the one who told me that the Aga wanted to learn the Charleston. Would I teach him? I was really flattered then. Teaching a three-hundred-pound man would have been a challenge. I was really sorry when he backed out of the lessons. He sent his driver with a very nice note calling the appointment off.

One of my first private pupils was Dolly O'Brien, a tall, handsome society woman who always wore white and lots of diamonds. She was once linked with Clark Gable. Too bad that relationship was only rumors. Her husband, Jay, was such a cracker that he said he resented seeing a Negro man in a smoking jacket.

One of my more intriguing Charleston pupils was a famous ballerina at the Paris Opera. There she was, a prima ballerina, and she wanted to learn how to do the Charleston!

Through the Charleston lessons I began to meet the top hosts and hostesses of Paris. This was a time when there were big, big parties. The best party-givers I knew were Cole; Elsa Maxwell;

Dolly O'Brien and her cracker husband; Arturo Lopez, the Chilean multimillionaire; the Rothschilds; Lady Mendl; Daisy Fellowes; Mrs. George Dixon; and Consuelo Vanderbilt, who had married the Duke of Marlborough. There were many others, of course, but these were the people I knew personally.

There were so many parties in those days in Paris—everything from garden affairs to lavish costume balls to formal dinners. The very exclusive dinners were for ten to fifty guests. At a buffet affair there might be as many as five hundred guests. In between, there were the big sit-down dinners for as many as a hundred and fifty people. The largest spring garden parties and winter balls had three hundred to five hundred people. I have no idea how expensive these parties were. Probably the hosts and hostesses didn't even know. Money was no object. I don't think those affairs could ever be reproduced today except by a government or one of those giant corporations.

When I was asked to do a party, we didn't usually discuss terms. Our fees were understood. I was paid fifty dollars for a party, and could expect another fifty or so as a tip. The piano player got twenty-five, and when I brought a combo along, the fee could be as high as three hundred dollars. I never stooped to negotiate with a host or hostess. No high-class woman ever lays down a price.

One of the first parties I did was given by Elsa Maxwell at the Ritz. I brought along the Three Eddys, a team of dancers who did a comedy act. Like many entertainers of the time, Negro and white, they blackened their faces with burnt cork, wore white gloves and big eyeglasses. It was a great party, and the Three Eddys thought they'd gone over well.

That night, however, Elsa came over to the club to say, "Brick, don't use the Three Eddys again."

My first thought was that they'd misbehaved. "Well, not exactly," said Elsa. "But when they saw all the men kissing women's hands, they must have decided that was the thing to do. About half a dozen women had their hands smeared with burnt cork. And, Brick, if you don't know how hard that is to clean off, I do. I used to wear cork in vaudeville."

I did many other parties for Elsa, and we kept in touch for years. I never got too close to Elsa, though. With her, the best thing to do was to be cordial. You could stay that way for a long time. I suppose that's why we remained casual friends and I never found myself on the wrong end of her sharp, cutting words. I could have gotten into a feud with her if I'd called her on her claim that she was responsible for my success. I could have reminded her that she took me up simply because Cole was interested. I decided it wasn't worth the trouble, however. She could be a formidable enemy.

In another time Elsa could never have made it the way she did. She was unique in a unique era. She came from nowhere and ended up on top because she managed to push herself forward without seeming brassy. That took real skill. She was a wonderful party-giver, a born hostess, a great organizer. She knew how to run things and how to give service. She also had a great imagination, and you needed that if you were going to be a top party-giver.

Hostesses stayed up all night dreaming up new party ideas. The Porters gave great affairs. For one party at the Ritz he wrote a Charleston song. The words were strung across the room so everybody could sing along with me: "A dark-eyed lady, not so shady, started winking her eye and saying Charleston . . ." Then we went into the dance.

You didn't go out just one or two nights a week in those days. You went out every night. If it wasn't to a party, it was to the opera or the theater or the Folies-Bergère, and afterward you went to one of the Montmartre clubs. Parties began at eleven, or even at midnight. I sometimes left the club to do a party, came back, and more often than not found the whole party moving into the club in the early hours of the morning. If I'd had the stamina, I could have been at a party every night.

[. . .]

Josephine came to Paris in the fall of 1925. She came with a whole bunch of American Negroes for a colored revue produced by André Devan called *La Revue Nègre*. By 1925 Paris was having its own version of the Harlem Renaissance. It was called *Le Tumulte Noir*. I may have benefitted from this great interest in Negro things, but Josephine became a star overnight.

Maude de Forrest was the original star of the revue, but Maude's voice was tricky. It could fail completely without a moment's warning. On the ship to Paris, Josephine was rehearsed secretly to take over from Maude, because the company was afraid Maude wouldn't make the important Paris opening. A hit in Paris opened the way to bookings all over the Continent.

Well, Maude's voice did fail, and Josephine Baker got her chance. She made her Paris debut wearing practically nothing, and the theater turned into a circus. Paris had never seen anything like Josephine. She was still a teenager, and the ovation scared her so that she ran off the stage.

Overnight, she was a star. Within a few nights after that, she was being dressed by Paul Poiret—and, oh, how she could wear clothes, although her fame would rest a lot on her ability to perform without them. Her reputation for performing nude too often overshadowed the fact that she was born to wear couturier styles, or the fact that she had a live, wonderful, natural talent.

Also overshadowed was the fact that she was still a kid, and she was one of the most vulnerable stars I've ever met. At the time, Negro female entertainers were still a rarity in Paris. Naturally, Josephine and I got together.

She was only about seventeen years old. She brought out the mother instinct in me, just as Scott Fitzgerald had. Only, Scott had a lot more going for him when I met him than Josephine had.

She hadn't had much schooling. She could hardly write her name and, suddenly, everyone wanted her autograph. I said, "Baby, get a stamp." I talked her into writing her name once, in the clearest and best script she could manage, and having it made into a rubber stamp. That saved her a lot of embarrassment.

She didn't know how to take care of nice things. She didn't know how to appreciate them. I arrived at her hotel room one day and found the floor covered with stacks of couturier clothes, mostly Poiret's. I'd been given couturier clothes, too, but I'd never piled them on the floor. I said, "Hang these dresses up, or have your maid do it." Josephine said, "But, Bricky, they're going to take them away tomorrow and bring me another pile." Everything was for the moment with Josephine. She couldn't see past today.

However, she was scared—and who wouldn't be? She was a star before she was even full-grown. She could put on couturier clothes and not know what she was wearing—but she had sense enough to know she was in over her head.

I became her big sister. She'd come into Le Grand Duc and ask me about everything. She'd say, "Bricky, tell me what to do." She wouldn't go around the corner without asking my advice.

A big sister doesn't get far when she gives advice about men, however, and when Josephine needed advice the most, I couldn't do much good.

She used to come into Le Grand Duc with a fellow named Zito, a caricaturist who worked at Zelli's across the street. Zito wasn't much of a date, but there are always times when a woman in the spotlight doesn't have much choice. Many boys who might have asked her out were too shy, and too frightened by all the publicity she was getting. When a gal hits the top, it's taken for granted that she's being wined and dined by some rich, handsome guy— and maybe a different one every night. The Josephine legend supports that idea about her, even though everyone knew she mostly went around with Zito.

One night Zito was sick. He got his cousin Pepito to take Josephine around. It turned out to be a fateful night.

Pepito had just arrived from Rome. His real name was Giuseppe Abatino and he was working as a gigolo at Zelli's. He and the others preferred to call themselves "dance instructors." He was good-looking, in his late thirties, and it hadn't taken him long to figure out that there were a lot of lonely women with money in Paris. In no time at all he was calling himself Count Pepito de Abatino. I called him the no-account count.

The night Josephine showed up at Le Grand Duc with Pepito, I couldn't believe my eyes. I didn't hesitate to tell Josephine how I felt. "What are you doing with this bum? He can't even pay for a glass of beer." Josephine explained that Zito was sick, but I didn't like the looks of things. I knew what Pepito was.

Zito may have seen Josephine again, but it was never the same between them. Pepito took over. He flattered Josephine, wrote her love notes, followed her around like a puppy. But he was slick. He had a plan, and part of it was to cut Josephine off from her old friends.

Being a kid and not knowing any better, Josephine told Pepito what I'd said about him. He started steering her away from the club and me. He kept her away from all the blacks in Paris. Pretty soon Spencer Williams, the musician, was the only old pal still allowed around. I guess he didn't present any threat.

With Pepito's encouragement, Josephine opened her own club, Chez Joséphine, on the Rue Fontaine in December 1926. It was an immediate success. That Christmas they came into the club and Pepito showed me the platinum watch studded with diamonds that Josephine had just given him. It was exactly like the watch I'd just given my "man of the moment." I blew up. In front of Pepito, I lit into Josephine and told her what a fool she'd become.

For some time afterward, whenever we met on the street, I found myself saying hello to her back.

Pepito came to control more and more of Josephine's life. He put a kind of guard around her. You couldn't get near her. Pepito especially didn't want Josephine to have anything to do with Bricktop, because I'd told her what he was from the beginning.

He talked her into putting all of her money in his name, in case she was ever sued. I have to give him credit for what he did for Josephine, though. She wasn't a hit in her second Paris show, and without Pepito she might have become a nobody. Pepito turned out to have a sharp business know-how. He manipulated her back into stardom. At the same time, he practically put her through school. He saw that she learned to read and write and speak proper French. He educated her in music and art and the social graces. Josephine was a smart kid, though. She could have picked a lot of that up on her own, or from someone else who wasn't so interested in using her.

I didn't lose complete contact with Josephine. We saw each other every once in a while. Since she was always in the papers, I couldn't help knowing about the progress of her career. Pepito made her a star, internationally famous, but Josephine always remained what she was—a great, great actress—and she played it, and she lived in another world. She had to live in another world. How else can you take a shirtwaist and skirt and make it into a Paris gown overnight? But she acted as if she'd been born to that gown. There was never anything vulgar about Josephine. If there had been, I would have been the first one to see it.

[...]

James Baldwin
(1924–1987)

JAMES BALDWIN wrote fiction, essays, and plays including the widely acclaimed works, *Go Tell It on the Mountain, Giovanni's Room, Another Country, Notes of a Native Son, The Fire Next Time,* and *No Name in the Street.* In 1942, he went to work at a New Jersey office in order to support his siblings and stepfather. The racism he encountered during this period made him determined to write full time. Despite some early successes in magazines and journals, however, he was unable to complete any long works of fiction. In 1948, he left Harlem for Paris, France. In the following excerpt, Baldwin wrote of this period in his life, "By this time, of course, I was mad, as mad as my dead father. If I had not gone mad, I could not have left." By his own accounts, and by many critics, it was a seminal journey—it gave him the distance to examine himself and his country with clarity. In Paris, he saw racism in another context and discovered what it meant to him to be *le noir Américain.* It was during this period that he began to publish the works for which he would be recognized. Perhaps because of the experiences he had abroad, Baldwin always called himself an American writer, rather than identifying himself solely by his race. He was criticized for this by writers in the Black Arts Movement, who felt that he wrote for a white audience. Nevertheless, Baldwin sat on the advisory board of the Congress on Racial Equality and actively lectured on race issues throughout the United States and Europe, speaking out against racism and discrimination.

He received the George Polk Memorial Award, the Foreign Drama Critics Award, and an honorary doctorate in literature from the University of British Columbia, Vancouver. For his love of France and his contributions to literature, France named him a Commander of the Legion of Honor. He died in St. Paul de Vence, France.

from

✦ No Name in the Street ✦

I left home—Harlem—in 1942. I returned, in 1946, to do, with a white photographer, one of several unpublished efforts; had planned to marry, then realized that I couldn't—or shouldn't, which comes to the same thing—threw my wedding rings into the Hudson River, and left New York for Paris, in 1948. By this time, of course, I was mad, as mad as my dead father. If I had not gone mad, I could not have left.

I starved in Paris for a while, but I learned something: for one thing, I fell in love. Or, more accurately, I realized, and accepted for the first time that love was not merely a general, human possibility, nor merely the disaster it had so often, by then, been for me—according to me—nor was it something that happened to other people, like death, nor was it merely a mortal danger: it was among *my* possibilities, for here it was, breathing and belching beside me, and it was the key to life. Not merely the key to *my* life, but to life itself. My falling in love is in no way the subject of this book, and yet honesty compels me to place it among the details, for I think—I know—that my story would be a very different one if love had not forced me to attempt to deal with myself. It began to pry open for me the trap of color, for people do not fall in love according to their color—this may come as news to noble pioneers and eloquent astronauts, to say nothing of most of the representatives of most of the American states—and when lovers quarrel, as indeed they inevitably do, it is not the degree of their pigmentation that they are quarreling about, nor can lovers, on any level whatever, use color as a weapon. This means that one must accept one's nakedness. And nakedness has no color: this can come as news only to those who have never covered, or been covered by, another naked human being.

In any case, the world changes then, and it changes forever. Because you love one human being, you see everyone else very differently than you saw them before—perhaps I only mean to say that you begin to *see*—and you are both stronger and more vulnerable, both free and bound. Free, paradoxically, because, now, you have a home—your lover's arms. And bound: to that mystery, precisely, a bondage which liberates you into something of the glory and suffering of the world.

I had come to Paris with no money and this meant that in those early years I lived mainly among *les misérables*—and, in Paris, *les misérables* are Algerian. They slept four or five or six to a room, and they slept in shifts, they were treated like dirt, and they scraped such sustenance as they could off the filthy, unyielding Paris stones. The French called them lazy because they appeared to spend most of their time sitting around, drinking tea, in their cafés. But they were not lazy. They were mostly unable to find work, and their rooms were freezing. (French students spent most of their time in cafés, too, for the same reason, but no one called them lazy.) The Arab cafés were warm and cheap, and they were together there. They could not, in the main, afford the French cafés, nor in the main, were they welcome there. And, though they spoke French, and had been, in a sense, produced by France, they were not at home in Paris, no more at home than I, though for a different reason. They remembered, as it were, an opulence, opulence of taste, touch, water, sun, which I had barely dreamed of, and they had not come to France to stay. One day they were going home, and they knew exactly where home was. They, thus, held something within them which they would never surrender to France. But on my side of the ocean, or so it seemed to me then, we had surrendered everything, or had had everything taken away, and there was no place for us to go: we *were* home. The Arabs were together in Paris, but the American blacks were alone. The Algerian poverty was absolute, their stratagems grim, their personalities, for me, unreadable, their present bloody and their future certain to be more so: and yet, after all, their situation was far more coherent than mine. I will not say that I envied them, for I didn't, and the directness of their hunger, or hungers, intimidated me; but I respected them, and as I began to discern what their history had made of them, I began to suspect, somewhat painfully, what my history had made of me.

The French were still hopelessly slugging it out in Indo-China when I first arrived in France, and I was living in Paris when Dien Bien Phu fell. The Algerian rug-sellers and peanut vendors on the streets of Paris then had obviously not the remotest connection with this most crucial of the French reverses; and yet the attitude of the police, which had always been menacing, began to be yet more snide and vindictive. This puzzled me at first, but it shouldn't have. This is the way people react to the loss of empire—for the loss of an empire also implies a radical revision of the individual identity—and I was to see this over and over again, not only in France. The Arabs were not a part of Indo-China, but they *were* part of an empire visibly and swiftly crumbling, and part of a history which was achieving, in the most literal and frightening sense, its *dénouement*—was revealing itself, that is, as being not at all the myth which the French had made of it—and the French authority to rule over them was being more hotly contested with every hour. The challenged authority, unable to justify itself and not dreaming indeed of even attempting to do so, simply increased its force. This had the interesting result of revealing how frightened the French authority had become, and many a North African then resolved, *coûte que coûte*, to bring the French to another Dien Bien Phu.

Something else struck me, which I was to watch more closely in my own country. The French were hurt and furious that their stewardship should be questioned, especially by those they ruled, and if, in this, they were not very original, they were exceedingly intense. After all, as they continually pointed out, there had been nothing in those colonies before they got there, nothing at all; or what meagre resources of mineral or oil there might have been weren't doing the natives any good because the natives didn't even know that they were there, or what they were there for. Thus, the exploitation of the colony's resources was done for the good of the natives; and so vocal could the French become as concerns what they had brought into their colonies that it would have been the height of bad manners to have asked what they had brought out. (I was later to see something of how this fair exchange worked when I visited Senegal and Guinea.)

It was strange to find oneself, in another language, in another country, listening to the same old song and hearing oneself condemned in the same old way. The French (for example) had always had excellent relations with their natives, and they had a treasure-house of anecdotes to prove it. (I never found any natives to corroborate the anecdotes, but, then, I have never met an African who did not loathe Dr. Schweitzer.) They cited the hospitals built, and the schools—I was to see some of these later, too. Every once in a while someone might be made uneasy by the color of my skin, or an expression on my face, or I might say something to make him uneasy, or I might, arbitrarily (there was no reason to suppose that they wanted me), claim kinship with the Arabs. Then, I was told, with a generous smile, that I was different: *le noir Americain est très évolué, voyons!* But the Arabs were not like me, they were not "civilized" like me. It was something of a shock to hear myself described as civilized, but the accolade thirsted for so long had, alas, been delivered too late, and I was fascinated by one of several inconsistencies. I have never heard a Frenchman describe the United States as civilized, not even those Frenchmen who like the States. Of course, I think the truth is that the French do not consider that the world contains any nation as civilized as France.

But, leaving that aside, if so crude a nation as the United States could produce so gloriously civilized a creature as myself, how was it that the French, armed with centuries of civilized grace, had been unable to civilize the Arab? I thought that this was a very cunning question, but I was wrong, because the answer was so simple: the Arabs did not wish to be civilized. Oh, it was not possible for an American to understand these people as the French did; after all, they had got on well together for nearly one hundred and thirty years. But they had, the Arabs, their customs, their dialects, languages, tribes, regions, another religion, or, perhaps, many religions—and the French were not *raciste*, like the Americans, they did not believe in destroying indigenous cultures. And then, too, the Arab was always hiding something; you couldn't guess what he was thinking and couldn't trust what he was saying. And they had a different attitude toward women, they were very brutal with them, in a word they were rapists, and they stole, and they carried knives. But the French had endured this for more than a hundred years and were willing to endure it for a hundred years more, in spite of the fact that Algeria was a great drain on the national pocketbook and the fact that any Algerian—due to the fact that Algeria was French, was, in fact, a French *département*, and was damn well going to stay that way—was free to come to Paris at any time and jeopardize the economy and prowl the streets and prey on French women. In short, the record of French generosity was so exemplary that it was impossible to believe that the children could seriously be bent on revolution.

Impossible for a Frenchman, perhaps, but not for me. I had watched the police, one sunny afternoon, beat an old, one-armed Arab peanut vendor senseless in the streets, and I had watched the unconcerned faces of the French on the café terraces, and the congested faces of the Arabs. Yes, I could believe it: and here it came.

Not without warning, and not without precedent: but only

poets, since they must excavate and recreate history, have ever learned anything from it.

I returned to New York in 1952, after four years away, at the height of the national convulsion called McCarthyism. This convulsion did not surprise me, for I don't think that it was possible for Americans to surprise me anymore; but it was very frightening, in many ways, and for many reasons. I realized, for one thing, that I was saved from direct—or, more accurately, public—exposure to the American Inquisitors only by my color, my obscurity, and my comparative youth: or, in other words, by the lack, on their parts, of any imagination. I was just a shade too young to have had any legally recognizable political history. A boy of thirteen is a minor, and, in the eyes of the Republic, if he is black, and lives in a black ghetto, he was born to carry packages; but, in fact, at thirteen, I had been a convinced fellow traveler. I marched in one May Day parade, carrying banners, shouting, *East Side, West Side, all around the town, We want the landlords to tear the slums down!* I didn't know anything about Communism, but I knew a lot about slums. By the time I was nineteen, I was a Trotskyite, having learned a great deal by then, if not about Communism, at least about Stalinists. The convulsion was the more ironical for me in that I had been an anti-Communist when America and Russia were allies. I had nearly been murdered on 14th Street, one evening, for putting down too loudly, in the presence of patriots, that memorable contribution to the War effort, the Warner Brothers production of *Mission To Moscow.* The very same patriots now wanted to burn the film and hang the filmmakers, and Warners, during the McCarthy era, went to no little trouble to explain their film away. Warners was abject, and so was nearly everybody else, it was a foul, ignoble time: and my contempt for most American intellectuals, and/or liberals dates from what I observed of their manhood then. I say most, not all, but the exceptions constitute a remarkable pantheon, even, or, rather, especially those who did not survive the flames into which their lives and their reputations were hurled. I had come home to a city in which nearly everyone was gracelessly scurrying for shelter, in which friends were throwing their friends to the wolves, and justifying their treachery by learned discourses (and tremendous tomes) on the treachery of the Comintern. Some of the things written during those years, justifying, for example, the execution of the Rosenbergs, or the crucifixion of Alger Hiss (and the beatification of Whittaker Chambers) taught me something about the irresponsibility and cowardice of the liberal community which I will never forget. Their performance, then, yet more than the combination of ignorance and arrogance with which this community has always protected itself against the deepest implications of black suffering, persuaded me that brilliance without passion is nothing more than sterility. It must be remembered, after all, that I did not begin meeting these people at the point that they began to meet *me*: I had been delivering their packages and emptying their garbage and taking their tips for years. (And they don't tip well.) And what I watched them do to each other during the McCarthy era was, in some ways, worse than anything they had ever done to me, for I, at least, had never been mad enough to depend on their devotion. It seemed very clear to me that they were lying about their motives and were being blackmailed by their guilt; were, in fact, at bottom, nothing more than the respectable issue of various immigrants, struggling to hold on to what they had acquired. For, intellectual activity, according to me, is, and must be, disinterested—the truth *is* a two-edged sword—and if one is not willing to be pierced by that sword, even to the extreme of dying on it, then all of one's intellectual activity is a masturbatory delusion and a wicked and dangerous fraud.

I made such motions as I could to understand what was happening, and to keep myself afloat. But I had been away too long. It was not only that I *could* not readjust myself to life in New York—

it was also that I *would* not: I was never going to be anybody's nigger again. But I was now to discover that the world has more than one way of keeping you a nigger, has evolved more than one way of skinning the cat; if the hand slips here, it tightens there, and now I was offered, gracefully indeed: membership in the club. I had lunch at some elegant bistros, dinner at some exclusive clubs. I tried to be understanding about my countrymen's concern for difficult me, and unruly mine—and I really *was* trying to be understanding, though not without some bewilderment, and, eventually, some malice. I began to be profoundly uncomfortable. It was a strange kind of discomfort, a terrified apprehension that I had lost my bearings. I did not altogether understand what I was hearing. I did not trust what I heard myself saying. In very little that I heard did I hear anything that reflected anything which *I* knew, or had endured, of life. My mother and my father, my brothers and my sisters were not present at the tables at which I sat down, and no one in the company had ever heard of them. My own beginnings, or instincts, began to shift as nervously as the cigarette smoke that wavered around my head. I was not trying to hold on to my wretchedness. On the contrary, if my poverty was coming, at last, to an end, so much the better, and it wasn't happening a moment too soon—and yet, I felt an increasing chill, as though the rest of my life would have to be lived in silence.

I think it may have been my own obsession with the McCarthy phenomenon which caused me to suspect the impotence and narcissism of so many of the people whose names I had respected. I had never had any occasion to judge them, as it were, intimately. For me, simply, McCarthy was a coward and a bully, with no claim to honor, nor any claim to honorable attention. For me, emphatically, there were *not* two sides to this dubious coin, and, as to his baleful and dangerous effect, there could be no *question* at all. Yet, they spent hours debating whether or not McCarthy was an enemy of domestic liberties. I couldn't but wonder what conceivable further proof they were awaiting: I thought of German Jews sitting around debating whether or not Hitler was a threat to their lives until the debate was summarily resolved for them by a knocking at the door. Nevertheless, this learned, civilized, intellectual-liberal debate cheerfully raged in its vacuum, while every hour brought more distress and confusion—and dishonor—to the country they claimed to love. The pretext for all this, of course, was the necessity of "containing" Communism, which, they unblushingly informed me, was a threat to the "free" world. I did not say to what extent this free world menaced me, and millions like me. But I wondered how the justification of blatant and mindless tyranny, on any level, could operate in the interests of liberty, and I wondered what interior, unspoken urgencies of these people made necessary so thoroughly unattractive a delusion. I wondered what they really felt about human life, for they were so choked and cloaked with formulas that they no longer seemed to have any connection with it. They were all, for a while anyway, very proud of me, of course, proud that I had been able to crawl up to their level and been "accepted." What *I* might think of *their* level, how *I* might react to this "acceptance," or what this acceptance might cost me, were not among the questions which racked them in the midnight hour. One wondered, indeed, if anything could ever disturb their sleep. They walked the same streets I walked, after all, rode the same subways, must have seen the same increasingly desperate and hostile boys and girls, must, at least occasionally, have passed through the garment center. It is true that even those who taught at Columbia never saw Harlem, but, on the other hand, everything that New York has become, in 1971, was visibly and swiftly beginning to happen in 1952: one had only to take a bus from the top of the city and ride through it to see how it was darkening and deteriorating, how human bewilderment and hostility rose, how human contact was endangered and dying. Of course, these liberals were not, as I was, forever being found by the police in the "wrong" neighborhood, and so could not have had firsthand knowledge of how gleefully a policeman translates his orders from above. But they had no right not to know that; if they did not know that, they knew nothing and had no right to speak as though they were responsible actors in their society; for their complicity with the patriots of that hour meant that the policeman was acting on *their* orders, too.

No, I couldn't hack it. When my first novel was finally sold, I picked up my advance and walked straight to the steamship office and booked passage back to France.

I place it here, though it occurred during a later visit: I found myself in a room one night, with my liberal friends, after a private showing of the French film, *The Wages of Fear.* The question on the floor was whether or not this film should be shown in the United States. The reason for the question was that the film contained unflattering references to American oil companies. I do not know if I said anything, or not; I rather doubt that I could have said much. I felt as paralyzed, fascinated, as a rabbit before a snake. I had, in fact, already seen the film in France. It had not occurred to me, or to anyone I knew, that the film was even remotely anti-American: by no stretch of the imagination could this be considered the film's *motif.* Yet, here were the autumn patriots, hotly discussing the dangers of a film which dared to suggest that American oil interests didn't give a shit about human life. There was a French woman in the room, tight-mouthed, bitter, far from young. She may or may not have been the widow of a Vichyite General, but her sympathies were in that region: and I will never forget her saying, looking straight at me, "We always knew that you, the Americans, would realize, one day, that you fought on the wrong side!"

I was ashamed of myself for being in that room: but, I must say, too, that I was glad, glad to have been a witness, glad to have come far enough to have heard the devil speak. That woman gave me something, I will never forget her, and I walked away from the welcome table.

Yet, hope—the hope that we, human beings, can be better than we are—dies hard; perhaps one can no longer live if one allows that hope to die. But it is also hard to see what one sees. One sees that most human beings are wretched, and, in one way or another, become wicked: because they are so wretched. And one's turning away, then, from what I have called the welcome table is dictated by some mysterious vow one scarcely knows one's taken—never to allow oneself to fall so low. Lower, perhaps, much lower, to the very dregs: but never there.

When I came back to Paris at the end of the summer, most of the Arab cafés I knew had been closed. My favorite money changer and low-life guide, a beautiful stone hustler, had disappeared, no one knew—or no one said—where. Another cat had had his eyes put out—some said by the police, some said by his brothers, because he was a police informer. In a sense, that beautiful, blinded boy who had been punished either as a traitor to France or as a traitor to Algeria, sums up the Paris climate in the years immediately preceding the revolution. One was either French, or Algerian; one could not be both.

There began, now, a time of rumor unlike anything I had ever been through before. In a way, I was somewhat insulated against what was happening to the Algerians, or was aware of it from a certain distance, because what was happening to the Algerians did not appear to be happening to the blacks. I was still operating, unconsciously, within the American framework, and, in that framework, since Arabs are paler than blacks, it is the blacks who would have suffered most. But the blacks, from Martinique and Senegal, and so on, were as visible and vivid as they had always been, and no one appeared to molest them or to pay them any particular attention at all. Not only was I operating within the American frame of reference, I was also a member of the American colony, and we were, in general, slow to pick up on what was going on around us.

Nevertheless, I began to realize that I could not find *any* of the Algerians I knew, not one; and since I could not find one, there was no way to ask about the others. They were in none of the dives we had frequented, they had apparently abandoned their rooms, their cafés, as I have said, were closed, and they were no longer to be seen on the Paris sidewalks, changing money, or selling their rugs, their peanuts, or themselves. We heard that they had been placed in camps around Paris, that they were being tortured there, that they were being murdered. No one wished to believe any of this, it made us exceedingly uncomfortable, and we felt that we should do something, but there was nothing we could do. We began to realize that there *had* to be some truth to these pale and cloudy rumors: one woman told me of seeing an Algerian hurled by the proprietor of a café in Pigalle *through* the café's *closed* plate-glass door. If she had not witnessed a murder, she had certainly witnessed a murder attempt. And, in fact, Algerians *were* being murdered in the streets, and corraled into prisons, and being dropped into the Seine, like flies.

Not only Algerians. Everyone in Paris, in those years, who was not, resoundingly, from the north of Europe was suspected of being Algerian; and the police were on every street corner, sometimes armed with machine guns. Turks, Greeks, Spaniards, Jews, Italians, American blacks, and Frenchmen from Marseilles, or Nice, were all under constant harassment, and we will never know how many people having not the remotest connection with Algeria were thrown into prison, or murdered, as it were, by accident. The son of a world-famous actor, and an actor himself, swarthy, and speaking no French—rendered speechless indeed by the fact that the policeman had a gun leveled at him—was saved only by the fact that he was close enough to his hotel to shout for the night porter, who came rushing out and identified him. Two young Italians, on holiday, did not fare so well: speeding merrily along on their Vespa, they failed to respond to a policeman's order to halt, whereupon the policeman fired, and the holiday came to a bloody end. Everyone one knew was full of stories like these, which eventually began to appear in the press, and one had to be careful how one moved about in the fabulous city of light.

I had never, thank God—and certainly not once I found myself living there—been even remotely romantic about Paris. I may have been romantic about London—because of Charles Dickens—but the romance lasted for exactly as long as it took me to carry my bags out of Victoria Station. My journey, or my flight, had not been *to* Paris, but simply *away* from America. For example, I had seriously considered going to work on a kibbutz in Israel, and I ended up in Paris almost literally by closing my eyes and putting my finger on a map. So I was not as demoralized by all of this as I would certainly have been if I had ever made the error of considering Paris the most civilized of cities and the French as the least primitive of peoples. I knew too much about the French Revolution for that. I had read too much Balzac for that. Whenever I crossed la place de la Concorde, I heard the tumbrils arriving, and the roar of the mob, and where the obelisk now towers, I saw—and see—*la guillotine*. Anyone who has ever been at the mercy of the people, then, knows something awful about us, will forever distrust the popular patriotism, and avoids even the most convivial of mobs.

Still, my flight had been dictated by my hope that I could find myself in a place where I would be treated more humanely than my society had treated me at home, where my risks would be more personal, and my fate less austerely sealed. And Paris had done this for me: by leaving me completely alone. I lived in Paris for a long time without making a single French friend, and even longer before I saw the inside of a French home. This did not really upset me, either, for Henry James had been here before me and had had the generosity to clue me in. Furthermore, for a black boy who had grown up on Welfare and the chicken-shit goodwill of American liberals, this total indifference came as a great relief and, even, as a mark of respect. If I could make it, I could make it; so much the better. And if I couldn't, I couldn't—so much the worse. I didn't want any help, and the French certainly didn't give me any—they let me do it myself; and for that reason, even knowing what I know, and unromantic as I am, there will always be a kind of love story between myself and that odd, unpredictable collection of bourgeois chauvinists who call themselves *la France*.

Permissions Acknowledgments

Grateful acknowledgment is made for the permission to use the following previously published materials.

John Adams: John Adams. Letters to Abigail Adams: April 12, 1778, and April 25, 1778; autobiography entry for May 27, 1778. Adams Family Papers, MHS. Reprinted with permission, courtesy of the Massachusetts Historical Society. Originally published in *The Book of Abigail and John: Selected Letters of the Adams Family, 1762–1784*, ed. L. H. Butterfield et al., Harvard University Press, 1975.

Jennifer Allen: "Euro Disney: A Postcard" by Jennifer Allen. Reprinted by permission of the author. Copyright © 1999 by Jennifer Allen. Originally published as "Tragic Kingdom: Euro Disney—A Postcard" in *The New Republic*, January 10, 1994.

Deborah Baldwin: "Paying the Way" by Deborah Baldwin. Reprinted by permission of the author. Copyright © 1999 by Deborah Baldwin. Originally published in *Paris Notes*, May 1999.

James Baldwin: Excerpt from *No Name in the Street* by James Baldwin (Dial Press). Reprinted by permission of the James Baldwin Estate. Copyright © 1972 by James Baldwin.